D1256418

JOHN DEWEY

THE MIDDLE WORKS, 1899–1924

Volume 12: 1920

Edited by Jo Ann Boydston
Textual Editor, Bridget A. Walsh
With an Introduction by Ralph Ross

Carbondale and Edwardsville
SOUTHERN ILLINOIS UNIVERSITY PRESS

Manufactured in the United States of America
Designed by George Lenox

CENTER FOR
SCHOLARLY EDITIONS
AN APPROVED TEXT
MODERN LANGUAGE
ASSOCIATION OF AMERICA

®

*Editorial expenses for this edition have been met
in part by grants from the National Endowment for the
Humanities. Publishing expenses have been met in part by
grants from the John Dewey Foundation and from Mr.
Corliss Lamont.*

Library of Congress Cataloging in Publication Data (Revised)

Dewey, John, 1859–1952.
  The middle works, 1899–1924.
  Vol. 12 has introd. by Ralph Ross
  Includes bibliographies and indexes.
    1. Dewey, John, 1859–1952. 2. Education—Philosophy. I. Title.
LB875.D34 1976   370'.1'0924   76–7231
ISBN 0–8093–1004-X (v. 12)

The Middle Works, 1899–1924

CONTENTS

INTRODUCTION

By Ralph Ross

I

When Oliver Wendell Holmes, Jr., wrote Sir Frederick Pollock about *Experience and Nature*, he said, "But although Dewey's book is incredibly ill written, it seemed to me after several re-readings to have a feeling of intimacy with the inside of the cosmos that I found unequalled. So methought God would have spoken had He been inarticulate but keenly desirous to tell you how it was." Holmes had grown up with William James; he was "Dear Wendy" in James's letters. He was prepared for a pragmatic philosophy. But *Experience and Nature*, for all its pragmatic base, moved on to kinds of speculation not even found in *The Quest for Certainty*. Much earlier, in *Reconstruction in Philosophy*, which is in this volume, Dewey summarized his version of pragmatism, or instrumentalism as it was being called, and placed it in the history of western thought and western civilization.

Reconstruction in Philosophy is a radical book. It is also a pugnacious book by a gentle man. A part of it sounds like an open-ended, undogmatic, but still vituperative Marx, who could no longer believe in historical materialism and who knew that ideas, though related to their times, moved men to action or complacency. Dewey's belief in his own thought here is rock-ribbed; other philosophies are wrong or they represent a bygone society and have little significance today. His attacks on them are so sharp they require explanation. Traditional social theory he calls an "idle luxury." And "Reason as employed by historic rationalism has tended to carelessness, conceit, irresponsibility, and rigidity— in short absolutism." There is much more of the same sort. Why so much gunfire, untypical and unexpected?

The answer may be—I can't say anything more sure than that—an old anger at the way William James had been treated by those rationalists and absolutists Dewey flays or ridicules throughout his book. That, and a similar attitude to F. C. S. Schiller and Dewey and all who spoke their language may have brought Dewey to hitting back. *Reconstruction in Philosophy*, as I read it, is a development in theory and an extension into society and history, of the Jamesian philosophy that Dewey had then accepted and helped grow. That philosophy had been abused and mocked. James wrote of his "enemies" to whom he once offered "a conciliatory olive branch," a gift they trampled under foot, "I had counted too much on their good will—oh for the rarity of Christian charity under the sun! Oh for the rarity of ordinary secular intelligence also!" The philosophical establishment's early verdict on pragmatism was that it meant believing anything one pleases and calling it truth. This was its understanding of (among others) James's italicized statement in *Pragmatism: "True ideas are those that we can assimilate, validate, corroborate and verify."* The heresy in what may seem obvious enough now was the introduction of "we" into so august a matter as truth. A true idea, as every honest thinker knew, was one that corresponded to reality, or perhaps one that fit into a logically coherent system of the whole. But validating or verifying were only human activities that helped us discover what was true, and always had been, quite apart from our clever monkey tricks.

James called Dewey and Schiller "humanists." They were pragmatists with new emphases and different horizons, so he did not claim them as mere followers. The name was apt. Dewey was making a revolution in philosophy, with Peirce and James behind him, and by the time he wrote *Reconstruction in Philosophy* he knew it. Humanism was the introduction of the human into philosophy, whose marble walls had traditionally housed forms, essences, archetypes, and reality, but not human activity. Dewey turned them all out. They were tenants surviving from antiquity and the Middle Ages and had to be replaced by people who acted on the strength of intelligence modeled on science. Henceforth, philosophy would be different and its results incalculable.

Reconstruction, not revolution, in philosophy was Dewey's phrase. Revolution had been claimed before, by Kant and for him, a Copernican Revolution in philosophy which, if put in a careless sentence, would seem to the layman to be the very revolution Dewey thought was his. At a guess, that is why Dewey is so hard on Kant, here and elsewhere. He would doubtless have said the same things anyway, but he might have said them less harshly. Kant had made knowledge dependent on the human mind and that, in a way, was what pragmatism seemed to be doing. The Kantian revolution is still enshrined: to many contemporaries we all inhabit a post-Kantian intellectual world in which we know that all our judgments are qualified by the nature of mind. But Kantianism was, for Dewey, a mistaken revolution, moving in the wrong direction, for it found the experienced world inchoate, unless compressed into the categories of mind. And Dewey was sympathetic to the upshot of James's "radical empiricism," which had moved in just the opposite direction: experience was comprehensible in itself and all things a philosopher could consider were definable in terms drawn from experience; further, the relations between things were matters of direct particular experience, as much as things themselves.

James complained, "The great obstacle to radical empiricism in the contemporary mind is the rooted rationalist belief that experience as immediately given is all disjunction, and no conjunction, and that to make one world out of this separation, a higher unifying agency must be there." It was this higher unifying agency, whether the structure of the human mind or the all-encompassing absolute, that neither James nor Dewey could tolerate. For such agencies were made necessary by refusing to accept the facts before every man's eyes, that is, a world which intelligence could pretty well grasp, but which it did not create. Indeed, to think that it did was to arrogate to man the powers of God.

Experience was richer and more complex for Dewey than for James. Observation was neither outside of nor prior to thinking. Even mathematics was based on observation, and to treat thinking apart from observation was "intellectual somnambulism." We do not, that is, think only in the course of experience but also with the materials of experience. James may have had things like this in mind when he commented about the universes of discourse of Schiller, Dewey, and himself. "Dewey's panorama, if I understand this colleague, is the widest of the three."

As *Reconstruction in Philosophy* shows so well, Dewey's panorama included the history and development of thought and its position in what later was apotheosized as "culture." Philosophy was always being redefined by Dewey because he did not see it as an attempt to know reality or to contemplate existence, but

as a vital and functional part of man's struggle to understand himself and his conditions in order to better his situation. Later, philosophy became for him a criticism of criticisms, an evaluation of
evaluations. In 1920, he was interested in philosophy as a way of
dealing fruitfully with the great problems of man and society. But
he never gave up one definition for another; rather he expanded
and clarified what he meant. For James, philosophy was an unusually strenuous attempt to think clearly. Dewey was not only
interested in thinking clearly; he was also concerned with philosophy as an instrument whose employment might bring a new
day. But that of course was not just philosophy but his philosophy,
which he hoped would be everybody's because it was a philosophy
for our time.

The origin of philosophy, which Aristotle had found in wonder, Dewey found in the attempt to reconcile social tradition and
reason. Early social tradition was, to him, belief based on memory
of the group past (association, suggestion, dramatic fancy), and
reason was a combination of factual knowledge and rationality.
Philosophers had an allegiance to both, so they could not oppose
the two; instead they tried to extract the moral kernel in tradition
and justify it rationally. Thus philosophy became a rational justification of tradition, or of its essence as philosophers understood
it, and that made it in part conventional and loyal (think of Socrates in the *Crito*) and in part critical (as the *Apology* and much
else shows) because the essence might not square with the facts.
Even the rational part was tinged by traditional attitudes, as it
usually is, and the office of reason itself was understood by its
devotees in the terms used to characterize society. Philosophy
bakes no bread and Reason does not get flour on its fingers.
Thought was for aristocrats and freemen. Practice was for artisans and workmen, and surely for slaves, whose lower offices kept
society's fires lit; theory, sheer understanding, was the higher office of philosophy, whose ultimate goal was contemplation of the
good or the real, but which, along the way, could lend its wisdom
to the supreme art, that of governing, itself an upper-class function. In the Italian Renaissance, in an echo of this distinction,
Leonardo praised the relatively immaculate painter at the expense of the laboring, sweating sculptor, thus putting Michelan-
gelo in his lower place.

The classical philosophic universe had an aristocratic structure which became quite feudal in the Middle Ages. Classes and species did not flow into each other or overlap, nor were they equal; they fit easily into a hierarchy. If there was a plurality of goods, there was always a highest good, a *summum bonum*. Political analogies were not always unconscious: ancient anatomists were capable of using political terms to describe organic structures. Alcmaeon of Croton, in the sixth century B.C., treated physical health as a balance of qualities, *isonomia*, a word which also meant equality of political rights. Disease, then, was domination by one quality, and Alcmaeon called it monarchy. Even in the nineteenth century Rudolf Virchow, who thought the cell the unit of life, said of the body, "It is a free state of individuals with equal rights though not with equal endowments."

Finally, the supernatural order in heaven in the Middle Ages was a kind of feudal hierarchy, meticulously arranged from lowest to highest. Not only did heaven mimic earth; earth also imitated heaven. In the ancient world, many kings became gods and in the feudal world they partook of divinity, having been chosen by the Lord and being especially responsible to Him, not to the people. Shakespeare's Richard II says:

> "Not all the water in the rough rude sea
> Can wash the balm off from an anointed king;
> The breath of worldly men cannot depose
> The deputy elected by the Lord;"

Shakespeare knew better, and there is irony in the scene because Richard is about to be deposed by worldly men, but Shakespeare also knew what kings claimed and what was claimed for them.

Dewey retains his image of a hierarchial society underlying the older philosophies, and sounds like Alcmaeon, when he speaks of modern science as bringing "the substitution of a democracy of individual facts equal in rank for the feudal system of an ordered gradation of general classes of unequal rank." At this point, and even before this, the image may feel strained because the relation of philosophy to the social and political order in which it is born may not seem so close as to warrant such images. Yet in our own more democratic day—the real test is how one talks and thinks in his own time—we have developed a philosophy of ordinary language. "Ordinary language" is not the technical usage of the scholar or the exact diction of the poet, but the speech and usage of the ordinary man. And what that man means when he uses words becomes the basis for an account of meaning. Are such ideas likely to develop in an aristocratic age in which the ordinary language of common men might be the subject of ridicule rather than respect? And if "ordinary language" is more likely to be used by a professor in his nontechnical moments than by a tailor, that only means that the professor, too, is regarded as an ordinary man.

When modern science shattered the mediaeval cosmos, it brought more than a new physical picture of the world. The sun ceased to be more important than the earth, man's place in the universe seemed changed, orthodox religion was troubled, and cause and effect replaced the symbolic Book of Nature. Philosophers tried to comprehend the new universe and to apply its meanings to politics, morals, and religion. Dewey honors this remarkable attempt, especially in his introduction to the second edition of *Reconstruction in Philosophy*, written twenty-five years after the original text. Descartes, Spinoza, Hobbes, Locke, and Leibniz are the great names. Yet one of philosophy's critical responses to science was an empirical theory of knowledge in which the basis of all knowing was human experience based on sensation. The seventeenth-century Locke and many Enlightenment thinkers in England and France developed an elaborate sensationalist philosophy which fell into skepticism of its own weight, but which keeps recurring.

For sensationalism, Dewey has as much scorn as for rationalism, but shows more unhappiness because it was thought of as empirical, and has been called the school of experience. Sensations were thought to infringe on the passive mind; they were not quite experience itself, but the "atoms" which were the building-blocks of experience, and it is as atomism that the twentieth century has usually encountered it. For Dewey, attention lights on sensations during the flow of experience. They are relative to other sensations, and we feel cold in transition from warmth, but the same cold may be warm in transition from colder. They are "signals to redirection of action," not knowledge. At most they provoke inquiry which leads to knowledge; they are the beginning of knowledge only in that sense.

Experience, for Dewey, is altogether another matter from sensation; it occurs in the interaction of organism and environment, in which adaptation of the one or adjustment of the other, or of course both, allows some use of the environment. Fundamentally, experience is activity and an awareness of it, a doing, a creature acting on its surroundings. In the nature of things, changes result from action, and they in turn react upon the creature and its activities. Thus every creature undergoes, or suffers, the consequences of its acts. Experience is this close connection between doing and undergoing. (A fuller explanation of doing and undergoing in the live creature can be found in *Art as Experience*.) There are, of course, doing and undergoing quite separate from each other, but then there is no instruction, no learning, no process of accumulation, and no experience, unless that word is used in a desultory fashion, and indicates nothing vital. Dewey's own example is of a man who is burned through none of his own doing, fire coming upon him while he is asleep. In contrast, there is the child who puts his finger in a flame, is burned, and learns to shun fire. The former, Dewey says, cannot "in any instructive way" be named experience, whereas the latter can.

From this account, it seems clear that Dewey either uses "experience" in an evaluative way, and not purely as designation, or else he admits two kinds: an experience which is just simple awareness, and is not vital or significant, and an experience in which doing and undergoing are closely connected, which is vital and significant. The distinguishing element in the consequences of these experiences would seem to be that in the first type there is no learning and in the second type there is. Experience in its full sense, then, includes learning, continuous observation shot through with thinking, and so is meaningful, and is constituted by a close connection between doing and undergoing. This is the basis for that relation between learning and doing in Dewey's theory of education which became both a battle cry and an object of ridicule for so many years; in both cases usually because of misunderstanding. It is also the reason that Dewey could treat art as experience (not experience as art), because art is meaningful and its meanings are not only in the responses of its audience, but in that kind of experience itself. Experience in Dewey's sense also permits his rejection of dualism in philosophy, which he thinks of as one heritage of class structure in society, because mind and matter, theory and practice, spirit and body, are all abstractions from the continuum of experience, within which we can find and name them as qualities or functions, though they do not have a separate, impermeable existence.

Dewey's writing shows little sense of self or of his own biography, and people have occasionally commented that he wrote as though he were describing the hang of the world but as though there were no describer. When this trait is attributed to an incapacity for introspection, as it sometimes is, one of Dewey's remarkable qualities is missed. Dewey might not have liked the word "introspection" applied to himself, for he commented, "while saints are engaged in introspection, burly sinners run the world." Still, when one examines experience, it is his own experience he examines; no other is accessible to him, except to some extent in the arts. One can also infer some things about other people's experiences from their behavior. Dewey was deeply interested in the arts and himself wrote poetry, he had been a professional psychologist, a student of human behavior, and he read a great deal of history. Whatever he learned about experience from those activities, he must also have scrutinized his own experience with fearful care and insight to have caught its parameters and organization as he did, and articulated them. And once he had an insight he never let it rest, but worried it and pushed it and tried it in new situations. Equally, he never let it go, if he thought it genuine, and it was always there when he needed it. Thus, he often treats the same topic in different places in the same book, a difficulty in exposition compensated for by the feel it gives of live thinking, thinking going on as the book proceeds; not thinking already done, discovery made in the past and systematic exposition the order of the present. In this, Dewey's practice was at one with Edmund Burke's advice about education, to show the order of discovery as it occurs.

An example of this practice is Dewey's return to the relation of thought and observation in experience, not only throughout his career, but later in this same book. His context is now the problematic situation encountered in the course of experience, a situation observed and felt, needing new thought to cope with it. Not only is that thought, when it comes, based on observation, but the initial observation, which contained a sense of the problem, also contained some vague sense of its meaning. That is, the recognition of the problem and a sense of its meaning do not wait on the thinking called forth to solve it and direct our action, as passengers in a station passively await a train, but significant observation demands more direct thought to clarify and expand it. In a horse race, a rider may see a horse moving in on his side, perhaps about to brush his own horse and cause him to lose his rhythm or his footing; at that instant there is an opening among the horses bunched ahead of him; instantly he spurs his horse into the opening, and avoids the possible collision. In retrospect, one can try to distinguish the rider's observation from his thought, but in the actual event the two flow into each other. The rider's observation is meaningful; it is not a bare looking devoid of significance. And his thought was and is correlative to observation. Observation and thought are emphases in an ongoing experience, not separate elements related within it.

When action is urgent, thought and observation are less separable than when there is no urgency and one can ruminate. Dewey regards thinking as a response to a difficulty we can perhaps resolve. When a difficulty is too great, and overwhelms us, then, he tells us, we fall into despair, or perhaps daydreams, but thought is paralyzed. And if we were omnipotent and omniscient, we would have no need of thought. Thinking, thus, is human, or animal, and not divine. Indeed, Aristotle's pure thought, an attribute of deity, would not be thinking in our sense because it would not be about anything. That is an implicit criticism of Aristotle from a man who often criticizes him explicitly. Yet in some ways Dewey is very Aristotelian, even apart from the biological inspiration that moved them both. They were deeply functionalist; in addition, what Dewey thinks is true is regularly explained as a mean between extremes, like Aristotle's virtues. One has only to compare Dewey's *Human Nature and Conduct* with Aristotle's *Nicomachean Ethics* to discover how far a similar vision moves Dewey along this path.

Because thinking arises in a problematic situation, it is not an end in itself, but the great instrument for dealing with life. Yet it has an aesthetic and intrinsic interest, which is why people can be so devoted to it. When we have time to think, a pattern emerges which can be described best by adding materials from works of Dewey's not in this volume. I think it can be stated something like this: we encounter a difficulty in ordinary experience or thought in that the simple, expected flow of events is impeded, things do not jibe, the way turns unexpectedly. Often we do not know what is wrong; the difficulty is felt and its meaning is dim, although we do have a sense of that meaning. We try to grasp what has happened, to clarify, and state it. In short, we think so that we can formulate the felt difficulty as a problem. A real problem can be more or less solved, and the better its formulation, the more the intimation of what the solution is. At this point, we have moved from a somewhat murky experience to a clearer one, more on the level of intellect. We proceed then in the fashion outlined by Dewey in *How We Think*, which was the basis for innumerable texts in logic and scientific method in which his name was never mentioned. In time we come, through inference and test, to a *solution* of our *problem*, which seems probable because of our procedure. Our next step is the application of our solution to the initial *difficulty*, in order to *resolve* it. And this application is a new test. Even if we solved the problem correctly, and we may have been wrong in thinking we did, that may not have helped us in applying the solution to the difficulty with which we started. The chief reason for this would be that the problem was a poor or incorrect formulation of the difficulty.

A traditional belief, widely held, is that one cannot quarrel with a problem, for it is a question, and so cannot be true or false. Of course, the question is easy, hard, or impossible to answer, and if one doesn't like it, he can avoid it, unless it must be met for practical reasons. But problems, as puzzles to be solved, are not simply encountered in experience. They are formulated to reveal the structure or meaning of a difficulty or trouble that is encountered. Problems, then, may or may not reveal the structure or meaning of the difficulties on which they are based. In that sense, they may be the wrong questions. Dewey uses the word "problem" casually in *Reconstruction in Philosophy* to mean a difficulty in experience or a question based on it, but when he writes more technically, he makes the distinction clear. All the same, the gist of the argument is here: "Thinking takes its departure," Dewey says, "from specific conflicts in experience that occasion perplexity and trouble."

To what I have just said must be added the instrumentalist view of things as they are and act in experience, which is not only the way in which we act in order to understand and cope with them. In this, Dewey was a forerunner of the enormous concern with function in American social science. It is not a fixed form, essence, or structure behind processes of change that is the key to knowledge, but the way change becomes evident as we experiment with things, putting them into different circumstances. Some of the changes we effect are intended and some are not. Things change in some ways under our pressure, and in other ways without it. Knowledge is not a matter of discovering what things "really are," as though they were unchanging and inhabited a universe without us. "They *are* what they can do and what can be done with them." And that is not itself final or static; in a changing world what can be done with things changes and so, in a sense, what they can do also changes. Science, as Dewey understood it, was revolutionized by the discovery that what was "universal" was process.

Dewey's instrumental philosophy, as I have been describing it, was not the reconstruction in philosophy of his title, but rather a preamble to that reconstruction. Reconstruction is preached in this book, not practiced, although Dewey did indeed practice it elsewhere. Reconstruction meant the application of intelligence (not Reason in the old sense, but the *kind* of observation, experiment, and reflection used in physical science) to human and moral subjects. Earlier philosophy had been pre-scientific, pre-technological, and pre-democratic. Now we can fashion a philosophy for our own day, one that is scientific, technological, and democratic. As early modern philosophy from, perhaps, the seventeenth century on, promoted and clarified scientific inquiry into physical and physiological conditions, philosophy today must inquire into human affairs, institutional arrangements and, above all, morals.

Dewey does not work out a moral theory here; rather he sounds the alarm: we are using advanced scientific techniques either blindly or to foster pre-scientific moral attitudes. This split between the scientific and the moral bolsters dualisms like matter and spirit, and it subordinates the scientific, as means, to fixed moral ends, echoing the old division of men into those who do servile and necessary work and those who have no need to labor. Reconstruction in philosophy must use all our intellectual methods (genetic, logical, and empirical) to deal with the governmental, economic, familial, and moral aspects of society. But there is more than a matter of method involved. We live in one atmosphere as we deal with technological and scientific matter, and in another atmosphere as we deal with our dearest human concerns. Philosophy provides a bridge and a general view. Its hypotheses are wider and more fundamental than those of science, it is more concerned with understanding and using the past, even while criticizing it, and it can blow new breezes through all aspects of life. It is reconstruction in *philosophy* that Dewey asks and that is neither deconstruction nor destruction of philosophy's history and tradition, although Dewey's rhetoric sometimes is excessive and makes it seem so. One constructs differently, rehabilitates what has already been constructed; one reorganizes existing organization.

In particular passages, Dewey calls for one reconstruction or another. Put them together and he is asking that we re-think our whole situation and bring it to critical awareness. He barely intimates in *Reconstruction in Philosophy* what he says at length in other places: significance is not identical with existence, or values with events, and science at best is one function of the imagination to enrich life with significance. Practical science must be reconciled with art, or it remains one-sided. Here he argues that we need reconstruction in our moral and psychological lives. Moral situations are not like grains of sand, but more like snowflakes: they may look alike to the casual and wandering eye, but on examination each turns out to be unique. Thus in some sense each moral situation has its own good, that which peculiarly satisfies its conditions and has the proper psychological quality. The things we think of as natural goods—justice, temperance, honesty, industry, health, wealth, learning, beauty—are generalized terms and are not to be possessed as if they were fixed ends. Rather, they are directions of change in the quality of experience. There is no *summum bonum* or highest good and, if there were, it could not be attained once and for all. All that we can think of as a moral or psychological "end" is growth, which is perhaps the human analogue of Nature's process.

Dewey ends his small book with high hopes for a world guided by intelligence. He speaks of a possible new birth of poetry, art, and religion, and of intelligence cooperating with social forces. Communication and shared experience can perhaps become everyday miracles, feeding the soul richly. Dewey never thought any of this was easy. Like James, he believed in and practiced the strenuous life. But he has been chided very severely of late for his optimism and, if any of his works gave his critics cause, it was *Reconstruction in Philosophy*. In his later works, some of the bloom is gone. He did not become a pessimist, surely, but he wrote rather about what could be done without intimating that it would be done. Much more than the existentialists, who nurtured a basic despair, Dewey kept to a world of open possibilities and great vistas, in which human striving could make a difference.

II

To what extent did Dewey apply the general ideas of *Reconstruction in Philosophy* to particular matters that fell under his scrutiny at that time? And how much of a simple optimist was he in practical affairs? His essays in this volume allow us to answer those questions.

"Our National Dilemma" alone shows that Dewey retained his point of view when he treated practical affairs and that he was not at all foolishly optimistic. Here Dewey is dealing with American participation in foreign affairs after World War I. He sees that American isolationism is over, that our internal policies are "invaded by foreign issues," and that the more we invest in European countries, the closer Europe is. Except for the Monroe Doctrine, we have had no foreign policy and, as the time comes to forge one, the problem is to ensure that it is a democratic policy, for we have not developed any techniques of popular control over foreign affairs. That is in the spirit of *Reconstruction in Philosophy*, and as for optimism about what might be done, our dilemma is that we have given up isolationism only to conduct international matters in a pre-democratic fashion, "a dilemma so serious," Dewey says, "that for the present there is no visible way out."

For all the charm and insight of Dewey's other essays on America, it is his writing on China that has the greater force. All of these pieces are awash in the flow of politics and economics just after World War I. The League of Nations is a divisive issue, the Red scare in the United States, following on the Russian Revolution, brings pressure on civil liberties, Europe and Japan squabble over China and try to dominate far eastern trade. As Dewey tries to find his bearings in this sea of issues, he manages to restate and refine some of his general views. His comments on civil liberties, though brief, are penetrating. Merely to defend civil liberties, so natural to him, is not enough; our Bill of Rights comes from another time and other circumstances, and has trouble surviving the contention that a new crisis demands new conduct. Dewey knows, of course, that without freedom of speech and press, we are not likely to solve our problems, and it is free inquiry and communication that he defends. But he goes further quickly, for it is one thing to be allowed to say what you believe, but quite another to believe anything worth saying. Although he touches the subject lightly, saying that liberty is mental, a matter of thought, he is not telling us that we are free when we think we are free, but that we are free when we think freely. A rejoinder seems simple; thinking freely is not enough; we must also be able to say and write freely what we think.

Dewey's fuller position is not stated here, but I think it is assumed. Everyone thinks, as he was fond of saying, for himself. Otherwise, he does not think, but parrots. Therefore, it is enough to say that he thinks. But without free and open communication, thought is stifled. It cannot feed on itself, unexpressed and unheard, while all that is expressed and heard is controlled or official. Thinking goes on when one can say what he thinks and hear others say what they think. Otherwise, even if one does not parrot what he hears, but tries to think secretly, his thought is uncriticized and untested, and readily goes askew. One remembers Milton's injunction that the scanning of error is necessary to the confirmation of truth. That is part of what Dewey means. In addition, he insists that thinking, like man himself, is social, not solitary. It follows that thinking and speaking, in some form, are not separable, and the defense of thought is also the defense of civil liberties.

As we think about civil liberties, we assume that political guarantees are a *sine qua non*. Unless the state limits its own powers and is prepared to intervene when private agencies or persons act to check our liberties, we cannot count on having them. In American history the words of the Declaration of Independence blaze with the fire of freedom, but until the Bill of Rights was adopted as amendments to the Constitution, nothing in the Declaration was the law of the land. How hard it is to realize that without public consensus, laws languish in books, quoted perhaps, but rusted in disuse. Even harder is the realization that, in the absence of law, deep and prevailing consensus can bring about what laws might not. Anthropology has taught us that pre-literate peoples, without written laws, can have laws graven on their hearts and that their "laws" are rarely violated. Yet civilization has seemed, in great part, a matter of law, and the names of the towering lawgivers—Moses, Solon, Hammurabi—are almost synonymous with the advent of civilization. It is startling, therefore, when foreign correspondents in the 1980s explain the lack of clear laws in Communist China on the grounds that the Chinese are, and have been, scornful of the West's reliance on law because it implies the absence of a morality so internalized that people can be expected to act on it. Sure of their own morality, the Chinese have felt little need of our sort of legalism.

Yet Dewey, in 1920, in a China ruled more by provincial governors than by a central state, had discovered the power of Chinese consensus and morality. In his "New Leaven in Chinese Politics," he wrote, "It is to be doubted whether China will ever make the complete surrender to legalism and formalism that western nations have done." Of course, "ever" is a long time, and Dewey does not usually use such words; that he does so here is a sign of how impressed he was. And he adds, "This may be one of the contributions of China to the world." It is a contribution of a model and an idea, for it points to a relation, or set of relations, between legal formalism and a living morality. I use the adjective "living" to mean regularly practiced, as distinct from a moral code to which people are committed verbally, but which may be more honored in the breach than the observance, that Sunday sermon morality by which we do not abide.

If people act as if there were laws they obey, and do not in fact have those laws, do they in any sense need them? Laws are backed by force and sanctions and one virtue of having them is that they may be enforced when conduct flags. But unless there is sufficient will on the part of authorities, they may not be enforced and, when there is mass apathy or hostility, strict enforcement may be folly. In a democratic country, people learn that if they do not want a law, they can change it. In a country like China they could change their behavior and that would have more than the force of a changed law. But it would mean a change in morality. In practice, Dewey did not find that all Chinese acted without friction, for they had different interests. When groups were in opposition, however, they settled their difficulties themselves, without appeal to officials, who were trusted less than rival groups. Individual persons, though, were punished if they tried to redress their own wrongs; that was a prerogative of organized groups—families, villages, clans.

Law can of course be enforced by violent action when there is a preponderance of force in official hands, even when the people as a whole is opposed. Government by terror is too common a phenomenon to doubt this. Yet a real divorce between government and the people makes government unstable, hence official lies, propaganda, and brainwashing. Some moral consensus, then, is indispensable to a functioning society, no matter how strong its government or how rigid its laws. Small groups, especially under critical conditions, may act on such a consensus without much need of law and punishment, but for the larger society to do nearly the same probably requires long tradition and not too much change in the consensus. New democracies, as Rousseau argued, are less stable than old ones. And an age-old civilization, like China's, surviving and absorbing its conquerors, and distinguished by a resistance to change (until the era of communism?) can develop a deep and abiding consensus.

That resistance to change, the "undoubted conservatism" of the Chinese which helped develop their moral consensus, is not easy to explain. A pat answer would be that they made an excellent adaptation to their geographic and social conditions and, since the conditions remained the same, their adaptation did too. Yet all manner of things have happened in the history of the Central Kingdom. One condition, however, has remained the same for a long time, what Dewey calls "continual living in a crowd," and that, he suggests, may explain Chinese conservatism—not political conservatism so much as retention of manners, customs, and morals. As Dewey puts it, "Until the recent introduction of rapid transportation, very few Chinese ever enjoyed even the possibility of solitude that comes from being in a crowd of strangers. Imagine all elbow-room done away with, imagine millions of men living day by day, year by year, in the presence of the same persons (a very close presence at that), and new light may be shed upon the conservatism of the Chinese people." Any initiative, any innovation, even a burst of energy, could make things worse. Easy courtesy, cheerfulness, and acceptance of fate take precedence over getting things done, in western fashion. Dewey's explanation may be right or wrong, but it bears consideration in these days of far eastern turmoil and change.

III

This volume contains a series of six lectures delivered in Peking in 1919, two lectures each on William James, Henri Bergson, and Bertrand Russell. The lectures were apparently translated as Dewey spoke, probably by Hu Shih, the eminent Chinese thinker who studied with Dewey for his doctorate at Columbia. Because, no doubt, of the Oriental audience listening to talks about western philosophers, and the added difficulty of translation, Dewey was extremely simple, so simple that his lectures give a general overview but avoid the density of their subjects' thought.

Still, there are many insights that are worth attention. James, Dewey tells us, was the first person to apply the idea of evolution to psychology. Quite properly, Dewey regards *Principles of Psychology* as James's most important work, but he goes on to say that James never really wrote a book in philosophy, that his philosophy appeared in the form of literary essays. That is a judgment by a master technician about the work of a writer of vision and genius who was less technically gifted, or less interested in technical precision. One qualification, though, must be added: *Principles of Psychology* is, among other things, a book of philosophy. In fact, Dewey treats it as such, starting with the idea of knowledge.

Knowledge, for James, is the mediating process that occurs between a stimulus coming from the environment and the human organism's response to it. Knowledge can scarcely intervene between a flicker of movement toward the head, and a resulting eye blink. But in less instantaneous action, knowledge may determine a response appropriate to a stimulus. Dewey gives the example of a man who knows enough to have water available where there is a fire hazard. Then, when there is a fire, he responds by using the water to put it out. Knowledge may also slow response, when there is not such urgency as a fire, and so give time to plan.

Or an imagined stimulus, like that of a fire itself, can bring us to store water or arrange a hydrant, preparing for a quick and adequate response when the stimulus occurs.

Within *Principles of Psychology*, Dewey finds what he regards as the most important single concept in James's philosophy, the stream of consciousness which, he says, is "uniquely Jamesian." It is an idea that permeated modern literature, was used brilliantly by Joyce and Faulkner, and had an important influence on clinical psychology and psychotherapy. Its effect on philosophy was, perhaps, not so widespread as a positive contribution, but it helped enormously in the criticism of other points of view. It had been common to treat consciousness as made up of isolated impressions, often thought of as passive or inert, with which the mind constructed objects. James's image instead is of a stream in constant motion, in which all impressions are connected to each other. The ceaseless flow is forward, carrying everything with it and, like Heraclitus's flow, it is always changing; indeed, *we* are changing because our consciousness is changing and so what we are conscious of is changing. One of the distinctions James makes is between physical objects and mental functions; the former can be divided into their parts, but in consciousness we experience wholes. James offers lemonade as an example: physically it is composed of lemon juice, water, and sugar, but as we drink it we are conscious simply of lemonade. This is a part of Gestalt psychological theory before the Gestalt psychologists. But it was not just Wertheimer and Köhler that James preceded in some respects; it was many schools of psychology, including the Freudian.

As for the relation between the conscious experiences and the physical object, James was not worried about the presumed need for the former to correspond to the latter, the traditional correspondence theory of truth. His concern was rather that one experience lead to other experience or, in Dewey's words, that perception produce anticipated consequences. This, of course, was central to the theory of pragmatism.

Although Dewey was devoted to William James and one could expect warm appreciation when he talked about him, it is a little surprising to see how much sympathy he had for Henri Bergson. Bergson was a systematizer and a Vitalist, even in some ways a mystic, traits that should not have endeared him to Dewey, but he was a man of extraordinary insight, who commanded a lucid and flexible prose, and he had many ideas in common with James; these matters Dewey saw clearly. Of course, Bergson's reputation has declined by now and, from Dewey's final comment about him, was not all that it should have been in 1919, when he was sixty years old, just Dewey's age, but it had been a formidable reputation and, for many, it remained that at least through his lifetime. What we also remember, I hope, Dewey could not have known until long after he gave these lectures: Bergson's great courage when the Nazis entered Paris.

What Dewey sees as Bergson's initial resemblance to James is that both men started with psychology and used psychological ideas in developing their philosophies. The same comment could be made about Dewey. But there is a more fundamental issue. Many philosophers, from Plato to Bertrand Russell, have mathematical leanings and tend to view mathematics as a model for philosophy, unattainable finally, but to be approximated. If the Socrates of *The Republic* is not just Plato in disguise, he was the great source of the mathematical model, demanding not just precision in thought, but the movement of mind from the materials of experience to the abstractions that he thought lay behind experience and made it intelligible. The nobility of this vision, as well as the brilliance of its detail, has captivated mankind, at least in the West, for its entire history since the fifth century B.C. We seldom notice the occasional descent into preposterous quantification, sheer bathos which chills the mind or weakens it with laughter. We are informed, for example, in Book IX of *The Republic*, that "the tyrant is removed from true pleasure by the space of a number which is three times three." This leads us to the further exact knowledge that the king lives 729 times more pleasantly than the tyrant, who lives more painfully by this same number. And in some wonderful fashion this "concerns human life," for 729 is *nearly* the number of days and nights in one year.

In contrast to the philosophers influenced by mathematics are those with a biological or bio-psychological cast, from Aristotle to John Dewey, and of course others with a social orientation, and a combination of all of these. Biological philosophers, too, have their triumphs; one has only to think of Aristotle's domination of western thought for centuries; to Dante, Aristotle was "the master of them that know." Yet the biological impulse in philosophy also has its ludicrous moments. Aristotle "knew" that the heart's temperature is the chief factor if one is to give birth to a boy. Imagine what some of our quantification and our knowledge of man will look like in a few hundred years.

As Dewey explains Bergson he, like James, views the mind as a stream in which nothing is repeated exactly and in which everything is connected. We are constantly changing, unable to step into the same river twice because the water is different each time and so are we. Bergson, too, thought physical objects could be separated into their parts but experience was of wholes. When Bergson asked himself why people insist on thinking about mind as if it were like a thing, he started an inquiry that took him far from James. His answer was that we must be able to talk to each other and this brought us to segment experience into units of a kind that can be portrayed in language. Linguistic symbols represent units, bits and pieces of the continuous experience, and we learn to think in the manipulation of words.

This leads Bergson to distinguish between time and duration. Time is an analogue of space; it is measured by the clock, and it has units of seconds, minutes, hours, years, and light-years. Time is necessary for dealing with the material world, which is a set of spatial relations, but it caricatures mental experience, which can be explained only by duration. Duration is the quality of the stream of consciousness, a continual forward motion which incorporates the past. Bergson's image is of a snowball rolling down a mountain, bringing its past with it, growing ever larger, and being transformed continually. Duration is a growing, maturing change, and that brings constant self-creation. The concept of self-creation is of particular significance to Bergson. It is the constant addition of new meaning to experience.

Because one is always adding meaning, he is continually creating, and what he is creating is a self, transformed by that meaning. No experience is predetermined, or even predictable. Of course, much in the material world is predictable, and we can deal with a great deal of that world mechanically, but that is because we have segmented it into discrete units the better to use it for our purposes. Before we did that, the material world was not different from the spiritual world and it is conceivable that in the future they will again be alike. At this time, we see the material world through the spectacles of interest and our interests are served by the application of knowledge, but the world of duration can be penetrated only by a high level of introspection and intuition. As Dewey understands it, Bergson's philosophy has attracted so many disciples because his epistemology is pragmatic whereas the rest of his philosophy is semi-mystical. Thus it offers something for people of very different kinds. To be fair, one should add that there is an inspiring quality in Bergson that is extremely rare in twentieth-century philosophy.[1]

I shall say little about Dewey's treatment of Russell, because Dewey says little about Russell's technical philosophy. He sees Russell as a mathematicizing philosopher ready, when the world is too much with him, to seek refuge in a quasi-Platonic realm of forms. (For an eloquent statement about this by Russell, one should read his essay "A Free Man's Worship.") Dewey finds Russell unique in one respect: his theoretical philosophy is aristocratic while his ethical and social philosophy is fairly democratic. Aristocratic tendencies, as Dewey wrote about them in *Reconstruction in Philosophy*, exalt reason at the expense of experience and universal principles at the expense of individual things. In particular, the aristocratic mode in thought always prefers pure reflection to practical life. Even time is to be transcended, for universal principles are eternal.

In his social philosophy at that time, Russell emphasized a distinction between creative and possessive impulses, although I have never been sure why one cannot be creative in acquiring possessions and possessive about his creativity. He believed that our institutions, which could foster creativity, have been corrupted by possessive characteristics and are now decadent. Education, which should be a creative adventure, has dwindled in the

---

1. What Dewey says in the lecture on Bergson (p. 221) about Plato and Kant is true about Kant but not about Plato. Had he said "Locke" the sentence would have been all right. Then he makes a similar mistake about Berkeley in the first lecture on Bertrand Russell. Something seems wrong textually because Dewey's knowledge of the history of philosophy was encyclopedic and one would never expect this kind of error.

It turns out that the text is more than dubious. Dewey spoke from notes and someone transcribed his statements. Then the lectures were translated into Chinese and printed in a Peking newspaper. Our text is a translation into English from the Chinese. Mark Twain, as I recall, printed a French translation of his "The Celebrated Jumping Frog of Calaveras County" and then translated it back into English. It was by then a caricature of the original. In Twain's case, there was a genuine original and it was translated into a language not too unlike English. In Dewey's case, there was no genuine original, and the transcription of what he said was translated into a language so different from English that it does not have an alphabet. And then it was translated into English. The possibility of error in this final text is beyond calculation.

school to a defense of property and compliance; it preserves the past and cheapens the future. Socialism as well as capitalism is concerned with mass production and increasing wealth. In order to succeed, socialism depends on a strong state which, by its nature, suppresses individuality and creativeness. Russell, Dewey thinks, believes in "creation, growth, change, and transformation" and in that he stands with Bergson and James.

I find it interesting that Dewey chose to introduce these three philosophers to a Chinese audience in 1919, calling them, in his title, "Three Contemporary Philosophers." James had been dead for nine years, and Dewey justified his inclusion by the comment that his works were having their greatest impact at the moment. Bergson was a logical choice; he was alive and famous. But so was Benedetto Croce, whose massive *Philosophy of the Spirit* had attracted many disciples and was translated into English as a series of books from 1909 to 1921. Yet, for all the Hegelian influence on him, Dewey did not find Idealists sympathetic, and Croce was an Idealist. The new English metaphysicians of genuine fame were Samuel Alexander and Alfred North Whitehead. Still, Alexander's chief work, *Space, Time and Deity*, was published in 1920, and Whitehead's *Process and Reality* came later; that was a reason not to choose them, although they were more than well-known in 1919. One might add that Dewey was not partial to metaphysicians, either. But I doubt that his choices were a matter of personal taste, because that might have led him to omit Russell, too, despite Russell's meteoric career and extraordinary brilliance. Perhaps Dewey was trying to show his Oriental audience what he believed and hoped about man and society and was talking about those fellow philosophers who shared the same beliefs and hopes.

Essays

OUR NATIONAL DILEMMA

Nothing is easier to say than that the period of our national isolation is past. Nothing is simpler to proclaim than that we are now called upon to assume the burden of sharing in the conduct of world affairs. Large words about these things make a double appeal. Our inherent idealism responds—and so does our vanity and our love of power. The two responses so intermingle, so cover each other, that the wonder is that the appeal has not been irresistible. Why has it failed? Under what conditions may it succeed?

Quite probably it is fortunate for us that nationalistic ambitions and imperialistic aggressions were so undisguisedly powerful in the peace negotiations. We owe monuments to Clemenceau, Sonnino and Balfour. Probably in our excited idealism nothing less flagrant than the exhibition they gave could have averted our becoming innocent and ignorant accomplices in the old world game of diplomacy. As it was, the contrast between prior professions and actual deeds was so obvious as to evoke revulsion.

That the revulsion should have found most articulate expression in narrowly nationalistic inhibitions and repudiations of foreign responsibilities may be unfortunate; but it was, possibly, in its after effects better than nothing. The terms in which Republican Senators articulated American selfishness in response to European selfishness would not of themselves have commanded the assent of the American people. There was a deeper instinct and emotion behind the rejection. Doubtless it was associated with our historic policy of no foreign entanglements. But it is desirable to clarify the emotion expressed in this attitude. What in addition to national egoism lies back of the instinct against being mixed up in the affairs of foreign nations?

The answer seems clear. We have a preference for democracy

[First published in *New Republic* 22 (1920): 117–18. Republished in *Characters and Events*, ed. Joseph Ratner (New York: Henry Holt and Co., 1929), 2:615–19.]

in politics. Our attachment is doubtless halting, and subject to deflections and corruptions, to say nothing of being not adequately enlightened. But it is genuine. Responsible government and publicity are our ideal, and upon the whole the ideal fares as well as most ideals in a rude and imperfect world. But, putting it roundly, democracy has never had even a look-in with respect to conducting the foreign affairs of peoples, and this is true even of nations that are democratic in their management of domestic affairs. By virtue of our geographical position and the fullness of our empire within, rather than by any moral virtue, we have maintained a state of relative innocence through abstention. We have had no foreign policy save to have none, barring the sacred Monroe Doctrine. We dwelt pleasantly enough in our Garden of Eden. During the war, we thought we could easily extend its blessings to the entire world. But the undisguised scramble after the armistice days reminded us of the Fall of Man, and we hurried back into our Paradise, though remaining on the lookout for remunerative investments in the outer world of sin and misery.

Yet it is true that a policy of isolation and non-participation is impossible. When we have invested enough in European countries they will be as near to us as Mexico now is. We may have the same tender interest in maintaining the stability of established powers, that democratic France has shown for the old autocratic regime of Russia. The war itself is sufficient demonstration that aloofness and neutrality have gone by the board; their day is over. We cannot longer piously inscribe the Open Door on parchments impressed with our national seal, and then complacently retire to such a distance that we can identify words with facts. But the most significant thing is not that our period of isolation is done with so that we must henceforth have foreign policies, League of Nations or no League. It is that henceforth our internal policies, our problems of domestic politics, are entangled with foreign questions and invaded by foreign issues.

It is not for us to choose whether we shall remain isolated. Who would have believed a few years ago that universal military service could be injected as a vital question into American politics? The problems of taxation that will come up in connection with our national debt will remind us that we cannot keep domestic politics pure and unspotted from the international world. We shall be fortunate if issues of bonuses and pensions do not become important partisan questions. The intimate connection of labor problems with immigration is another reminder. Pro-Irish, pro-British, or Jewish questions suggest another side of our entanglement.

Economic reactionaries have succeeded in creating a Bolshevist issue among us, the most contentedly middle class nation on earth. They are trying to "sell" this issue to the American people by wholesale advertising through news and editorial columns. Sixteen per cent of Americans raise the issue of one hundred per cent Americanism in behalf of policies that judged by all sane American history are anti-American. Yes, wherever we turn we find plenty of reminders that the angel with a flaming sword forbids our return into the Garden of innocence and isolation.

The net effect, however, is a dilemma, a dilemma so serious that for the present there is no visible way out. We must guard ourselves against the idealizations with which we customarily protect ourselves from seeing the realities of an unpleasant situation. The dilemma is that while our day of isolation is over, international affairs are still conducted upon a basis and by methods that were instituted before democracy was heard of as a political fact. Hence we engage in foreign policies only at the risk of harming even such imperfect internal democracy as we have already achieved.

There is no use in blinking the non-democratic foreign policy of the democratic nations, of France and Great Britain. The Versailles Conference was not an untoward exceptional incident. It was a revelation of the standing realities. To recognize this fact is the sole guarantee that as we surrender our innocence we may yet be able to retain our integrity.

For example, as I write, a copy of the *New Republic* comes to hand with a discussion from a contributor and in an editorial of a naval alliance between Great Britain and the United States. A residence in the Far East makes one aware of the possibilities of such an alliance; it makes one almost ready to cheer for it on any terms. A Chinese owned newspaper in Shanghai carries at the top of its front page a standing slogan: "British-American cooperation in China is the A B C of safety and progress for China." And most Americans and British add a hearty amen.

And yet, and yet—an alliance, but an alliance for what? Just an alliance, without any definition or discussion of ends and methods which will make democratic control a reality and not a name? All treaties relating to the Far East are designed, if we trust their makers, to maintain the peace of the Orient, the territorial integrity of China and the Open Door. The additional expense of engrossing upon them that they are designed to promote the welfare of humanity would be slight. Now the main fact about British policy in China, in fact in Asia, is that it is conducted with one eye upon India, or rather with both eyes upon India and an occasional look elsewhere.

Is there as a matter of fact any use in discussing a naval alliance with Great Britain if we have not faced what our relation, say, to Britain's Indian policy is to be? Suppose that an economic blockade of India should become as desirable as that of Russia seemed lately to be;—are we to be accomplices in that also? The reverberation of our surrender of the Philippines upon all problems of the Far East, from Korea to India, will be great. What would be the effect of a formal alliance upon our Philippine policy? Would it not inevitably strengthen the propaganda that we retain them, lest their surrender "endanger the peace of the Far East"—as the phrase always goes?

The case is not even as if we had any guarantee that we are going to have democratic control of our own foreign policies when we enter upon them. And I am speaking generally, not of the special instance just mentioned. Congress must indeed share in the opening of war and the Senate in its concluding. But it is an elementary fact that we have not developed a technique of popular control. How was the Russian adventure of Great Britain finally halted? Partly, of course, by the common sense of diplomats who concluded it wouldn't pay. But from the popular side not by an effective check such as we take for granted in domestic affairs, but by fear of mutinies abroad and strikes at home. Would we be better off?

It is easier to state the dilemma that isolation is impossible and participation perilous than to state any solution. But meantime we should certainly tread warily. We should avoid all general commitments, and confine ourselves to the irreducible minimum, and that most specifically stated. "Meantime," until what? Until the labor parties of European democracies, or some other liberal organization, supervise and direct the foreign policies of those nations with jealous regard for democratic principles, and until we have ourselves attained not merely greater knowledge of foreign and international politics but have developed the sure means of popular control. Diplomacy is still the home of the exclusiveness, the privacy, the unchecked love of power and prestige, and one may say the stupidity, characteristic of every oligarchy. Democracy has not touched it. Beware of contamination through contact. That, I think, is the sound instinct, behind our aversion to foreign entanglements.

We are not holier than other nations, but there is an obligation upon us not to engage too much or too readily with them until there is assurance that we shall not make themselves and ourselves worse, rather than better, by what is called sharing the common burdens of the world, whether it be through the means of a League of Nations or some special alliance.

FREEDOM OF THOUGHT AND WORK

An American liberal, a man of wealth, has recently conceded that existing industrial institutions are to a considerable extent unjust. This injustice he admits to be one great cause in the existing unrest of the world. The remedy is a more equitable distribution of the material products of industry. Yet in fundamental directions he thinks something like the present system is permanently necessary to get the work of the world done. Such a position is inevitable in times of transition. Practically it is to be welcomed as a step forward. It seems ungenerous to criticize.

Yet the step forward will be awkwardly taken and, quite probably, futile in its avowed object of dealing with unrest unless it is frankly recognized that it is only a step. Its significance is that it will make easier a further and much more far-reaching movement. If not taken with a more distant object in view it may easily intensify class hostility. It will strengthen the power of wage-earners to make demands for a still larger share in material products, without creating among them a feeling of responsibility for industry itself. It will increase the bitterness of employers regarding the unreasonable, unintelligent and ungrateful disposition of labor, its willingness in its own selfish interest to throw a monkey-wrench into the entire industrial machine. As a "solution," the proposed remedy not only does not go to the root of the matter, but it tends away from it.

Would Mr. Hoover, to whom this point of view is attributed, be contented under the charge that the animating spring of his own activities had been the material products of his work? Men of large wealth are justly contemptuous of the idea that they have been dollar-chasers, or that acquisitiveness or security has been their moving principle even in collecting securities. It is a mischievous mistake to suppose that wage-earners are differently

[First published in *New Republic* 22 (1920): 316–17. Republished in *Characters and Events*, ed. Joseph Ratner (New York: Henry Holt and Co., 1929), 2:522–25.]

made. Not idealism but human psychology proclaims the fact that man does not live by wages alone. What men need is an outlet for what is human in them. Not for any long period can they be bribed to be quite lacking such an outlet. At present, the period is almost zero. For the workers realize that increase in wages is now a testimony to their power; and an awakened sense of power is just what demands opportunity for exercise. And this means a responsible share in the management of activities.

In every new crisis it seems to be forgotten that the demand for freedom means a reaching out for mental activity, for greater scope of thought. This is the reason why the battle for freedom is never won, and why its ancient guarantees always fail in a crisis. They are outworn for conservative and radical alike. The former sees them used for purposes which he is sure were never intended, and the latter is interested in something deeper. Apply this statement to the present situation as to freedom of speech. The old legal guarantees of freedom of speech and publication are, of course, sacred, thinks the reactionary, but they have no bearing upon the existing situation. The authors of the bills of rights had no experience with the contemporary labor situation, and never contemplated the existence and spread of sovietism. Hence the ease with which civil rights, complacently supposed to be settled, are trampled upon. And if the masses take attacks upon these rights with less resentment than we would have thought possible, it is because after all they have an instinctive feeling that the centre of the present struggle for freedom of mind lies somewhere else.

The hang-over of a war psychology of suspicion and fear is, of course, a large factor in the campaign for intimidation of free social thinking. The desire of a ruling class to utilize this hang-over to create a psychological reign of terror which will infect the timid among sympathizers with liberty and which will invade the courts is a large factor. But the existing situation cannot be explained by these factors alone. They need something else to give them full operative force. And this something else is the fact that freedom of mind no longer finds an adequate expression in political action, or in speech and writing. Large numbers of men have reached the point where they feel, and are beginning to see, that they can get true freedom of mind only when they can exercise their minds in connection with their daily occupations. Executives, managers, scientific men, artists have such freedom. Why not the others? This is the consciousness which cannot be bought off with an increased share of the material products of industry. And it also accounts for the thinness of the old guarantees of freedom of speech, publication and political agitation.

This is a new struggle. It cannot be cramped within the limits of old law. The conservatives are the first to learn this lesson, and it is they who are teaching it to others who, without their teaching, would probably have remained inert for a much longer time. By the nature of the case it is always the conservative who is most sensitive to the meaning of any new tendency, and it is he who by his attacks upon the new movement, instructs the masses as to its real significance. What he is now shouting at the top of a frenzied voice is that freedom of mind can be achieved only with the exercise of control over one's work, and that in comparison with this, freedom of speech and the right to vote are of superficial importance.

Like other advocates of freedom of speech, the writer has upon occasion used the safety-valve argument. A social crisis, a social turning point, gives the argument an ironic turn. That is just what a great new force should not want—a cheap safety-valve. Steam is needed to overcome obstacles, and it should not be wasted in talk that merely blows it off. Shooting off the mouth is an easy way in which to dissipate force. The reactionary with his predestined assistance to the radical, can be trusted, when any matter is really important, to prevent this cheap and easy road from being taken. He makes it necessary for men to seek for the reality of freedom instead of being contented with an inflated sense that it is attained when talk is unconfined.

Because liberty is essentially mental, a matter of thought, and because thought is free only as it can manifest itself in act, every struggle for liberty has to be reenacted on a different plane. The old struggle for liberty of speech, assemblage and publication was significant because it was part of a struggle for liberty of worship, and security of property. It is stupid to suppose that the older fight is cheapened when the presence of economic motives is pointed out. Men who had won their property by honest industry and enterprise wanted security against other men who had won their property by conquest and who wished to continue their predatory career. Their fight demands respect, not disparagement or denial.

But it is equally stupid to suppose that thought and effort will always circulate in the channels then marked out.

Freedom of speech and of the franchise is now significant because it is part of the struggle for freedom of mind in industry, freedom to participate in its planning and conduct. Were not republics proverbially ungrateful, it would be safe to predict the erection of future monuments to Mr. Palmer, Mr. Sweet and others who have taken such seemingly gratuitous pains to make this fact clear to masses of people who otherwise would hardly have seen this fact for a long time to come. For we may be sure that the old guarantees of civil liberty would not have cracked so easily, even with the assistance of a war psychology of fear and excitement, unless something vital was going on underneath the shell. While the reactionary thinks he is shackling a dangerous foe, he is really demonstrating how superficial is a freedom of thought that can manifest itself only in speech and not in work.

AMERICANISM AND LOCALISM

When one is living quite on the other side of the world, the United States tend to merge into a unit. One thinks largely in terms of national integers, of which the United States is one. Like a historian of the old school or a writer of diplomatic notes, one conceives of what the United States is doing about this or that. It is taken, as schoolmen say, as an entity. Then one happens to receive a newspaper from one of the smaller towns, from any town, that is, smaller than New York—and sometimes Chicago. Then one gets a momentary shock. One is brought back to earth. And the earth is just what it used to be. It is a loose collection of houses, of streets, of neighborhoods, villages, farms, towns. Each of these has an intense consciousness of what is going on within itself in the way of fires, burglaries, murders, family jars, weddings, and banquets to esteemed fellow citizens, and a languid drooping interest in the rest of the spacious land.

Very provincial? No, not at all. Just local, just human, just at home, just where they live. Of course, the paper has the Associated Press service or some other service of which it brags. As a newspaper which knows its business, it prints "national" news, and strives assiduously for "national" advertisements, making much on provocation of its "national" circulation. But somehow all this wears a thin and apologetic air. The very style of the national news reminds one of his childhood text-book in history, or of the cyclopaedia that he is sometimes regretfully obliged to consult. Let us have this over as soon as possible and get to something interesting, it all seems to say. How different the local news. Even in the most woodenly treated item there is flavor, even if only of the desire to say something and still avoid a libel suit.

Yet there is a strange phenomenon noted. These same papers that fairly shriek with localisms devote a discreet amount of space to the activities of various Americanization agencies. From time

[First published in *Dial* 68 (1920): 684–88. Republished in *Characters and Events*, ed. Joseph Ratner (New York: Henry Holt and Co., 1929), 2:537–41.]

to time, with a marked air of doing their duty, there are earnest editorials on the importance of Americanization and the wickedness of those who decline to be either Americanized or to go back where they came from. But these weighty and conscientious articles lack the chuckle and relish one finds in the report of the increase of the population of the town and of its crime wave.

One vaguely wonders whether perhaps the recalcitrants who are denounced may not also be infected by the pervading spirit of localism. They decline to get Americanized for the same reason they put up with considerable annoyance rather than go back. They are chiefly concerned with what goes on in their tenement house, their alley, their factory, their street. If a "trained mind"—like the writer's, for example—can't tell very well from these articles just what Americanization is, probably the absorbed denizens of the locality are excusable for not trying to find out more about it. One gathers of course that Americanization consists in learning a language strangely known as English. But perhaps they are too busy making the American language to devote much time to studying the English.

In any case, the editorial emphasis on Americanism stands in extraordinarily vivid contrast to the emphasis in the news columns on local interests. The only things that seem to be "nationwide" are the high cost of living, prohibition, and devotion to localisms. A Pacific Coast newspaper just reaching Peking contains on its front page the correspondence between President Wilson and Secretary Lansing about the latter's resignation. Doubtless in London the news was of the first importance. The San Francisco editor was too good a journalist not to print the entire correspondence faithfully. But it was entirely overshadowed by a local graft case as to head-lines, space given, and editorial comment.

This remark is not a complaint. It is merely a record of a fact easily verified in almost any city in the United States. The editor doubtless sympathized with the feeling of the mass of the readers that a civic reformation at home was more important than a cabinet revolution in Washington; certainly more important for the "home town," and quite likely for the country—the country, mind you, not the nation, much less the state. For the country is a spread of localities, while the nation is something that exists in Washington and other seats of government.

Henry Adams somewhere remarks in effect that history is a

record of victories for the principle of unity in form and of plurality in effect. The wider the formal, the legal unity, the more intense becomes the local life. The defeat of secession diversified the South even more than the North, and the extension of the United States westward to the ocean rendered New England less exclusively a New Englandish homogeneity and created a unique New York, a New York clustering about Wall Street. When we have a United States of the World, doubtless localism will receive its last release—until we federate with the other planets. And yet there are those who fear internationalism as a menace to local independence and variety!

I am not, however, essaying a political treatise. The bearing of these remarks is upon the literary career of our country. They perhaps explain why the newspaper is the only genuinely popular form of literature we have achieved. The newspaper hasn't been ashamed of localism. It has revelled in it, perhaps wallowed is the word. I am not arguing that it is high-class literature, or for the most part good literature, even from its own standpoint. But it is permanently successful romance and drama, and that much can hardly be said for anything else in our literary lines.

The exception, as usual, proves the fact. There are journals of hundreds of thousands—nay, millions of circulation, which claim to be national, and which certainly are not local, even when they locate their stories in New York. This seeming exception is accounted for by the simple fact that localities in the United States are connected by railways and roads upon which a large number of passenger trains and motor cars are moving from one place to another. There is an immense population constantly in transit. For the time being they are not localists. But neither are they nationalists. They are just what they are—passengers. Hence the S——— E——— P——— and other journals expressly designed for this intermediate state of existence. Besides, the motor car fugitives must have advertisements and pictures of their cars. What becomes of all these periodicals? The man who answered this question would be the final authority on literature in America. Pending investigation, my hypothesis is that the brakeman, the Pullman porter, and those who clean out the street-cars inherit them.

Now the thing that makes these periodicals somewhat thin as literature (even if they provide exciting reading matter for those in a state of passage from one locality to another) is that they have to eliminate the local. They subsist for those who are going from one place and haven't as yet arrived at another. They cannot have depth or thickness—nothing but movement. Take all the localities of the United States and extract their greatest common divisor, and the result is of necessity a crackling surface. The bigger and more diversified the country, the thinner the net product.

Isn't this the explanation also of the "serious" novel, of its comparative absence and its comparative failure when it does come into existence? It aims at universality and attains technique. Walt Whitman exhausted the cataloguing of localities, and it hasn't occurred to the novel writer to dig down in some locality mentioned in the gazetteer till he strikes something. The writers of short stories have done something but they have hardly got beyond what is termed local color. But a locality exists in three dimensions. It has a background and also extensions. I haven't read Mary Wilkins's stories of New England life for many years, but I have only to think of them to recover the whole feel of the life. They are local with a faithfulness that is beyond admiration. But they lack background.

To invert a sentence of Mr. Oppenheim's: The persons in them are characters but they have no manners. For manners are a product of the interaction of characters and social environment, a social environment of which the background, the tradition, the descent of forces, is a part. And in Mary Wilkins's stories, as in the New England she depicts, the traditions are the characters. They have become engrained. There is no background with which they may interact. There are only other characters and the bleak hills and the woods and fields. All, people and nature alike, exist, as the philosophers say, under the form of eternity. Like Melchizedek, they have no ancestry or descent—save from God and the Devil. Bret Harte and Mark Twain have dimensions as well as color. But the former never attained adequate momentum for lack of a suitable audience. The latter had an audience when he came East but it was an alien one. He tamed himself lest he should shock it too much. His own, his real, locality could not be projected on the Eastern locality without reserve. He believed in his locality, but he believed in his audience more.

We are discovering that the locality is the only universal.

Even the suns and stars have their own times as well as their own places. This truth is first discovered in abstract form, or as an idea. Then, as Mr. Oppenheim points out in the February *Dial*, its discovery creates a new poetry—at least so I venture to paraphrase him. When the discovery sinks a little deeper, the novelist and dramatist will discover the localities of America as they are, and no one will need to worry about the future of American art. We have been too anxious to get away from home. Naturally that took us to Europe even though we fancied we were going around America. When we explore our neighborhood, its forces and not just its characters and color, we shall find what we sought. The beginning of the exploring spirit is in the awakening of criticism and of sympathy. Heaven knows there is enough to criticize. The desired art is not likely to linger long, for the sympathy will come as soon as we stay at home for a while. And in spite of the motor car, moving about is getting difficult. Things are getting filled up—and anyway we only move to another locality.

HOW REACTION HELPS

Is freedom possible only in periods of transition from one economic era to another? Does it flourish only because of the relaxation of old economic ties and endure only as long as the new economic regime is not consolidated? Was the democratic movement, the liberal movement—or whatever name it should go by—not a general and inherently steady development but merely a temporary episode attending the shifting of control from agrarian feudalism to privileged capitalism?

Five years ago such questions seemed absurd to the vast majority of people, especially to middle class people. Today these same questions, though of course in a much less abstract form, are entertained by a steadily increasing number of these same people. The thinking among them have always recognized in a way that eternal vigilance is the price of liberty. But they thought this vigilance should be exercised in keeping the ways open, in preventing and removing the obstacles by which losing interests strove to slow down on moving progress. Today they are asking whether the vigilance that secures freedom must not be exercised in altering the conditions which determine the direction of social forces. They are solicitous not about obstructions to democratic progress but about its foundations.

Consideration of the growing change of temper will throw some light on the question of the relation of reactionaryism to social progress. There is a general belief, supposedly justified by history, that in the long run every exhibition of reactionary conservatism (such as we have experienced in America since the 11th of November 1918) ends by strengthening the cause of progress. But the means by which the reactionary helps do not seem to have received analysis. If the technique of the process were known possibly it would cease to be true that nothing is ever

[First published in *New Republic* 24 (1920): 21–22. Republished in *Characters and Events*, ed. Joseph Ratner (New York: Henry Holt and Co., 1929), 2:815–19.]

learned from history. Certainly it is not instructive to say that a
social movement to one extreme always ends by calling out a
swing of the pendulum in the other direction, that there are radical as well as conservative reactions. The question is one of specific fact. How does the reactionary release progressive forces?

The question can be answered only by careful historic study
guided by knowledge of human psychology. But a hypothesis may
be ventured. The reactionary helps by clarifying the issue, by revealing obscure facts, uncovering hidden forces. History itself
gives the lie to the idea that oppression by itself arouses an effective love of liberty. The worst thing about any form of enslavement is that it tends to make the oppressed content in their enslavement. It dulls perception of the possibility of another state of
affairs and it destroys the energy which is required to effect
change. To apply to the relation of oppression and freedom in politics the physical law of equal action and reaction is to delude ourselves with foolish magical formulae. Reactionaryism helps only
when it awakens men's minds, only when it makes them see
things they didn't see before, only when it focusses attention. The
cause of the reactionary depends upon the immense inertia of
human stupidity. But the stupidity of the reactionary is that at
critical junctures he strives to entrench himself by doing things
which force attention to facts that he has every interest in keeping concealed; by doing things which crystalize forces that work
in his behalf only as long as they remain diffused and obscure.

The madness with which the gods afflict those whom they
would destroy is precisely the temptation to use a temporary possession of strategic power so as to make that power permanent.
In this effort they necessarily exaggerate evils that had existed
previously but that were tolerated in part because they were not
perceptible and in part because they had not as yet become intolerable. The excess, the exaggeration, makes the evil obvious, conspicuous, and it adds force to old and neglected criticism by leading men to believe that the evil had always been there in the same
intense form which it assumes under the exaggeration of the moment.

The terms of the peace settlement, for example, are such as
to emphasize the desire of Great Britain to obtain a monopoly of
oil, and of France to keep Germany in permanent industrial subjection. Such things lie so obviously upon the surface as to con-

vince multitudes of what they never had believed—that the main
if not the sole cause of the war was greed for economic supremacy, and that most of the talk about justice and self-determination
was bunk. The multitude is in no condition to discriminate. It
does not reflect that the outcome of the war exaggerated the significance of certain economic factors, and put a few men in a
position where they could make an excessive unrelieved assertion
of this exaggeration. The outcome is read back into the antecedent state of things, and it is concluded that these forces were
working in the same intensified fashion all the time.

They were indeed working and working powerfully. But it
was a condition of their continued working that they should not
be intense and concentrated, but diffused and thus bound up
with many genuinely idealistic factors. Their exaggeration con-
denses, concentrates, crystalizes them, and in so doing strips
them bare of all the humane associations which were indispensable to their smooth working. At the same time millions are induced to believe the worst that radical extremists had ever said
about the economic determination of society. The reactionary, not
the socialistic critic, has supplied the object lesson in the alliance
of politics with privileged control of land and its natural resources.

Another way in which the reactionary helps is by the advertising he gratuitously gives radicalism. This enables us to understand why terms given in objurgation and scorn become the honored names of parties and movements. It is not the fault of
American reactionaries that an actual Bolshevism has not been
created by them. If conditions had been at all propitious the myth
of the extraordinary power and unceasing activity of extreme
Reds would have ended in a fact. Where there is such fear, it is
only proper that there should be something to be afraid of. As it
is, the effort to render everything that departs from laudatory acceptance of existing capitalism into a dangerous and sinister radicalism can only terminate in making radicalism respectable and
honorable. Men of honesty and spirit who are at all dissatisfied
with the existing regime will be ashamed of calling themselves
anything else. Already there are signs that liberalism will be es-
chewed as a milk and water term. At the close of every vehement
reactionary movement in history, the commonplaces of thought
and discussion which form the plane of action have moved to the
left. Vice is not the only thing that becomes tolerable through

familiarity. If the reactionary were wise he would show confidence in his strength by leaving the ideas he dislikes in a region of vague and unmentionable mystery. Too much ghost talk creates a desire to see ghosts, until finally the men are willing to pay good money to see the spirits which had once been the source of panicky terrors.

The reactionary also serves by forcing the radical to abandon the cloudland of dreams and come to closer grip with realities. As long as "scientific" socialism lived upon the revolutionary formulae of '48 it was either 75 years behind or ahead of the times. It certainly was not in touch with them in America. But when the Hessians of reactionary capitalism discovered these rhetorical flourishes and took them seriously enough to send men to jail for indulging in them, it was a signal that it was no longer necessary to take refuge in millennial dreams. The current facts of particular economic transformation were substituted for prophetic hopes of a universal transformation. Dream psychology is always evidence of impotence. But the dreamer who is prodded into wakefulness faces the facts that enter into action.

For the violence of the reactionary shows prescience of actual tendencies. It reveals the movement of actual forces. As long as socialism accepted the Marxian doctrine of a sudden revolution which was to be the result of the universal misery, poverty and weakness of the laborer, it was practically negligible. Every such doctrine expresses a compensatory psychology. It is the proof of weakness. Any real "revolution" will proceed from strength, from increased strength of capacity and position. The war gave labor precisely this access of strength. Yet it might, in the United States at least, have remained largely unconscious and unconcentrated, ready to be dissipated with the inevitable oncoming of hard times and unemployment, if the reactionary had not forced its recognition. His irrational violence of fear revealed the strength that was there. Labor can never entirely forget the instruction it has received as to its potential power. It is the reactionary who has turned prophet, and his prophecy is based on a frightened perception of the actual movement of forces. Thus he helps. He spreads enlightenment by his endeavors to establish obscurantism. There is just one passing period in which he succeeds. There is a stage of development in which a vague and mysterious feeling of uncertain terror seizes the populace. During this time the reactionary has things all his own way. Deceived by this success, his movements become noisy; his intentions obvious. He attracts attention away from the terror to himself. The twilight clears and objects are again seen in their natural proportions. Discussion and free speech are suppressed. But the means taken to suppress them become more enlightening than normal discussion and free speech would have been. Timid souls have been cowed into a permanent acquiescence; but they never counted anyway except as a passive weight. Suppression of truth and circulation of lies permanently twisted some facts. But the loss as far as progress is concerned is more than made up for by the revelation of motives and objects through which the reactionary permanently weakened his power. Thus he helps.

THE SEQUEL OF THE STUDENT REVOLT

As I write, in late November, the Sino-Japanese fracas in Foo-chow (in which several Chinese students lost their lives and in consequence of which the Japanese landed marines who have stationed themselves in the Chinese city as well as in the foreign concession), is inflaming public feeling in China as it has not been stirred since last May. The students are again engaging in public demonstrations, and are joining with Chinese Chambers of Commerce in demanding that the people cease all social and economic intercourse with the Japanese until the latter change their course. The waning boycott is revived. It is demanded that the government declare a policy of economic non-intercourse and an embargo on imports and exports, until Japan has radically altered its policies. It is impossible to forecast the outcome. Pessimists declare that Japan is taking advantage of the situation to bring Fukien directly within her sphere of influence—an intention expressed in the Twenty-one Demands, but temporarily held in abeyance.

There are no optimists in China in the extreme sense, but the more hopeful assert that in the present state of affairs, with the Shantung question unsettled, the Consortium in its bearing upon Manchuria under discussion, and with an acute Siberian trouble on hand, the Japanese government is not looking for more trouble—especially with the eyes of the world in general upon it, and those of the American Senate in particular. Pessimists counter with the remark that it is precisely the growing influence and prestige of the United States in China that has forced the hand of the Japanese militarist expansionists to take an aggressive step, and face the world with a fait accompli; that Japan will make use of the difficulty to demand that the Chinese government put a stop, once for all, to the boycott movement; that Japanese troops, once having obtained a footing, will never be with-

[First published in *New Republic* 21 (1920): 380–82.]

drawn, and that Fukien is now to go the way of Manchuria and Shantung.

Perhaps the most sinister feature is the semi-official report from Tokyo that the disturbance was deliberately started by the Chinese in order to force the Japanese to land troops, and thereby increase the prejudice against them now existing throughout the world. Official reports from the American consulate agree with Chinese reports that unarmed Chinese students were attacked by armed Japanese and Formosans under conditions which give an appearance of a planned and organized movement with at least the connivance of local Japanese authorities. Judging from the past, the chief outcome will not be immediately to establish Japan in the Province of Fukien, but to strengthen her hands in other controversies by injecting an element to be reckoned with in making a "compromise." Such is Oriental diplomacy. The gathering, as I write, of ten thousand Pekingese students for a demonstration, after a period of quiescence, gives a good opportunity to take stock of what the Student Movement has accomplished in the six months of its existence.

As an immediate political movement it has accomplished nothing beyond preventing the signing of the Peace Treaty by China. The reasons for the relative political failure are not hard to see in retrospect, however difficult it was to perceive them in the excitement and stir of last May and June. The youth and inexperience of the students; the fear of some excess which would undo what had been effected; the fear in Peking, where the movement began, that government officials (who regarded the movement not as patriotic but as a pestilential disturbance headed toward Bolshevism) would make demonstrations an excuse for abolishing the University and the Higher Schools that are the centres of liberal thought; the difficulty in maintaining continuous organized cooperation with the mercantile guilds; the natural waning of enthusiasm when the crisis was past—all these things entered in.

But it would be a great mistake to think the movement died. The active current was diverted from breaking against the political and militaristic dam. It was drawn into a multitude of side streams and is now irrigating the intellectual and industrial soil of China. In Canton and Foochow the economic boycott has been active; in Tientsin, the political ferment has retained its vitality.

Otherwise the students' organizations have gone into popular
education, social and philanthropic service and vigorous intellectual discussion. China has never been anything but apathetic towards governmental questions. The Student Revolt marked a
temporary exception only in appearance. The hopelessness of the
political muddle, with corrupt officials and provincial military
governors in real control, is enough to turn the youth away from
direct politics. In addition a universal feeling operates that the
comparative failure of the Revolution is due to the fact that political change far outran intellectual and moral preparation; that political revolution was formal and external; that an intellectual
revolution is required before the nominal governmental revolution can be cashed in. Patriotism in China has centered about the
maintenance of the existence of the nation against external
aggression. The Student Revolt holds that national existence can
best be secured by building up China from within, by spreading
a democratic education, raising the standard of living, improving
industries and relieving poverty.

The external phase of the movement centres in the creation
of new schools supported and taught by the students, schools for
children and adults; popular lectures and direct "social service"
movements; cooperation with shops to supply technical advice
and expert assistance in improving old processes and introducing
new arts. These activities protect the intellectual movement in
getting away from all practical affairs, in getting away from politics, and guarantee it against becoming a cultural and literary
side-show.

What is termed the literary revolution was under way before
the Student Revolt. It aimed at a reform of the language used in
books, magazines, newspapers, and public discussion. The outsider will jump to the conclusion that this means an attempt to
encourage a phonetic substitute for ideographic characters. Not
at all. There is a movement to supplement ideographs with phonetic signs to show their pronunciation, the aim being quite as
much to standardize pronunciation as to make it easier to learn to
read. But this movement arouses no such interest and excitement
as the literary revolution. The latter is an attempt to make the
spoken language the standard language for print. Literary Chinese
is as far away from the vernacular as Latin is from English, perhaps further. It is the speech of two thousand years ago, adorned

and frozen. To learn it is to learn another language. The reformers were actuated by the practical impossibility of making education really universal when in addition to the difficulties of mastering the ideographs, children in the elementary schools are compelled to get their education in terms of a foreign language. They are actuated even more by the belief that it was not possible to develop a literature which shall express the life of today unless the spoken language, the language of the people, is used. Apart from employing and enriching the vulgar tongue, it is not possible to develop general discussion of the issues of today, social, moral, economic.

Fortunately the new movement was "advertised by its loving enemies." The literary classicists saw in it the deathblow to the old moral classics, upon which China was built. They argued that the history of China is the history of its literary classics. Its unity resides in acceptance of the moral traditions they embody. To neglect them is to destroy China. The fight merged into one between conservatives and liberals in general, between the representatives of the old traditions and the representatives of western ideas and democratic institutions. Young China rallied as one man to the support of the literary revolution. It is stated that whereas two years ago there were but one or two tentative journals in the vulgar tongue, today there are over three hundred. Since last May the students have started score upon score of journals, all in the spoken tongue and all discussing matters in words that can be understood by the common man. In the columns of one of the older Chinese dailies in Peking there has lately been a discussion carried on by voluntary correspondents about a single particle that is used freely in colloquial speech—a discussion already running into ten thousands of words.

Those who know what the change from a learned language to the vernacular meant for the transition from medieval to modern Europe will not despise this linguistic sign of social change. It is more important by far than the adoption of a new constitution. Conservatism in China is not native or natural. It is largely the product of an inelastic system of memoriter education. This education has its roots in the use of a dead language as the medium of instruction. A national education conference held in October last passed a resolution in favor of having all text-books hereafter composed in the colloquial language. After this course

has been followed for a generation, the judicious historian may
see in it an event of greater importance than the downfall of the
Manchu dynasty.

According to published summaries, social questions are up-
permost in the new press. Eloquent testimony to the new-found
unity of the world is seen in the amount of discussion devoted to
economics and labor questions, which as yet do not exist in any
acute form in China itself. Although Marx is hardly more perti-
nent to the present industrial situation in China than Plato, he is
translated and much discussed. All the new 'isms are discussed.
Ideal anarchism has many followers partly because of the historic
Chinese contempt for government, partly because of the influence of French returned students who came in contact with com-
munistic ideas in Paris. A friend who made a careful study of
some fifty of the students' papers says that their first trait is the
question mark, and the second is the demand for complete freedom of speech in order that answers may be found for the questions.

In a country where belief has been both authoritatively dogmatic and complacent, the rage for questioning is the omen of a
new epoch. More than westerners realize, the interest of the Orient in the west has centered in the material progress of Europe
and America, in machines for industry and war. There was no
belief that the west was superior in other respects. Only within
the last year or two has the idea become general that western
ideas and modes of thought are more important than western
battle-ships and steam-engines. This belief is concentrated in the
intellectual side of the Student Movement, though it shows itself
not in any great zeal for western ideas, as such, but in a desire for
such knowledge of them as will facilitate discussion and criticism
of typical Chinese creeds and institutions. One incident out of a
multitude must suffice to show that the demand for freedom of
thought and speech has a definite practical significance. China
took over from Japan the law for assemblies which Japan had
taken over from Germany. A discussion club applied to the Peking
police authorities for a permit, stating that the object was consideration of the newer currents of world thought. The authorities
refused the permit on the ground that newer currents must mean
Bolshevism, anarchism and communism and that consideration
of such topics was dangerous.

As is always the case, official opposition stimulates the movement of ideas. The menace of autocracy from within and without gives edge and fire to the hunger for new ideas. The eagerness grows for knowledge of the thought of liberal western countries in just the degree in which the powers near at hand in Tokyo and Peking seem to symbolize an intellectual creed which the world has outgrown. The more the so-called political revolution exhibits itself as a failure, the more active is the demand for an intellectual revolution which will make some future political revolution a reality. The thing that time makes stand out most in the Student Revolt is its spontaneity. The students met discouragement on all sides. Even their teachers and advisers among the returned students from America were inclined at first to wet-blanket their ardor. Its spontaneity is the proof of its genuine and inevitable nature. When most political in its outward expression, it was not a political movement. It was the manifestation of a new consciousness, an intellectual awakening in the young men and young women who through their schooling had been aroused to the necessity of a new order of belief, a new method of thinking. The movement is secure no matter how much its outward forms may alter or crumble.

SHANTUNG, AS SEEN FROM WITHIN

I

American apologists for that part of the Peace Treaty which relates to China have the advantage of the illusions of distance. Most of the arguments seem strange to anyone who lives in China even for a few months. He finds the Japanese on the spot using the old saying about territory consecrated by treasure spent and blood shed. He reads in Japanese papers and hears from moderately liberal Japanese that Japan must protect China as well as Japan, against herself, against her own weak or corrupt government, by keeping control of Shantung to prevent China from again alienating that territory to some other power.

The history of European aggression in China gives this argument great force among the Japanese, who for the most part know nothing more about what actually goes on in China than they used to know about Korean conditions. These considerations, together with the immense expectations raised among the Japanese during the war concerning their coming domination of the Far East and the unswerving demand of excited public opinion in Japan during the Versailles Conference for the settlement that actually resulted, give an ironic turn to the statement so often made that Japan may be trusted to carry out her promises. Yes, one is often tempted to say, that is precisely what China fears, that Japan will carry out her promises, for then China is doomed. To one who knows the history of foreign aggression in China, especially the technique of conquest by railway and finance, the irony of promising to keep economic rights while returning sovereignty lies so on the surface that it is hardly irony. China might as well be offered Kant's *Critique of Pure Reason* on a silver plat-

[First published in *New Republic* 21 (1920): 12–17. Revised and republished in *China, Japan and the U.S.A.* (New York: Republic Publishing Co., 1921), pp. 9–21.]

ter as sovereignty under such conditions. The latter is equally metaphysical.

A visit to Shantung and a short residence in its capital city, Tsinan, made the conclusions, which so far as I know every foreigner in China has arrived at, a living thing. It gave a vivid picture of the many and intimate ways in which economic and political rights are inextricably entangled together. It made one realize afresh that only a President who kept himself innocent of any knowledge of secret treaties during the war, could be naïve enough to believe that the promise to return complete sovereignty retaining *only* economic rights is a satisfactory solution. It threw fresh light upon the contention that at most and at worst Japan had only taken over German rights, and that since we had acquiesced in the latter's arrogations we had no call to make a fuss about Japan. It revealed the hollowness of the claim that pro-Chinese propaganda had wilfully misled Americans into confusing the few hundred square miles around the port of Tsing-tao with the Province of Shantung with its thirty millions of Chinese population.

As for the comparison of Germany and Japan one might suppose that the objects for which America nominally entered the war had made, in any case, a difference. But aside from this consideration, the Germans exclusively employed Chinese in the railway shops and for all the minor positions on the railway itself. The railway guards (the difference between police and soldiers is nominal in China) were all Chinese, the Germans merely training them. As soon as Japan invaded Shantung and took over the railway, Chinese workmen and Chinese military guards were at once dismissed and Japanese imported to take their places. Tsinan-fu, the inland terminus of the ex-German railway, is over two hundred miles from Tsing-tao. When the Japanese took over the German railway business office, they at once built barracks, and today there are several hundred soldiers still there—where Germany kept none. Since the armistice even, Japan has erected a powerful military wireless within the grounds of the garrison, against of course the unavailing protest of Chinese authorities. No foreigner can be found who will state that Germany used her ownership of port and railway to discriminate against other nations. No Chinese can be found who will claim that this ownership was used to force the Chinese out of business, or to extend

German economic rights beyond those definitely assigned her by treaty. Common sense should also teach even the highest paid propagandist in America that there is, from the standpoint of China, an immense distinction between a national menace located half way around the globe, and one within two days' sail over an inland sea absolutely controlled by a foreign navy, especially as the remote nation has no other foothold and the nearby one already dominates additional territory of enormous strategic and economic value—namely, Manchuria.

These facts bear upon the shadowy distinction between the Tsing-tao and the Shantung claim, as well as upon the solid distinction between German and Japanese occupancy. If there still seemed to be a thin wall between Japanese possession of the port of Tsing-tao and usurpation of Shantung, it was enough to stop off the train in Tsinan-fu to see the wall crumble. For the Japanese wireless and the barracks of the army of occupation are the first things that greet your eyes. Within a few hundred feet of the railway that connects Shanghai, via the important centre of Tientsin, with the capital, Peking, you see Japanese soldiers on the nominally Chinese street, guarding their barracks. Then you learn that if you travel upon the ex-German railway towards Tsing-tao, you are ordered to show your passport as if you were entering a foreign country. And as you travel along the road (remembering that you are over two hundred miles from Tsing-tao) you find Japanese soldiers at every station, and several garrisons and barracks at important towns on the line. Then you realize that at the shortest possible notice, Japan could cut all communications between southern China (together with the rich Yangtze region) and the capital, and with the aid of the Southern Manchurian Railway at the north of the capital, hold the entire coast and descend at its good pleasure upon Peking.

You are then prepared to learn from eye-witnesses that when Japan made its Twenty-one Demands upon China, machine guns were actually in position at strategic points, throughout Shantung, with trenches dug and sandbags placed. You know that the Japanese liberal spoke the truth, who told you, after a visit to China and return to protest against the action of his government, that the Japanese already had such a military hold upon China that they could control the country within a week, after a minimum of fighting, if war should arise. You also realize the efficiency of official control of information and domestic propaganda as you recall that he also told you that these things were true at the time of his visit, under the Terauchi cabinet, but had been completely reversed by the present Hara ministry. For I have yet to find a single foreigner or Chinese who is conscious of any difference of policy, save as the end of the war has forced the necessity of more caution, since other nations can now look China-wards as they could not during the war.

An American can get an idea of the realities of the present situation if he imagines a foreign garrison and military wireless in Wilmington, with a railway from that point to a fortified sea-port controlled by the foreign power, at which the foreign nation can land, without resistance, troops as fast as they can be transported, and with bases of supply, munitions, food, uniforms, etc., already located at Wilmington, at the sea-port and several places along the line. Reverse the directions from south to north, and Wilmington will stand for Tsinan-fu, Shanghai for New York, Nanking for Philadelphia with Peking standing for the seat of government at Washington, and Tientsin for Baltimore. Suppose in addition that the Pennsylvania road is the sole means of communication between Washington and the chief commercial and industrial centres, and you have the framework of the Shantung picture as it presents itself daily to the inhabitants of China. Upon second thought, however, the parallel is not quite accurate. You have to add that the same foreign nation controls also all coast communications from, say, Raleigh southwards, with railway lines both to the nearby coast and to New Orleans. For (still reversing directions) this corresponds to the position of Imperial Japan in Manchuria with its railways to Dairen and through Korea to a port twelve hours sail from a great military centre in Japan proper. These are not remote possibilities nor vague prognostications. They are accomplished facts.

Yet the facts give *only* the framework of the picture. What is actually going on within Shantung? One of the demands of the "postponed" group of the Twenty-one Demands was that Japan should supply military and police advisers to China. They are not so much postponed but that Japan enforced specific concessions from China during the war by diplomatic threats to reintroduce their discussion, or so postponed that Japanese advisers are not already installed in the police headquarters of the city of Tsinan,

the capital city of Shantung of three hundred thousand population where the Provincial Assembly meets and all the Provincial
officials reside. Within recent months the Japanese consul has
taken a company of armed soldiers with him when he visited the
Provincial Governor to make certain demands upon him, the visit
being punctuated by an ostentatious surrounding of the Governor's yamen by these troops. Within the past few weeks, two
hundred cavalry came to Tsinan and remained there while Japanese officials demanded of the Governor drastic measures to suppress the boycott, while it was threatened to send Japanese troops
to police the foreign settlement if the demand was not heeded.

A former consul was indiscreet enough to put into writing
that if the Chinese Governor did not stop the boycott and the students' movement by force if need be, he would take matters into
his own hands. The chief tangible charge he brought against the
Chinese as a basis of his demand for "protection" was that
Chinese store-keepers actually refused to accept Japanese money
in payment for goods, not ordinary Japanese money at that, but
the military notes with which, so as to save drain upon the bullion
reserves, the army of occupation is paid. And all this, be it remembered, is more than two hundred miles from Tsing-tao and from
eight to twelve months after the armistice. Today's paper reports
a visit of Japanese to the Governor to inform him that unless he
should prevent a private theatrical performance from being given
in Tsinan by the students, they would send their own forces into
the settlement to protect themselves. And the utmost they might
need protection from, was that the students were to give some
plays designed to foster the boycott!

Japanese troops overran the Province before they made any
serious attempt to capture Tsing-tao. It is only a slight exaggeration to say that they "took" the Chinese Tsinan before they took
the German Tsing-tao. Propaganda in America has justified this
act on the ground that a German railway to the rear of Japanese
forces would have been a menace. As there were no troops but
only legal and diplomatic papers with which to attack the Japanese, it is a fair inference that the "menace" was located in Versailles rather than in Shantung, and concerned the danger of
Chinese control of their own territory. Chinese have been arrested
by Japanese gendarmes in Tsinan and subjected to a torturing

third degree of the kind that Korea has made sickeningly familiar. The Japanese claim that the injuries were received while the men were resisting arrest. Considering that there was no more legal ground for arrest than there would be if Japanese police arrested Americans in New York, almost anybody but the pacifist Chinese certainly would have resisted. But official hospital reports testify to bayonet wounds and the marks of flogging. In the interior where the Japanese had been disconcerted by the student propaganda they raided a High School, seized a school boy at random, and took him to a distant point and kept him locked up several days. When the Japanese consul at Tsinan was visited by Chinese officials in protest against these illegal arrests, the consul disclaimed all jurisdiction. The matter, he said, was wholly in the hands of the military authorities in Tsing-tao. His disclaimer was emphasized by the fact that some of the kidnapped Chinese were taken to Tsing-tao for "trial."

The matter of economic rights in relation to political domination will be discussed in part two of this article. It is no pleasure for one with many warm friends in Japan, who has a great admiration for the Japanese people as distinct from the ruling military and bureaucratic class, to report such facts as have been stated. One might almost say, one might positively say from the standpoint of Japan itself, that the worst thing that can be charged against the policy of Japan in China for the last six years is its immeasurable stupidity. No nation has ever misjudged the national psychology of another people as Japan has that of China. The alienation of China is widespread, deep, bitter. Even the most pessimistic of the Chinese who think that China is to undergo a complete economic and political domination by Japan do not think it can possibly last, even without outside intervention, more than half a century at most.

Today, at the beginning of a new year (1920), the boycott is much more complete and efficient than in the most tense days of last summer. Unfortunately, the Japanese policy seems to be under a truly Greek fate which drives it on. Concessions that would have produced a revulsion of feeling in favor of Japan a year ago will now merely salve the surface of the wound. What would have been welcomed even eight months ago would now be received with contempt. There is but one way in which Japan can now restore herself. It is nothing less than complete withdrawal from Shantung, with possibly a strictly commercial concession at Tsing-tao and a real, not a Manchurian, Open Door.

According to the Japanese-owned newspapers published in Tsinan, the Japanese military commander in Tsing-tao recently made a speech to visiting journalists from Tokyo in which he said:

The suspicions of China cannot now be allayed merely by repeating that we have no territorial ambitions in China. We must attain complete economic domination of the Far East. But if Sino-Japanese relations do not improve, some third party will reap the benefit. Japanese residing in China incur the hatred of the Chinese. For they regard themselves as the proud citizens of a conquering country. When the Japanese go into partnership with the Chinese they manage in the greater number of cases to have the profits accrue to themselves. If friendship between China and Japan is to depend wholly upon the government it will come to nothing. Diplomatists, soldiers, merchants, journalists should repent the past. The change must be complete.

But it will not be complete until the Japanese withdraw from Shantung leaving their nationals there upon the footing of other foreigners in China.

II

In discussing the return to China by Japan of a metaphysical sovereignty while economic rights are retained, I shall not repeat the details of German treaty rights as to the railway and the mines. The reader is assumed to be familiar with those facts. The German seizure was outrageous. It was a flagrant case of Might making Right. As von Buelow cynically but frankly told the Reichstag, while Germany did not intend to partition China, she also did not intend to be the passenger left behind in the station when the train started. Germany had the excuse of prior European aggressions, and in turn her usurpation was the precedent for further foreign rape. If judgments are made on a comparative basis, Japan is entitled to all of the white-washing that can be derived from the provocations of European imperialistic powers, including those that in domestic policy are democratic. And every fairminded person will recognize that, leaving China out of the reckoning, Japan's proximity to China gives her aggressions the color of self-defence in a way that cannot be urged in behalf of any European power.

It is possible to look at European aggressions in, say, Africa as incidents of a colonization movement. But no foreign policy in Asia can shelter itself behind any colonization plea. For continental Asia is, for practical purposes, India and China, representing two of the oldest civilizations of the globe and presenting two of its densest populations. If there is any such thing in truth as a philosophy of history with its own inner and inevitable logic, one may well shudder to think of what the closing acts of the drama of the intercourse of the West and East are to be. In any case, and with whatever comfort may be derived from the fact that the American continents have not taken part in the aggression and hence may act as a mediator to avert the final tragedy, residence in China forces upon one the realization that Asia is, after all, a large figure in the future reckoning of history. Asia is really here after all. It is not simply a symbol in western algebraic balances of trade. And in the future, so to speak, it is going to be even more here, with its awakened national consciousness of about half the population of the whole globe.

Let the agreements of France and Great Britain made with Japan during the war stand for the measure of western consciousness of the reality of a small part of Asia, a consciousness generated by the patriotism of Japan backed by its powerful army and navy. The same agreement measures western unconsciousness of the reality of that part of Asia which lies within the confines of China. An even better measure of western unconsciousness may be found perhaps in such a trifling incident as this:—An English friend long resident in Shantung told me of writing indignantly home concerning the British part in the Shantung settlement. The reply came, complacently stating that Japanese ships did so much in the war that the Allies could not properly refuse to recognize Japan's claims. The secret agreements themselves hardly speak as eloquently for the absence of China from the average western consciousness. In saying that China and Asia are to be enormously significant figures in future reckonings, the spectre of a military Yellow Peril is not meant nor even the more credible spectre of an industrial Yellow Peril. But Asia has come to consciousness, and her consciousness of herself will soon be such a massive and persistent thing that it will force itself upon the re-

luctant consciousness of the west, and lie heavily upon its conscience. And for this fact, China and the western world are in-
debted to Japan.

These remarks are more relevant to a consideration of the
relationship of economic and political rights in Shantung than
they perhaps seem. For a moment's reflection will call to mind
that all political foreign aggression in China has been carried out
for commercial and financial ends, and usually upon some economic pretext. As to the immediate part played by Japan in bringing about a consciousness which will from the present time completely change the relations of the western powers to China, let
one little story testify. Some representatives of an English mis-
sionary board were making a tour of inspection through China.
They went into an interior town in Shantung. They were received
with extraordinary cordiality by the entire population. Some time
afterwards some of their accompanying friends returned to the
village and were received with equally surprising coldness. It
came out upon inquiry that the inhabitants had first been moved
by the rumor that these people were sent by the British government to secure the removal of the Japanese. Later they were
moved by indignation that they had been disappointed.

It takes no forcing to see a symbol in this incident. Part of it
stands for the almost incredible ignorance which has rendered
China so impotent nationally speaking. The other part of it stands
for the new spirit which has been aroused even among the common people in remote districts. Those who fear, or who pretend
to fear, a new Boxer movement, or a definite general anti-foreign
movement, are, I think, mistaken. The new consciousness goes
much deeper. Foreign policies that fail to take it into account and
that think that relations with China can be conducted upon the
old basis will find this new consciousness obtruding in the most
unexpected and perplexing ways.

One might fairly say, still speaking comparatively, that it is
part of the bad luck of Japan that her proximity to China, and the
opportunity the war gave her to outdo the aggressions of European powers, have made her the first victim of this disconcerting
change. Whatever the motives of the American Senators in completely disassociating the United States from the peace settlement as regards China, their action is a permanent asset to
China, not only in respect to Japan but with respect to all Chinese

foreign relations. Just before our visit to Tsinan, the Shantung Provincial Assembly had passed a resolution of thanks to the American Senate. More significant is the fact that they passed another resolution to be cabled to the English Parliament, calling attention to the action of the American Senate and inviting similar action. China in general and Shantung in particular feels the reenforcement of an external approval. With this duplication, its national consciousness has as it were solidified. Japan is simply the first object to be affected.

The concrete working out of economic rights in Shantung will be illustrated by a single case which will have to stand as typical. Po-shan is an interior mining village. The mines were not part of the German booty; they were Chinese owned. The Germans, whatever their ulterior aims, had made no attempt at dispossessing the Chinese. The mines, however, are at the end of a branch line of the new Japanese owned railway—owned by the government, not by a private corporation, and guarded by Japanese soldiers. Of the forty mines, the Japanese have worked their way, in only four years, into all but four. Different methods are used. The simplest is, of course, discrimination in the use of the railway for shipping. Downright refusal to furnish cars while competitors who accepted Japanese partners got them, is one method. Another more elaborate method is to send but one car when a large number is asked for, and then when it is too late to use cars, send the whole number asked for or even more, and then charge a large sum for demurrage in spite of the fact the mine no longer wants them or has cancelled the order. Redress there is none.

Tsinan has no special foreign concessions. It is, however, a "treaty port" where nationals of all friendly powers can do business. But Po-shan is not even a treaty port. Legally speaking no foreigner can lease land or carry on any business there. Yet the Japanese have forced a settlement as large in area as the entire foreign settlement in the much larger town of Tsinan. A Chinese refused to lease land where the Japanese wished to relocate their railway station. Nothing happened to him directly. But merchants could not get shipping space, or receive goods by rail. Some of them were beaten up by thugs. After a time, they used their influence with their compatriot to lease his land. Immediately the persecutions ceased. Not all the land has been secured by threats or coercion; some has been leased directly by Chinese moved by high prices, in spite of the absence of any legal sanction. In addition, the Japanese have obtained control of the electric light works and some pottery factories, etc.

Now even admitting that this is typical of the methods by which the Japanese plant themselves, a natural American reaction would be to say that, after all, the country is built up industrially by these enterprises, and that though the rights of some individuals may have been violated, there is nothing to make a national, much less an international fuss about. More or less unconsciously we translate foreign incidents into terms of our own experience and environment, and thus miss the entire point. Since America was largely developed by foreign capital to our own economic benefit and without political encroachments, we lazily suppose some such separation of the economic and political to be possible in China. But it must be remembered that China is not an open country. Foreigners can lease land, carry on business, and manufacture only in accord with express treaty agreements. There are no such agreements in the cases typified by the Po-shan incident. We may profoundly disagree with the closed economic policy of China, or we may believe that under existing circumstances it represents the part of prudence for her. That makes no difference. *Given the frequent occurrence of such economic invasions, with the backing of soldiers of the Imperial Army, with the overt aid of the Imperial Railway, and with the refusal of Imperial officials to intervene, there is clear evidence of the attitude and intention of the Japanese government in Shantung.*

Because the population of Shantung is directly confronted with an immense amount of just such evidence, it cannot take seriously the professions of vague diplomatic utterances. What foreign nation is going to intervene to enforce Chinese rights in such a case as Po-shan? Which one is going effectively to call the attention of Japan to such evidences of its failure to carry out its promise? Yet the accumulation of precisely such seemingly petty incidents, and not any single dramatic great wrong, will secure Japan's economic and political domination of Shantung. It is for this reason that foreigners resident in Shantung, no matter in what part, say that they see no sign whatever that Japan is going to get out; that, on the contrary, everything points to a determination to consolidate her position. How long ago was the Portsmouth Treaty signed, and what were its nominal pledges about evacuation of Manchurian territory?

Not a month will pass without something happening which will give a pretext for delay, and for making the surrender of Shantung conditional upon this, that and the other thing. Meantime the penetration of Shantung by means of railway discrimination, railway military guards, continual nibblings here and there, will be going on. It would make the chapter too long to speak of the part played by manipulation of finance in achieving this process of attrition of sovereignty. Two incidents must suffice. During the war, Japanese traders with the connivance of their government gathered up immense amounts of copper cash from Shantung and shipped it to Japan against the protests of the Chinese government. What does sovereignty amount to when a country cannot control even its own currency system? In Manchuria the Japanese have forced the introduction of several hundred million dollars of paper currency, nominally, of course, based on a gold reserve. These notes are redeemable, however, only in Japan proper. And there is a law in Japan forbidding the exportation of gold. And there you are.

Japan itself has recently afforded an object lesson in the actual connection of economic and political rights in China. It is so beautifully complete a demonstration that it was surely unconscious. Within the last two weeks, Mr. Obata, the Japanese minister in Peking, has waited upon the government with a memorandum saying that the Foochow incident was the culminating result of the boycott; that if the boycott continues, a series of such incidents is to be apprehended, saying that the situation has become "intolerable" for Japan, and disavowing all responsibility for further consequences unless the government makes a serious effort to stop the boycott. Japan then immediately makes certain specific demands. China must stop the circulation of handbills, the holding of meetings to urge the boycott, the destruction of Japanese goods that have become Chinese property—none have been destroyed that are Japanese owned. Volumes could not say more as to the real conception of Japan of the connection between the economic and the political relations of the two countries. Surely the pale ghost of "Sovereignty" smiled ironically as he read this official note. President Wilson after having made in the case of Shantung a sharp and complete separation of economic and political rights, also said that a nation boycotted is within sight of surrender. Disassociation of words from acts has gone so far in his case that he will hardly be able to see the meaning of Mr. Obata's communication. The American sense of humor and fair-play may however be counted upon to get its point.

THE NEW LEAVEN IN CHINESE POLITICS

To the student of political and social development, China presents a most exciting intellectual situation. He has read in books the account of the slow evolution of law and orderly governmental institutions. He finds in China an object lesson in what he has read. We take for granted the existence of government as an agency for enforcing justice between men and for protecting personal rights. We depend upon regular and orderly legal and judicial procedure to settle disputes as we take for granted the atmosphere we breathe. In China life goes on practically without such support and guarantees. And yet in the ordinary life of the people peace and order reign.

If you read the books written about China, you find the Chinese often spoken of as the "most law-abiding people in the world." Struck by this fact, the traveler often neglects to go behind it. He fails to note that this law-abidingness constantly shows itself in contempt for everything that we in the West associate with law, that it goes on largely without courts, without legal and judicial forms and officers; that, in fact, the Chinese regularly do what the West regards as the essence of lawlessness—enforce the law through private agencies and arrangements. In many things the one who is regarded as breaking the real law, the controlling custom, is the one who appeals to the "law"—that is, to governmental agencies and officers. A few incidents of recent history may illustrate the point.

The Peking Government University students started the agitation last May which grew into that organized movement which in the end compelled the dismissal of some pro-Japanese members of the cabinet and forced the refusal to sign the peace treaty. The movement started with a procession. The parade passed by the house of an offensive member who was ordinarily referred to

[First published in *Asia* 20 (1920): 267–72. Republished in *Characters and Events*, ed. Joseph Ratner (New York: Henry Holt and Co., 1929), 1:244–54, with the title "Justice and Law in China."]

as "traitor." And the Chinese equivalent of the word traitor literally means thief-who-sells-his-country. In a fit of absent-mindedness the policeman on guard opened the gate into the compound. The leading students took this as a hint or an invitation. They rushed in. During the following scrimmage, the offender was beaten severely and his house was set afire.

This incident is now ancient history. What is not so well known is that public opinion compelled the release of the students who were arrested. To have tried and condemned them for crime would have had more serious consequences than the government dared face. The heads of the schools gave assurance the students would not engage in further disorder; and they were let go, nominally subject to summons later. But when in the autumn the government, having recovered its nerve somewhat, made a demand upon the heads of the schools to submit the students for trial, their action was regarded as a breach of faith. When the school officials replied that the students had not returned to their respective schools, nothing further happened. There was a general feeling that the summons for trial did not represent the real wish of the officials, but was taken because of pressure exercised by some vengeful person.

To western eyes, accustomed to the forms of regular hearings and trials, such a method seems lawless. In China, however, the moral sense of the community would have been shocked by a purely legal treatment. What in western law is compounded felony is frequently a virtue in China. The incident also illustrates the principle of corporate solidarity and responsibility which plays such a large part in Chinese consciousness. The school group to which the students belonged assumed liability for their future conduct, and gave guarantees for their proper behavior.

As the Peking students were the authors of the movement, they were regarded as its chief abettors. It was desirable for the militaristic reactionaries to discredit them. A meeting of a few actual students, together with some old students and some who intended entering the University, was planned. Resolutions had been prepared which stated that a few noisy, self-seeking students, anxious for notoriety, had fostered the whole movement, coercing their weaker fellows. The resolutions declared, in the alleged name of a thousand students, that the real student body was opposed to the whole agitation. The liberal students got wind of this meeting, entered with a rush, took the thirty dissenters prisoner, obtained from them a written statement of the instigation of the meeting by the reactionary clique, and then locked them up as a punishment. When they were released from confinement by the police, warrants were sworn out and the ringleaders of the invading liberal students were arrested. Great indignation was aroused by this act, which was regarded as highly unsportsmanlike—not playing the game. An educational leader, a returned student, said to me that officials had no business interfering in a matter that concerned only the students.

Yet this seeming absence of public law—this apparent lack of concern for the public interest in peace and orderly procedure—does not mean that opinion would support any individual in starting out to redress his own wrongs. It means that troubles of importance are regarded as between groups, and to be settled between them and by their own initiative.

It is easy to imagine the denunciation of lawlessness that a report of such acts may excite in clubs and editorial rooms. They are here related, however, neither to condemn nor to approve. They are illustrative incidents, fairly typical. They show that the entire legal and judicial background which we take for granted in the West is rudimentary in China. Law and justice, as they should be, are not deliberately challenged in such episodes. There is merely a recurrence to traditional methods of settling disputes. The incidents are also instructive because they suggest the underlying cause. There is no confidence in government, no trust in the honesty, impartiality or intelligence of the officials of the state. Families, villages, clans, guilds—every organized group—has more confidence in the willingness of an opposed group to come to some sort of reasonable settlement than it has in the good faith or the wisdom of the official group.

The following incident illustrates one reason for the lack of confidence in the government. One of the new liberal weeklies in Peking was a thorn in the side of the reactionary officials. Not that it was a political journal, but it was an organ of free discussion; it was connected through its editorial staff with the intellectual element in the Government University which the reactionaries feared, and it was serving as a model for starting similar journals all over the country. The gendarmerie in Shanghai complained to the Provincial Military Governor in Nanking that the journal was creating unrest. Bolshevism has become the technical term in China as well as elsewhere for any criticism of authority. The Military Governor reported this statement to the Minister of War in Peking, who reported it to his colleague the Minister of Justice, who reported it to the local police, who took possession of the newspaper office and shut down the paper.

Note the official House That Jack Built, and the impossibility of locating responsibility anywhere in any way that would secure the shadow of legal redress. Vagueness, overlapping authority, and consequent evasion and shifting of responsibility are typical of inherited governmental methods. Back of the incident lies, of course, the fact that government in China is still largely personal—a matter of edicts, mandates, decrees, rather than of either common or statute law. If we in the West sometimes suffer from the extreme to which the separation of administrative from legislative and judicial powers has gone, a slight study of oriental methods will reveal the conditions which created the demand for that separation. A few days ago, for example, the Minister of Justice in the Peking Cabinet issued a decree that all printed matter whatsoever must be submitted to the police for censorship before publication. There was no crisis, political or military. There was no legislative enabling act. It suited his personal wishes and his factional plans. The order was calmly received with the comment that it would be obeyed in Peking, because the government controlled the Pekingese police, but no attention would be paid to it in the rest of China. In many cases, the Republic's writ does not run beyond the city walls of the capital.

It has been repeatedly pointed out that the acute problems of Chinese existence and reconstruction are due to the fact that methods which worked well enough in the past are now sharply challenged by the changes that have linked China up to the rest of the world. China faces a world that is differently organized from itself in almost every regard; a world, for example, that prizes the forms of justice even when it neglects its substance; a world in which governmental action is the source and standard of redress of wrongs and protection of rights. The habitual method of China, though it has accomplished a great measure of law-abidingness among the Chinese in their own affairs, appears from without as total absence of law, when foreign relations come under consideration.

This is true of China's relations to practically all foreign nations. But Japan lies closest and has the most numerous and varied contacts, and hence has the most sources of complaint. She has borrowed and improved the technique of other nations in making these causes of friction the basis for demands for all sorts of concessions and encroachments, to the constant bewilderment and growing resentment of China. In enforcing the boycott against Japan, for example, the student unions have frequently taken matters into their own hands. They have raided stores in which Japanese goods are sold, carried the stocks off and burned them. When these things are reported in Japan, there is no scrupulous care taken to say that the goods are always the property of Chinese dealers, and that the Japanese themselves are not interfered with.

A succession of such incidents skilfully handled by the Japanese government through the press has bred among the mass of the Japanese people a sincere belief that the Chinese people are lawless, irresponsible and aggressively bumptious in all their dealings with the Japanese, who, considering their provocations, have acted with great forbearance. Thus the Imperial Government assembles behind it the public opinion that is necessary to support a policy of aggression. The feeling that China is in a general state of lawlessness is used, for example, as a reason for keeping Shantung.

The matter is further complicated by the large measure of autonomy enjoyed by the provinces, which historically are principalities rather than provinces. A well-informed English resident writing shortly before the downfall of the Manchu dynasty said: "Each of China's eighteen provinces is a complete state in itself. Each province has its own army and navy, its own system of taxation, and its own social customs. Only in connection with the salt trade and the navy do the provinces have to make concessions to one another under a modicum of Imperial control." In spite of nominal changes, the situation is not essentially different today. The railways and telegraphs have brought about greater unity; but on the other hand the system of military governors, one for each province, has in some respects increased the effective display of States' rights.

During the last few months there have been repeated rumors of the secession of the three Manchurian provinces, of the Southern provinces, and of the Yangtze provinces. These rumors, like the threats of governors here and there to withdraw when matters are not going to suit them, are largely part of the game for political prestige and power. But we know in the United States how our measure of independent action on the part of one state in the Union may complicate foreign relations. Given a greater measure of independence and a weak central state, it is easy to see how many cases of foreign friction may arise which give excuse for an aggressive policy.

Moreover, there is a constant temptation for an unscrupulous foreign power to carry on intrigues and bargains with provincial officials and politicians at the expense of the National State. The recent history of China is largely a history of this sort of foreign intervention, which naturally adds to dissension and confusion and weakens the national government still more. Whether justly or not, the Chinese believe that militaristic Japan has deliberately fomented every movement that would keep China divided. As I write, rumors are current of an attempt to restore the monarchy with Japanese backing.

The bearing of neglect of legal process and judicial forms upon the problem of extra-territoriality is obvious. At present, if commercial and other relations between China and foreign powers are to continue, some kind of extra-territoriality is a necessity, and this involves the existence of "concessions." Nevertheless, their existence is galling to national pride. Returned students have brought the idea and the word "sovereignty" home with them. No word issues more trippingly from the lips.

Yet the existing system has its present advantages for the Chinese themselves. The concessions in Shanghai and Tientsin, which are under foreign jurisdiction, are veritable cities of refuge for Chinese liberals and for political malcontents. As censorship and suppression of newspapers have increased under the present reactionary Ministry of Justice, there is a marked tendency for newspapers to form corporations under nominal foreign ownership and with foreign charters in order to get legal protection. Progressive Chinese business houses flock to the concessions. At present, without the Chinese element they would be mere shells. It is said that 90 per cent of the population of the International Settlement in Shanghai is Chinese and that Chinese pay 80 per cent of its taxes. Tares proverbially grow with the wheat. Corrupt officials protect their funds from confiscation by keeping them in foreign banks. As you ride through the Tientsin concessions, you have pointed out to you the houses of various provincial governors and officials who have thoughtfully provided a place of safety against the inevitable, though postponed, tide of popular indignation.

A Chinese friend said to me that one of the next patriotic movements on the part of the Chinese would be a wholesale exodus from foreign concessions. Except for investors in foreign real estate, it will be amusing to watch when it occurs. The concessions will be left a mere shell. The foreign interest in the maintenance of concessions would completely disappear in this contingency were there some other way of maintaining consular jurisdiction.

I would not give the impression that nothing is going to change the legal situation. The contrary is the case. There is a competent law codification bureau, presided over by a Chinese scholar whose works on some aspects of European law are standard texts in foreign law schools. A modern system is building up. An effort is being made to secure well trained judges and to reform and standardize judicial procedure. The desire for the abolition of extra-territoriality is hastening the change. But it is one thing to introduce formal changes and another to change the habitudes of the people. Contempt for politics and disregard of governmental jurisdiction in adjusting social and commercial disputes will die hard.

It is to be doubted whether China will ever make the complete surrender to legalism and formalism that western nations have done. This may be one of the contributions of China to the world. There is little taste even among the advanced elements, for example, for a purely indirect and representative system of legislation and determination of policy. Repeatedly in the last few months popular opinion has taken things into its own hands and, by public assemblies and by circular telegrams, forced the policy of the government in diplomatic matters. The personal touch and the immediate influence of popular will are needed. As compared with the West, the sphere of discretion will always be large in contrast with that of set forms. Western legalism will be short-circuited. Along with apathy on the part of the populace at large to political matters, there is extraordinary readiness to deal with such questions as a large number are interested in, without going through the intermediaries of political formality.

The liberals in the existing national Senate and House of Representatives make no pretense of attending meetings and trying to influence action by discussion and voting. They make a direct appeal to the country. And in effect this means appeal to a great variety of local organizations: provincial educational associations to reach scholars and students, industrial and mercantile guilds, chambers of commerce (whose powers are much larger than those of like bodies in our country), voluntary unions and societies, religious and other.

It is not at all impossible that, in its future evolution, China will depart widely from western constitutional and representative models and strike out a system combining direct expression of popular will by local group-organizations and guilds with a large measure of personal discretion in the hands of administrative officials as long as the latter give general satisfaction. Personal government by decrees, mandates and arbitrary seizures and imprisonments will give way. Its place will be taken by personal administration such as already exists in the railway, post office, customs, salt administration, etc., where the nature of the constructive work to be done furnishes standards and tests, rather than by formal legislation.

Roughly speaking, the visitor in China is likely to find himself in three successive stages. The first is impatience with irregularities, incompetence and corruptions, and a demand for immediate and sweeping reforms. Longer stay convinces him of the deep roots of many of the objectionable things, and gives him a new lesson in the meaning of the words "evolution" and "development." Many foreigners get stranded in this stage. Under the guise of favoring natural and slow evolution, they become opponents of all things and of any development. They even oppose the spread of popular education, saying it will rob the Chinese of their traditional contentment, patience and docile industry, rendering them uneasy and insubordinate. In everything they point to the evils that may accompany a transitional stage of development. They throw their weight, for example, against every movement for the emancipation of women from a servile status. They enlarge upon the dignity and power some women enjoy within the household and expatiate upon the evils that will arise from a relaxation of present taboos, when neither the old code nor that existing in western countries will apply. Many western business men especially deplore the attempts of missionaries to introduce new ideas. But the visitor who does not get arrested in this second stage emerges where he no longer expects immediate sweeping changes, nor carps at the evils of the present in comparison with an idealized picture of the traditional past. Below the surface he sees the signs of an intellectual reawakening. He feels that while now the endeavors for a new life are scattered, yet they are so numerous and so genuine that in time they will accumulate and coalesce. He finds himself in sympathy with Young China. For Young China also passed through a state of optimism and belief in wholesale change; a subsequent stage of disillusionment and pessimism; and, in a third stage, has now settled down to constructive efforts along lines of education, industry and social reorganization.

In politics, Young China aims at the institution of government by and of law. It contemplates the abolition of personal government with its arbitrariness, corruption and incompetence. But it realizes that political development is mainly indirect; that it comes in consequence of the growth of science, industry and commerce, and of the new human relations and responsibilities they produce; that it springs from education, from the enlightenment of the people, and from special training in the knowledge and technical skill required in the administration of a modern state.

The more one sees, the more one is convinced that many of the worst evils of present political China are the result of pure ignorance. One realizes how the delicate and multifarious business of the modern state is dependent upon knowledge and habits of mind that have grown up slowly and that are now counted upon as a matter of course. China is only beginning to acquire this special experience and knowledge. Old officials brought up in the ancient traditions, and new officials brought up in no traditions at all, but who manage to force themselves into power in a period of political break-up, will gradually pass off the scene. At present the older types of scholars, cultivated, experienced in the archaic tradition, are usually hesitant, if not supine. They are largely puppets in the hands of vigorous men who have found their way into politics from the army, or from the ranks of bandits;

men without education, who know for a large part no law but that of their own appetite, and who lack both general education and education in the management of the complex affairs of the contemporary state.

But in the schools of the country, in the Student Movement, now grown politically self-conscious, are the forces making for a future politics of a different sort.

WHAT HOLDS CHINA BACK

The longer one stays in China, the more the question of what holds China back impresses itself, and the more difficult it becomes to answer. There is "if" in almost every answer which your Chinese friends give to the question; and the "if" generally only restates the difficulty.

The remark heard most often is perhaps the most superficial of all. "If we had a stable government we could do this and that." But why isn't there a stable government? Its absence is much more of an effect than a cause. The country is still divided, both north and south having their own government, and each at loggerheads with the other. Yet every Chinese friend tells you the country is united although the government is divided, and everything you can learn confirms the statement. Why do not the people then enforce their feeling and will? Japanese intrigue and interference is an obvious answer. But again you are given an effect, a symptom, instead of a cause. Others tell you that the source of the difficulty is lack of ability and experience in organization. This answer goes further below the surface. But it still needs explanation. The Chinese have both experience and ability in some kinds of organization, as the long history of the guilds and of village self-government shows. Why should they not show at least as much capacity for organization as the Japanese, who have only recently emerged from feudalism with all the personal suspicions, jealousies and class division that feudalism opposes to organization? And no one who knows the Chinese can believe that the difficulty is intellectual, that the people have not the mental gifts required in successful organization.

To say (as is so often said) that the Chinese do not progress more systematically and rapidly because they are a conservative people is clearly repeating in other words the thing that needs to

[First published in *Asia* 20 (1920): 373–77. Republished in *Characters and Events*, ed. Joseph Ratner (New York: Henry Holt and Co., 1929), 1:211–21, with the title "Chinese Social Habits."]

be explained. Conservative they doubtless are. But nevertheless their history is not a history of stagnation, of fixity, as we are falsely taught, but of social as well as dynastic changes. They have tried many experiments in their day. Centuries ago they had a statesman who induced the emperor to commit the kingdom to something as near to modern socialism as was possible considering the absence of steam and electricity. China has undergone as many barbarian invasions as any country in Europe. Its survival and its absorption of its invaders do not argue conservatism of the inert kind. No country whose conservatism came from sheer routine, from lack of imagination, from mental rigidity, could have maintained and extended its civilization as China has done. And experience shows that the Chinese are supple, pliant, accommodating and adaptive—neither rigid nor dull.

It may strike the western reader as simply funny, but more than one Chinese friend has assured me that it is the Japanese people who are really conservative. And they back up their assertion by evidence other than the way in which Japan has clung, through all historic vicissitudes, to a primitive theocracy. They point out, for example, that a thousand years ago the Japanese borrowed their present style of clothing and of household furnishings, of sitting and sleeping on mats, from China; that China has changed several times, moving constantly in the direction of practical utility, of ingenious adaptation of means to needs. The Chinese cuisine is another argument. It is doubtless the most extensive in the world in the variety of material employed for food, and also the most varied in its combinations. Academic analysis may despise arguments drawn from food, clothing, shelter and furnishings. But when one notes the variety and ingenuity of the processes and appliances used in daily life and in the crafts, one is certain that the Chinese mind is naturally observant and adaptive. But it seems unnecessary to labor the question. Many charges have been brought against the Chinese, but no one has ever accused them of stupidity. Their undoubted conservatism is something to be explained rather than an explanation of anything.

It may well be doubted whether there is any single key to the mystery. Certainly the present observer has no final solution to proffer. But there is one fact which I am quite sure must be taken into the reckoning and which counts for much. It is beyond question that many traits of the Chinese mind are the products of an extraordinary and long-continued density of populations. Psychologists have discovered, or possibly invented, a "psychology of the crowd" to account for the way men act in masses, as a mob at a lynching bee. They have not inquired as to the effect upon the mind of constant living in close contact with large numbers, of continual living in a crowd. Years ago an enthusiastic American teacher of the Chinese in Honolulu told me that when the Chinese acquired Anglo-Saxon initiative they would be the greatest people in the world. I wonder whether even the Anglo-Saxons would have developed or retained initiative if they had lived for centuries under conditions that gave them no room to stir about, no relief from the unremitting surveillance of their fellows? Possibly they would then have acquired a habit of thinking of their "face" before they thought of the thing to be done. Perhaps when they thought of a new thing they would have decided discretion and hesitation to be the better part of invention. If solitude or loneliness exists in China it is only among the monks who have retired into the mountain fastnesses; and until I have ocular evidence to the contrary I shall believe that even monks in China are sociable, agglutinative beings. Until the recent introduction of rapid transportation, very few Chinese ever enjoyed even the possibility of solitude that comes from being in a crowd of strangers. Imagine all elbow-room done away with, imagine millions of men living day by day, year by year, in the presence of the same persons (a very close presence at that), and new light may be shed upon the conservatism of the Chinese people.

An English author, long resident in China, wrote a book which, aside from a wealth of picturesque incident, gossip and rumor, was a long diatribe against Young China—against, that is, the Chinese who favor the introduction of western institutions, inventions, methods. His way of arguing was sufficiently simple. China suffers from an excess of population. Great masses live just on the edge of subsistence. A flood, a disabling pestilence, a season's bad weather, plunges millions over the edge. Equilibrium is then restored. But a long succession of prosperous years produces an over-population which finds vent in rebellion, civil war, a killing off of a very large number, and possibly the overthrow of a dynasty. Chinese history is and must be a succession, a cycle, of such episodes. Meantime Confucian ideas, ancestor worship,

family and clan organization, transmit Chinese civilization intact.
This, Young China would destroy, robbing China of its moral
foundations. Since it cannot alter the basic facts of the struggle
for existence, Young China therefore offers nothing of value to
the country.

The logic is not close-knit; *non sequiturs* abound. But it is a
good example of the way in which foreigners become infected
with a belief that in China things must in the future be about as
they have been in the past, and that efforts to make a change only
result in making things worse. In my experience, most foreigners
who have been long in China and who think at all, acquire this
attitude in some degree. You hear solemn warnings on every hand
that this and that cannot be done, although next day you learn
from some Chinese friend that it is being done and the heavens
have not fallen. Many are more Confucianist—in a kind of vague
belief that Confucius contributed something without which
China cannot endure—than the younger generation of Chinese.
After a few years some foreigners find themselves hypnotized by
the thickness, the compactness, of a civilization forced upon
people living closely crowded together. They acquire the fear that
if one strand is touched, the whole will unravel, and the belief
that the safe thing is to leave things alone. Young American
teachers and social workers, recently over from America, tell me
that the older missionaries frequently admonish them against
their innovating zeal, and tell them that as they grow older and
wiser they will learn conservatism. Most of the older British resi-
dents are reported to have no sympathy with the Revolution, to
mourn the departed days of monarchy, and to point to many increased present evils as proofs of their belief that as China has
been, so she must be.

If China "gets" so many foreigners who come with the opposed tradition of the initiative of Anglo-Saxons, then what must
be the case with those brought up from infancy in thick, dense,
inbred civilization? Live and let live is the response to crowded
conditions. If things are fairly well off, then let well enough alone.
If they are evil, endure them rather than run the risk of making
them worse by interference. In western countries, the doctrine of
laissez faire has flourished because a policy of hands off was
thought to encourage individual energy and enterprise. In China
it flourishes because any unusual energy or enterprise on the part

of anybody may work untoward results. Not to rock the boat is wisdom the world over. In a crowded country, not organized along the lines of utilization of natural resources, any innovation is likely to disturb the balance of the social boat.

The reformer does not even meet sharp, clear-cut resistance. If he did, he might be stimulated to further effort. He simply is smothered. Stalling has become a fine art. At a recent national educational conference a returned student holding an official position moved that the public middle schools (corresponding to our high schools) be made co-educational. He was inspired by sound consideration. China suffers from lack of educated women. Funds are short. The effective thing is to admit girls to the schools already existing. But the proposition was a radical innovation. Yet it was not opposed. A resolution in favor was duly passed. But at the same time it was made subtly understood that this was done out of courtesy to the mover, and that no steps to carry the resolution into effect need be expected. This is the fate of many proposed social reforms. They are not fought, they are only swallowed. China does not stagnate, it absorbs. It takes up all the slack till there is no rope left with which to pull.

The weak points of a people, like those of an individual, are the defects of their qualities. Vices are not far removed from virtues; they are their reverse side. The Chinese believe themselves the politest people on earth. They are probably right in their belief. In comparison even the best of western manners often appear either crude or else overdone, affected. Nothing can exceed the amenity of the Japanese in personal intercourse. But they learned their etiquette as well as so much else from China, and it remains somewhat formal, a cultivated art. In China the ages have toned down and mellowed the forms of intercourse till they no longer seem forms. High and low are so easy and unconstrained in their bearing toward one another, that one is tempted, in spite of scientific authority, to believe in the inheritance by later generations of the manners acquired by previous generations. Cheerfulness and contentment amid the most trying conditions are a part of good manners. Yet there is none of that rigidity, to say nothing of glumness and fanaticism, which we ordinarily associate with stoicism or fatalism. There is no flourish of self-control which betrays that the self-control is maintained with difficulty. Fate is welcomed with a smile, perhaps a jest, not

with a frown, nor yet with heroics. Such courtesy and cheerfulness are undoubted products of long-continued close face-to-face
crowded existence. The unremitting impact of a thick civilization
has impressed the folly of adding to the burdens of life by friction
or repining. Politeness and cheerfulness are the lubricants by
which the closeness and constancy of personal contacts are made
endurable. Circumstances admit of but two alternatives: either
ruthless competition, war to the bone, or an easygoing peace.
Having chosen the latter way out, the Chinese have carried it to
its logical conclusion.

Yet personal consideration for others in direct face-to-face intercourse is quite compatible with what in the western world
would be regarded as unfeeling cruelty and lack of active aid to
others. The other day in Peking a passing carriage knocked down
a man in the street, and rolled by unheeding. The man was so
badly injured that he was unable to rise. No passer-by made a
move; all literally passed by on the other side, until some foreigners came to the rescue. A few months ago Mr. Baillie was set upon
by bandits in Manchuria. The other persons present not only offered no aid, but they ran aside and shut their eyes so that they
could not be called upon to testify. The further point of this incident lies in the fact that Mr. Baillie had taken poor and miserable
persons from the more crowded parts of China to Manchuria
where there was plenty of land, and by colonizing them had
greatly improved their conditions. These men who closed their
eyes that they might not know what was going on were men
whom he had aided; they were personal friends.

This does not mean that Chinese habitual politeness is insin-
cere. I have never heard the Chinese accused of hypocrisy,
though I have heard of many bitter complaints of their unwillingness to carry things through. I have never seen anyone who did
not regard genuine friendliness as one of the chief Chinese traits.
But where there is a complete manifestation of the Malthusian
theory of population, friendliness develops with great difficulty to
the point of active effort to relieve suffering. Where further increase in population means increase in severity of the struggle for
subsistence, aggressive benevolence is not likely to assume large
proportions. On the contrary, when the cutting off of thousands
by plague or flood or famine means more air to breathe and more
land to cultivate for those who remain, stoic apathy is not hard to

attain. A foreigner interested in the prevention of cruelty to animals after many discouragements approached with some hopefulness a Buddhist monk. He thought that the doctrine of universal pity would have prepared the way for sympathetic reception. But his message was coldly greeted. He was told that the animals, when they were abused, were justly suffering for the sins of some ancestor and that it was not for man to interfere. Such Buddhism only formulates the fatalism which is a general natural response to surroundings.

Most of the oriental traits of lack of active sympathy and relief which missionaries have cited as due to heathenism seem to have a simpler explanation. On the other hand, western philanthropy makes a great appeal. Missionaries and Y.M.C.A. workers took a large part of the burden of recent flood-relief work. The Chinese in the devastated region who had remained calmly impervious to prior preaching, were so impressed with the exhibition of kindness that was gratuitous that they flocked into the churches. The latter had to sift and choose very carefully to keep from being themselves flooded. And this result was not a "lively expectation of favors to come." The population had been deeply touched by the unprecedented display of sympathy and help. I was told on good authority that the Governor of Shansi, the most respected provincial governor in China, said that up to the time of the outbreak of bubonic plague, he had thought that western civilization was good only for battleships and machinery. But the unpaid devotion of physicians, teachers and missionaries, at the risk of their own lives, had convinced him that there was another side to western civilization.

The incidents of personal disregard of others have the same spring as the absence of organized relief. To do anything is to assume a responsibility. To have helped the man knocked down would have done more than involve a loss of time. Those helping would have implicated themselves with the authorities. They might be accused of complicity. Mind your own business, don't interfere, leave things to those whose express business it is to look after them, is the rule of living. Don't make a nuisance of yourself by meddlesomeness, to say nothing of getting yourself into incalculable trouble by leaving the beaten track. Practical indifference in matters that do not directly concern one is but the obverse side of exquisite consideration in immediate personal relations. Where the latter are concerned everything suggests the superior claims of an immediate smoothing over of things rather than an adjustment on the basis of actual objective consequences. Effect on "face" is more significant than consequences upon outer facts. It is contrary to the proprieties, for instance, for a government school to accept private gifts. It reflects upon the government, which then loses "face." The head of a Peking school recently said he would accept gifts, that he was willing to sacrifice his "face" to the good of his school and the country. This was a more genuine sacrifice than westerners might believe.

When people live close together and cannot get away from one another, appearances, that is to say the impression made upon others, become as important as the realities, if not more so. The ulterior consequences of, let us say, a diplomatic transaction with a foreign nation seem of less consequence than the immediate conduct of negotiations in such a way as to avoid present trouble and graciously to observe all the proprieties. When evasion and delay no longer suffice, it is better to surrender and to permit the other side to be rude and brusque than to lose "face" one's self. The Japanese knowledge of this trait accounts very considerably for their diplomatic methods with China. It is known as the policy of the strong hand. Concede anything to the Chinese and they think you are afraid of them, and they at once become presumptuous and demand more—this is a commonplace in Japanese newspaper discussion of Chinese affairs. So far as immediate dealings with officials are concerned, the Japanese seem to have decided wisely as to the methods which give results. What they failed to count upon was the immense backwash of resentment among the people at large.

In fine, the crowded population has bred those habits of mind, which, as the common saying goes, make the Chinese individually so companionably agreeable and attractive and collectively so exasperating to the outsider. Innovation, experimentation, get automatically discouraged, not from lack of intelligence, but because intelligence is too keenly aware of the mistakes that may result, the trouble that may arise. "Keep out of trouble" comes to be the guiding principle. In an evening pleasantly spent with ex-President Sun Yat-sen, he set forth his theory as to the slow change of China as compared with the rapid advance of Japan. It seems some old Chinese sage once said, "To know is easy;

to act is difficult." The Chinese had taken this adage to heart, so Mr. Sun explained. They did not act because they were afraid of making mistakes; they wanted to be guaranteed in advance against any failure or serious trouble. The Japanese, on the other hand, realized that action was much easier than knowing; they went ahead and did things without minding mistakes and failures, trusting to a net balance on the side of achievement. I am inclined to think the old sage was influential because his teaching was reinforced by effects of the ever-close and ever-thick environment.

Only the superficial think that to give the causes of an unfortunate state of affairs is to excuse them. Any state of affairs has to be judged on the basis of the consequences it produces, not on the basis of the causes that explain its existence. But if the causes are those described, they cannot be remedied by expostulation, exhortation and preaching. A change of conditions, an alteration of the environment, is needed. This cannot take place by reducing the population, although part of Young China is now shocking archaic China by preaching birth-control. An introduction of modern industrial methods is the only thing that will profoundly affect the environment. Utilizing energy and resources now untouched will produce an effect that will be the same as an enlargement of the environment. Mining, railways and manufacturing based upon China's wealth of unused resources will give a new outlet for energies that now cannot be used without the risk of causing "trouble." The impersonal and indirect effects of modern production and commerce will create habits that will lessen the importance of appearances and "face," and increase the importance of objective consequences of facts. A way will be discovered with the increase of wealth and of constructive appliances to turn personal friendliness, unfailing amiability and good-humor into general channels of social service.

CHINA'S NIGHTMARE

The world has been so satiated with extraordinary events in the last few years, that what would have been a miracle five years ago now hardly attracts attention. What a sensation would once have been created by an announcement that Russia was offering to return to China without compensation all Russian interest in the Chinese Eastern Railway, all mining and timber concessions in Manchuria or other Chinese territory; to renounce all extra-territorial rights as well as all further payments of the Boxer indemnity account! Make all the discount you wish on the ground that the offer comes from the Soviet government; and the transformation is still as extraordinary as if the Germans had without war offered France the voluntary return of Alsace-Lorraine and the return of the war indemnity of 1870. In many respects the proposal is even more sensational than that would have been; more indicative of the incredible levity of history. Twenty years ago no one doubted the intention of Russia to control the entire northern part of China and the Asiatic sea coast at least as far south as Tsingtao; and until Russia's defeat by Japan few doubted the success of her plans.

Read almost any of the books about China written twenty years ago, and you will find that you have only to substitute Japan for Russia, in order to have a fairly accurate description of the situation of today, so far as its spirit is concerned. Geographical details vary, but the objects and general technique of exploitation are the same. Lord Beresford visited China on a commercial mission in 1898. His report is contained in his book on *The Break-up of China*. In it he says: "I hardly ever made a suggestion to any prominent Chinese official which I thought might tend to the security of British trade and commerce, that I was not met with the question, 'But what would Russia say to that?' or words to that

[First published in *New Republic* 23 (1920): 145–47. Republished in *Characters and Events*, ed. Joseph Ratner (New York: Henry Holt and Co., 1929), 1:193–98.]

effect. The idea is gaining ground all over China that Great Britain is afraid of Russia."

In the Willy-Nicky letters are found the congratulations of the Kaiser to the Tsar upon having established himself as the dominant power in Peking. In the biography of John Hay there is an account of the denials by Cassini, then Russian minister at Washington, of the report of demands made by Russia upon China which were at the expense of other nations as well as of China. The denials were positive. At the same time Hay, as Secretary of State, was in possession from three different capitals of transcripts of the demands. One might readily imagine that he was reading the diplomatic history of the Twenty-one Demands. Both the wholesale critics of Japan and the wholesale apologists for her would probably change their tone if they realized how closely copied after the Tsarism of Russia is the imperialism of Japan.

The imitative capacity of the Japanese is notorious. Is there anything surprising that Japan should have followed in the wake of Russia in that feature of foreign policy which is most vital to her—the control of China? I have not the slightest doubt that the great part of the militarists and bureaucrats who have dictated her Chinese policy sincerely believe, with the pattern of Russia always before their eyes, that they are conforming strictly to the proper models of western diplomacy. Wholesale bribery, secrecy, force and fraud were regular parts of the Oriental diplomacy of Russia. It is natural for Japanese officials to believe that the outcry from America or England against similar methods on the part of Japan, is purely hypocritical or else itself a part of the regular diplomatic game.

The more thoroughly the history of the international relations of China for the last twenty years is studied the more apparent is it that Japan has been the heir of Russian aims and methods as well as of, since the great war, Russian achievements. It was Russia that evolved the technique of conquest by railway and bank. She consolidated if she did not wholly originate the sphere of influence politics with its favoritism and its dog-in-the-manger tactics. Russia discovered the value of police boxes as a means of insinuating semi-military and semi-civil administrative control in territory over which her legitimate claims, stretched to the utmost, were purely economic. Many of the Twenty-one Demands are almost verbatim copies of prior Russian requests, such as the exclusive right to train the army, etc. Russia evolved to the uttermost the doctrine of military occupation as a means of protecting nationals. She posed as the protector of China against "western" Powers, and prided herself (strangely enough with better reason and more success than Japan) upon understanding Chinese psychology, and knowing how to manage the Chinese. In the secret Cassini protocol made at St. Petersburg in 1896 with Li Hung Chang (the prototype of Chinese statesmen bought with foreign money) will be found the magna charta of subsequent Japanese diplomacy. It even includes a conditional provision for the Russian naval and military occupation of Kiaochou Bay.

In the earlier period of Chino-Russian-Japanese relations, that is up to the Treaty of Portsmouth in 1905, Japan could use in good faith the claim of self-defense in her dealings with China. For certainly Russia with her enormous undeveloped territory had much less excuse for aggression in Korea and northern China than had Japan. Moreover, every new aggressive step of Russia in China was followed at once by demands for compensating concessions and spheres by other Powers, especially by Great Britain and France. There is every reason for thinking that Germany's claim to Kiaochou was stimulated by Russia to give a colorable pretext to her claim for Port Arthur and Dalny, while the yielding of China in both these matters was immediately followed by demands from Great Britain in the Yangtze region and from France in the south.

This was the period which gave Beresford's book its title of *Break-up* though he himself was an ardent expositor of the doctrine of the Open Door. And it was this situation which enabled Japan in reasonable good faith to set herself up as the defender of the integrity and sovereignty of China against European aggression. Such feelings and claims have a remarkable historic inertia. There is nothing surprising in the fact that they still persist among the mass of the Japanese people, and supply the conditions which enable Japan to continue a policy of aggressive exploitation of China with popular support and sanction. There was a time when the Japanese had every reason to feel that their future destiny depended upon getting enough power to control China as the only sure way to keep China from falling into European hands. Times have changed; the sentiment of the Japanese people lags behind the change in facts and can still be exploited by the militarist party. And in the meantime (especially after the outbreak of the great war) Japan's own policy became less and less defensive and more and more flagrantly offensive.

If there had been in the United States an adequate knowledge of Russian diplomatic methods in their Oriental aspect and in their bearing upon Japan's fortunes and her Asiatic aims and methods, American gullibility would never have fallen an easy victim to Japan's propaganda for western consumption. As it was, American ignorance secured almost universal approval for the Portsmouth Treaty with its "supplementary clauses" which in spite of their innocent appearance meant that the settlement was really a truce concluded at the expense of China's rights in Manchuria. One foreign publicist in China is inclined to hold President Roosevelt responsible for China's international ills since 1905. He takes the ground that he ought to have insisted that since the war had been practically fought on Chinese territory, China should have been a party to the settlement, and that the peace conference was the one great opportunity for effective foreign protection of China against both aggressors. As a matter of fact, the actual outcome was certainly to make both Russia and Japan interested in trading with each other at China's expense. If it had not been for Great Britain's navy, it would doubtless have long ago led to a definite Russo-Japanese understanding regarding the division of northern China. But hindsight is proverbially easy, and it must be doubted whether President Roosevelt is to blame for a lack of foresight which no one else possessed at that date.

All this matter is by way of merely sketching the background of the next important epoch probable in Chinese foreign relations. It is not likely that China will accept the Soviet's offer in its present form. It is not probable the Allies will permit it even if China wanted to assume the risks of such a course. But none the less the offer symbolizes the opening of a new era. Even if the present Russian government is overthrown, any new government that takes its place will have every reason for coming to some good understanding with China. After all, their territories are contiguous for three thousand miles. Both countries are on a continental scale. Japan, when all is said and done, is an island, and the history of insular conquests on a continent afford no very good au-

gury for Japan's future success in Asia. The Siberian situation is
still confused. But to all appearances the Japanese militarist party
that favors a forward policy of adventure in Siberia is for the time
being dominant. China can again chuckle about the Providence
that always seems to come to her rescue when things are at the
worst. The Russians are not pacifists; they are still expansive, and
they have an enormous land hunger, due to the agrarian history
of Russia. The deeper the Japanese get themselves involved in
Siberia, the surer, in Chinese opinion, is her final checkmate,
even though for some years she may get virtual possession of
Eastern Siberia even up to Lake Baikal. There is much to be said
for the belief that China's international future is to be decided in
Siberia. The situation shifts rapidly. The idea, already broached
privately, of an armed conflict between Japan on one side and
Russia, Korea and China on the other, may have nothing in it.
But whether Russia returns to monarchy or becomes an established republic, it seems a safe prophecy that China's Russian
relations will be the ultimate decisive factor in her international
status. The diversion of Japan from China into Siberia probably
marks the culmination of her influence in China. It is not improb-
able that the last five years will soon, as history counts years, be
looked back upon as the years of China's nightmare.

A POLITICAL UPHEAVAL IN CHINA

Even in America we have heard of one Chinese revolution, that which thrust the Manchu dynasty from the throne. The visitor in China gets used to casual references to the second revolution, that which frustrated Yuan Shih-kai's aspirations to be emperor, and the third, the defeat in 1917 of the abortive attempt to put the Manchu boy emperor back into power. And within the last few weeks the (September 1920) fourth upheaval has taken place. It may not be dignified by the name of the fourth revolution, for the head of the state has not been changed by it. But as a manifestation of the forces that shape Chinese political events, for evil and for good, perhaps this last disturbance surpasses the last two "revolutions" in significance.

Chinese politics in detail are highly complicated, a mess of personalities and factions whose oscillations no one can follow who does not know a multitude of personal, family and provincial histories. But occasionally something happens which simplifies the tangle. Definite outlines frame themselves out of the swirling criss-cross of strife, intrigue and ambition. So, at present, the complete collapse of the Anfu clique which owned the central government for two years marks the end of that union of internal militarism and Japanese foreign influence which was, for China, the most marked fruit of the war. When China entered the war a "War Participation" army was formed. It never participated; probably it was never meant to. But its formation threw power wholly into the hands of the military clique, as against the civilian constitutionalists. And in return for concessions, secret agreements relating to Manchuria, Shantung, new railways, etc., Japan supplied money, munitions, instructors for the army and a benevolent supervision of foreign and domestic politics. The war came to an unexpected and untimely end, but by this time the offspring of

[First published in *New Republic* 24 (1920): 142–44. Revised and republished in *China, Japan and the U.S.A.* (New York: Republic Publishing Co., 1921), pp. 27–32.]

the marriage of the militarism of Yuan Shih-kai and Japanese money and influence was a lusty youth. Bolshevism was induced to take the place of Germany as a menace requiring the keeping up of the army, and loans and teachers. Mongolia was persuaded to cut her strenuous ties with Russia, to renounce her independence and come again under Chinese sovereignty.

The army and its Japanese support and instruction was, accordingly, continued. In place of the "War Participation" army appeared the "Frontier Defense" army. Marshal Tuan, the head of the military party, remained the nominal political power behind the presidential chair, and General Hsu (commonly known as little Hsu, in distinction from old Hsu, the president) was the energetic manager of the Mongolian adventure which, by a happy coincidence, required a bank, land development companies and railway schemes, as well as an army. About this military centre as a nucleus gathered the vultures who fed on the carrion. This flock took the name of the Anfu Club. It did not control the entire cabinet, but to it belonged the Minister of Justice, who manipulated the police and the courts, persecuted the students, suppressed liberal journals and imprisoned inconvenient critics. And the Club owned the ministers of finance and communications, the two cabinet places that dispense revenues, give out jobs and make loans. It also regulated the distribution of intelligence by mail and telegraph. The reign of corruption and despotic inefficiency, tempered only by the student revolt, set in. In two years the Anfu Club got away with two hundred millions of public funds directly, to say nothing of what was wasted by incompetency and upon the army. The Allies had set out to get China into the war. They succeeded in getting Japan into control of Peking and getting China, politically speaking, into a seemingly hopeless state of corruption and confusion.

The militaristic or Pei-Yang party was, however, divided into two factions, each called after a province. The Anwhei party gathered about little Hsu and was almost identical with the Anfus. The Chili faction had been obliged, so far as Peking was concerned, to content itself with such leavings as the Anfu Club tossed to it. Apparently it was hopelessly weaker than its rival, although Tuan, who was personally honest and above financial scandal, was supported by both factions and was the head of both. About three months ago there were a few signs that, while the

Anfu Club had been entrenching itself in Peking, the rival faction had been quietly establishing itself in the provinces. A league of Eight Tuchuns (military governors of the provinces) came to the assistance of the president against some unusually strong pressure from the Anfu Club. In spite of the fact that the military governor of the three Manchurian provinces, Chang Tso Lin, popularly known as the Emperor of Manchuria, lined up with this league, practically nobody expected anything except some maneuvering to get a larger share of the spoils.

But late in June the president invited Chang Tso Lin to Peking. The latter saw Tuan, told him that he was surrounded by evil advisers, demanded that he cut loose from little Hsu and the Anfu Club, and declared open war upon little Hsu—the two had long and notoriously been bitter enemies. Even then people had great difficulty in believing that anything would happen except another Chinese compromise. The president was known to be sympathetic upon the whole with the Chili faction, but the president, if not a typical Chinese, is at least typical of a certain kind of Chinese mandarin, non-resistant, compromising, conciliating, procrastinating, covering up, evading issues, face-saving. But finally something happened. A mandate was issued dismissing little Hsu from office, military and civil, dissolving the frontier defense corps as such, and bringing it under the control of the Ministry of War (usually armies in China belong to some general or Tuchun, not to the country). For almost forty-eight hours it was thought that Tuan had consented to sacrifice little Hsu and that the latter would submit, at least temporarily. Then with equally sensational abruptness Tuan brought pressure to bear on the president. The latter was appointed head of a national defense army, and rewards were issued for the heads of the chiefs of the Chili faction, nothing, however, being said about Chang Tso Lin, who had meanwhile returned to Mukden and who still professed allegiance to Tuan. Troops were mobilized; there was a rush of officials and of the wealthy to the concessions of Tientsin and to the hotels of the legation quarter.

This sketch is not meant as history, but simply as an indication of the forces at work. Hence it is enough to say that two weeks after Tuan and little Hsu had intimidated the president and proclaimed themselves the saviors of the Republic, they were in hiding, their enemies of the Chili party were in complete control of Peking, and rewards from fifty thousand dollars down were offered for the arrest of little Hsu, the ex-ministers of justice, finance and communications, and other leaders of the Anfu Club. The political turnover was as complete as it was sensational. The seemingly impregnable masters of China were impotent fugitives. The carefully built up Anfu Club, with its military, financial and foreign support, had crumbled and fallen. No country at any time has ever seen a political upheaval more sudden and more thoroughgoing. It was not so much a defeat as a dissolution like that of death, a total disappearance, an evaporation.

Corruption had worked inward, as it has a way of doing. Japanese-bought munitions would not explode; quartermasters vanished with the funds with which stores were to be bought; troops went without anything to eat for two or three days; large numbers, including the larger part of one division, went over to the enemy en masse; those who did not desert had no heart for fighting and ran away or surrendered on the slightest provocation, saying they were willing to fight for their country but saw no reason why they should fight for a faction, especially a faction that had been selling the country to a foreign nation. In the manner of the defeat of the Anfu clique at the height of its supremacy, rather than in the mere fact of its defeat, lies the credit side of the Chinese political balance sheet. It is a striking exhibition of the oldest and best faith of the Chinese—the power of moral considerations. Public opinion, even that of the coolie on the street, was wholly against the Anfu party. It went down not so much because of the strength of the other side as because of its own rottenness.

So far the results are to all appearances negative. The most marked is the disappearance of Japanese prestige. As one of the leading men in the War Office said: "For over a year now the people have been strongly opposed to the Japanese government on account of Shantung. But now even the generals do not care for Japan any more." It is hardly logical to take the easy collapse of the Japanese-supported Anfu party as a proof of the weakness of Japan, but prestige is always a matter of feeling rather than of logic. Many who were intimidated to the point of hypnotism by the idea of the irresistible power of Japan are now freely laughing at the inefficiency of Japanese leadership. It would not be safe to predict that Japan will not come back as a force to be reckoned with in the internal as well as external politics of China, but it is safe to say that never again will Japan figure as superman to China. And such a negation is after all a positive result.

And so in its way is the overthrow of the Anwhei faction of the militarist party. The Chinese liberals do not feel very optimistic about the immediate outcome. They have mostly given up the idea that the country can be reformed by political means. They are sceptical about the possibility of reforming even politics until a new generation comes on the scene. They are now putting their faith in education and in social changes which will take some years to consummate themselves visibly. The self-styled southern republican constitutional party has not shown itself in much better light than the northern militarist party. In fact, its old leader Sun Yat Sen now cuts one of the most ridiculous figures in China, as shortly before this upheaval he had definitely aligned himself with Tuan and little Hsu.[1]

This does not mean, however, that democratic opinion thinks nothing has been gained. The demonstration of the inherent weakness of corrupt militarism will itself prevent the development of any militarism as complete as that of the Anfus. As one Chinese gentleman said to me: "When Yuan Shih-kai was overthrown, the tiger killed the lion. Now a snake has killed the tiger. No matter how vicious the snake may become, some smaller animal will be able to kill him, and his life will be shorter than that of either lion or tiger." In short, each successive upheaval brings nearer the day when civilian supremacy will be established. This result will be achieved partly because of the repeated demonstrations of the uncongeniality of military despotism to the Chinese spirit, and partly because with every passing year education will have done its work. Suppressed liberal papers are coming to life, while over twenty Anfu subsidized newspapers and two subsidized news agencies have gone out of being. The soldiers, including many officers in the Anwhei army, clearly show the effects of student propaganda. And it is worth while to note down the name

1. This was written of course several months before Sun Yat Sen was reinstated in control of Canton by the successful revolt of his local adherents against the southern militarists who had usurped power and driven out Sun Yat Sen and his followers. But up to the time when I left China, in July of this year, it was true that the liberals of northern and central China who were bitterly opposed to the Peking Government, did not look to the Southern Government with much hope. The common attitude was a "plague upon both of your houses" and a desire for a new start. The conflict between North and South looms much larger in the United States than it did in China.

of one of the leaders on the victorious side, the only one whose troops did any particular fighting, and that against great odds in numbers. The name is Wu Pei Fu. He at least has not fought for the Chili faction against the Anwhei faction. He has proclaimed from the first that he was fighting to rid the country of military control of civil government, and against traitors who would sell their country to foreigners. He has come out strongly for a new popular assembly, to form a new constitution and to unite the country. And although Chang Tso Lin has remarked that Wu Pei Fu as a military subordinate could not be expected to intervene in politics, he has not as yet found it convenient to oppose the demand for a popular assembly. Meanwhile the liberals are organizing their forces, hardly expecting to win a victory, but resolved, win or lose, to take advantage of the opportunity to carry further the education of the Chinese people in the meaning of democracy.

INDUSTRIAL CHINA

Nowhere in the world is the difference between industrious and industrial as great as in China. The industriousness of the Chinese is proverbial. Industrially, they are in the earliest stages of the revolution from domestic to machine production, and from transportation on the necks of men (and women and children) to the freight car. The necks of men:—for while the bulk of goods in central China is doubtless carried by its marvellous system of water-ways, yet whenever winds fail the boats are towed with ropes attached to the shoulders of men—and women and children. On the Grand Canal, you can sometimes count forty persons from ten years up tugging at a rope attached to the mast of some clumsy junk. Even a Ruskin if abruptly placed in strictly mediaeval economic conditions might be forced to admit that there are two sides to the humanity of the steam locomotive. And the indiscriminate admirers of the mediaeval guild might learn something from a study of the workings of its Chinese counterpart.

My last six weeks have been spent in travelling through the Province of Kiangsu. Shanghai is located in this province and it is industrially and commercially the most advanced in China, the one with the most mills, railways and foreign trade. For details and statistics the reader may go to consular reports, trade journals, etc. This article has a humbler task. Its aim is merely to record impressions which seem to me to be indicative of the problems China has to face during the years of its oncoming accelerated industrial transformation.

The fifteen towns visited are scattered from the extreme north to the extreme south of the province; strictly speaking, two of them lie in the Province of Chekiang to the south. The towns fall into four groups. The first contains the treaty ports, where

[First published in *New Republic* 25 (1920): 39–41. Revised and republished in *Impressions of Soviet Russia and the Revolutionary World: Mexico—China—Turkey* (New York: New Republic, Inc., 1929), pp. 237–51.]

foreign merchants have come in, where foreign capital is concentrated, and where foreign methods, though usually subjected to
Chinese conditions in the form of acceptance of the compradore
as a middleman, set the pace. For technical commercial purposes,
from a statistical point of view, these towns of which Shanghai is
the most important, are doubtless the most interesting. From a
social point of view they are the least interesting, except as one
may want to make a study of the contact of two civilizations meeting with but one common object—the making of money.

Otherwise they are chiefly significant as revealing an increasing ability of the Chinese to adopt the joint-stock and mana-
gerial system without coming to grief—as did most of the early
companies that were exclusively Chinese. The reasons are worth
recording, because they affect the entire problem everywhere of
the introduction of modern industrialism. The speculative element, the promoter element, was at first most marked. The general psychology was that of gold mine promoting. After an early
furore in which most "investors" lost their money, the bitten became wary, and even legitimate enterprises could not secure attention, except in the case of a very small number of persons who
had made a success of their joint-stock mills. In the next place,
the Chinese family system with the obligation it puts upon the
prosperous member of the family to carry all his relatives who
wish to be carried made nepotism so common as to be an impossible burden. And in the third place, most of the earlier enterprises scorned the technique of putting aside reserve funds in a
prosperous season, and of writing off for depreciations. A short
life and a merry one was the usual motto. Now, however, business
methods have developed to the point where many Chinese mills
are successfully competing with foreign capital and foreign management. In fact many Chinese think that the latter will soon be
at a disadvantage because of the diversion of profits to the compradore, and the lack of personal contact with workmen. But
upon this point it is not possible to get facts that can be depended
upon.

The second class includes towns at the opposite extreme of
development, towns that are not only non-treaty ports but that are
only beginning to be touched. The northern part of the province,
for example, is almost as primitive as it was five hundred years
ago. The building of a railway has created some flour mills, and

since the war egg-factories have made a new market. Eggs that used to sell for a third of a cent apiece now bring three times that, and the producer gets most of the increase. In all of the towns and villages, the number of hens any one family can keep is limited by communal action, as otherwise hens would poach. The extraordinary cumulative effect of large numbers so characteristic of China is nowhere better demonstrated than in the hundred thousands of eggs that nevertheless are daily brought by hand, or rather by neck, to the factories. Such an impression may seem too slight to be recorded. But it is typical of the kind of happening that is still most significant for the larger part of industrial China. Even this fact is increasing the value of land, raising the standard of living so that rural families that had only one bedding now have two, and is changing the attitude toward railways from one of hostility to one of favor.

In these primitive districts one realizes also the immense odds that have to be overcome. There are districts of a million population that a few years ago had no public schools whatever, no public press, no postoffices, and where these facilities are still most scanty. The great positive obstacle is the activity of bandits. Being a robber is a recognized profession like being a merchant. The well-to-do live in constant fear of being looted so that their homes are almost as bare as those of beggars and in fear of being kidnapped for ransom. The professions of soldier and bandit are interchangeable, and upon the whole the peasants prefer the latter. One hears the story of the traveller who met a whole village in flight with their household goods on mules and in wheelbarrows, because the soldiers were coming to protect them from bandits.

It is such facts as these that lead many to assert that any genuine industrial development of China must wait upon the formation of a strong and stabilized government. The significance of the political factor is evidenced in the province of Anwhei which juts into the northern part of Kiangsu. Here is seen the perfect flower of militarism. The military governor recently closed all schools in the province for a year in order to spend the money on his army. He has been getting personal possession of all the mines in the province and recently diverted a river from two cities in order to make a canal to some of his mines. This is only an extreme case of the effect of present political conditions upon the industrial growth of China. Almost everywhere officials use their power, based on control of soldiers, to exact tribute. They levy blackmail on mills and mines; use the control of railways to manipulate the supply of cars until they can force an interest to be given them. Then they reinvest their funds in pawn shops, banks and other agencies of economic domination. Thus a new kind of feudalism is growing up in which militarism is a direct adjunct to capitalism. These men keep their spare millions in foreign banks and have places of refuge in foreign concessions. The control of the Ministries of Communications and of Finance is equivalent to an economic overlordship of China, and the effects ramify everywhere. The station master has to pay several thousands of dollars to get his job, and he recoups by charging fifty or a hundred dollars when a shipper wants a car. Yet industry and commerce are advancing, and there is probably as much reason for thinking that in the end their growth will reform government as that a stabilized government will permit the normal growth of industry.

The third class of towns consists of cities that also represent old China, but the prosperous and cultivated side of old China, cities that are now lazy, luxurious and refined along with extreme poverty and ignorance; towns that are slowly degenerating, for they want none of the new methods while at the same time the new methods are diverting industry and trade from them. To these cities go many retired officials with their stolen funds. As one moves about near the clubhouses and gilded house boats one hears everywhere the click of the gambling dominoes. There is money for dissipation and opium, but little for new industrial developments. Surplus funds are invested in neighboring rice lands; old small owners are crowded out, and a large class of tenant farmers is being created where family ownership has been the rule. Where the northern towns are merely primitive and backward, these once rich cities of the southern part of the province are reactionary and corrupt.

Finally there are industrial towns where foreigners cannot own land or trade, and where the chimneys of cotton and flour mills and silk filatures are as numerous and smoky as in the factory districts of Shanghai—a development mostly of the last ten years, and indeed largely post-war. As it happens, the two most important of these towns present opposite types. In one of them the entire development has been in the hands of a single family, two brothers. And the leading spirit is one of a small group of men who vainly and heroically strove for the reformation of the Manchu dynasty from within. Finding his plans pigeon-holed and his efforts blocked, he retired to his native town and began almost single-handed a course of industrial and economic development. He has in his record the fact that he established the first strictly Chinese cotton mill in China and also the first normal school. And since both were innovations, since China had never had either of these things, he met with little but opposition and prophecies of disaster to himself and the district. Now the district is known popularly as the model town of China, with its good roads, its motor buses for connecting various villages, its technical schools, its care of blind and deaf, its total absence of beggars. But the method is that of old China at its best, a kind of Confucian paternalism; an exhibition on the small scale of the schemes for the reformation of the country which were rejected on the large scale. The combination of the new in industry and the old in ideas is signalized in the girl and woman labor in the factories, while the magnate finds it "inconvenient" that boys and girls should be educated together after the age of ten years, with the usual result that most of the girls receive no schooling. The other town represents a go-as-you-please competitive development. There is less symmetry but more vitality. Many deplore the absence of cooperation and organization in developing civic life. But it is characteristic of young China that it regards the greater individualism with all its lack of system as more promising than what it terms the benevolent autocracy of the model town.

But all of the industrial towns have one problem in common, and it is the problem of China. Is the industrial development of China to repeat the history of Great Britain, the United States and Japan until the evils of total laissez faire bring about a labor movement and a class struggle?[1] Or will the experience of other countries be utilized and will the development be humanized? China is the land of problems, of problems so deadlocked and interlocked that one is constantly reminded of the Chinese puzzles of his childhood days. But for China and for the whole world this problem of the direction to be taken by its industrial evolution is the one of chief importance. Outwardly all the signs as yet point

1. The nationalistic revolution which has occurred since this was written has brought with it a development of labor unions, and also at times a class-war.

to movement in the inhuman direction, to blind repetition of the worst stages of the western industrial revolution. There are no factory laws, and if there were, no government capable of administering and enforcing them. You find silk filatures in which children of eight and ten are working fourteen hours a day for a pittance, and twelve hours is the regular shift in all the mills. And these establishments have many of them for the last few years paid dividends of from fifty to two hundred and fifty per cent a year. Superficially China looks at the outset of its industrial career like the paradise of the socially unrestrained exploiter. The case however is not so simple or so certain. It is still conceivable that the future historian will say that the resistance of China to the introduction of the agencies of modern production and distribution, the resistance which was long cited as the classic instance of stupid conservatism, was in truth the manifestation of a mighty social instinct which led China to wait until the world had reached a point where it was possible for society to control the industrial revolution instead of being its slave. But the tail of an article is no place even to list the conditions and forces which make such a history conceivable, and only conceivable at the best.

Reconstruction in Philosophy

Prefatory Note

Being invited to lecture at the Imperial University of Japan in Tokyo during February and March of the present year, I attempted an interpretation of the reconstruction of ideas and ways of thought now going on in philosophy. While the lectures cannot avoid revealing the marks of the particular standpoint of their author, the aim is to exhibit the general contrasts between older and newer types of philosophic problems rather than to make a partisan plea in behalf of any one specific solution of these problems. I have tried for the most part to set forth the forces which make intellectual reconstruction inevitable and to prefigure some of the lines upon which it must proceed.

Any one who has enjoyed the unique hospitality of Japan will be overwhelmed with confusion if he endeavors to make an acknowledgment in any way commensurate to the kindnesses he received. Yet I must set down in the barest of black and white my grateful appreciation of them, and in particular record my ineffaceable impressions of the courtesy and help of the members of the department of philosophy of Tokyo University, and of my dear friends Dr. Ono and Dr. Nitobe.

1. CHANGING CONCEPTIONS OF PHILOSOPHY

Man differs from the lower animals because he preserves his past experiences. What happened in the past is lived again in memory. About what goes on today hangs a cloud of thoughts concerning similar things undergone in bygone days. With the animals, an experience perishes as it happens, and each new doing or suffering stands alone. But man lives in a world where each occurrence is charged with echoes and reminiscences of what has gone before, where each event is a reminder of other things. Hence he lives not, like the beasts of the field, in a world of merely physical things but in a world of signs and symbols. A stone is not merely hard, a thing into which one bumps; but it is a monument of a deceased ancestor. A flame is not merely something which warms or burns, but is a symbol of the enduring life of the household, of the abiding source of cheer, nourishment and shelter to which man returns from his casual wanderings. Instead of being a quick fork of fire which may sting and hurt, it is the hearth at which one worships and for which one fights. And all this which marks the difference between bestiality and humanity, between culture and merely physical nature, is because man remembers, preserving and recording his experiences.

The revivals of memory are, however, rarely literal. We naturally remember what interests us and because it interests us. The past is recalled not because of itself but because of what it adds to the present. Thus the primary life of memory is emotional rather than intellectual and practical. Savage man recalled yesterday's struggle with an animal not in order to study in a scientific way the qualities of the animal or for the sake of calculating how better to fight tomorrow, but to escape from the tedium of today by regaining the thrill of yesterday. The memory has all the excitement of the combat without its danger and anxiety. To revive it and revel in it is to enhance the present moment with a new meaning, a meaning different from that which actually belongs either to it or to the past. Memory is vicarious experience in which there are all the emotional values of actual experience without its strains, vicissitudes and troubles. The triumph of battle is even more poignant in the memorial war dance than at the moment of victory; the conscious and truly human experience of of the chase comes when it is talked over and re-enacted by the camp fire. At the time, attention is taken up with practical details and with the strain of uncertainty. Only later do the details compose into a story and fuse into a whole of meaning. At the time of practical experience man exists from moment to moment, preoccupied with the task of the moment. As he resurveys all the moments in thought, a drama emerges with a beginning, a middle and a movement toward the climax of achievement or defeat.

Since man revives his past experience because of the interest added to what would otherwise be the emptiness of present leisure, the primitive life of memory is one of fancy and imagination, rather than of accurate recollection. After all, it is the story, the drama, which counts. Only those incidents are selected which have a present emotional value, to intensify the present tale as it is rehearsed in imagination or told to an admiring listener. What does not add to the thrill of combat or contribute to the goal of success or failure is dropped. Incidents are rearranged till they fit into the temper of the tale. Thus early man when left to himself, when not actually engaged in the struggle for existence, lived in a world of memories which was a world of suggestions. A suggestion differs from a recollection in that no attempt is made to test its correctness. Its correctness is a matter of relative indifference. The cloud suggests a camel or a man's face. It could not suggest these things unless some time there had been an actual, literal experience of camel and face. But the real likeness is of no account. The main thing is the emotional interest in tracing the camel or following the fortunes of the face as it forms and dissolves.

Students of the primitive history of mankind tell of the enormous part played by animal tales, myths and cults. Sometimes a mystery is made out of this historical fact, as if it indicated that primitive man was moved by a different psychology from that which now animates humanity. But the explanation is, I think, simple. Until agriculture and the higher industrial arts were developed, long periods of empty leisure alternated with comparatively short periods of energy put forth to secure food or safety from attack. Because of our own habits, we tend to think of people as busy or occupied, if not with doing at least with thinking and planning. But then men were busy only when engaged in the hunt or fishing or fighting expedition. Yet the mind when awake must have some filling; it cannot remain literally vacant because the body is idle. And what thoughts should crowd into the human mind except experiences with animals, experiences transformed under the influence of dramatic interest to make more vivid and coherent the events typical of the chase? As men in fancy dramatically re-lived the interesting parts of their actual lives, animals inevitably became themselves dramatized.

They were true *dramatis personae* and as such assumed the traits of persons. They too had desires, hopes and fears, a life of affections, loves and hates, triumphs and defeats. Moreover, since they were essential to the support of the community, their activities and sufferings made them, in the imagination which dramatically revived the past, true sharers in the life of the community. Although they were hunted, yet they permitted themselves after all to be caught, and hence they were friends and allies. They devoted themselves, quite literally, to the sustenance and well-being of the community group to which they belonged. Thus were produced not merely the multitude of tales and legends dwelling affectionately upon the activities and features of animals, but also those elaborate rites and cults which made animals ancestors, heroes, tribal figure-heads and divinities.

I hope that I do not seem to you to have gone too far afield from my topic, the origin of philosophies. For it seems to me that the historic source of philosophies cannot be understood except as we dwell, at even greater length and in more detail, upon such considerations as these. We need to recognize that the ordinary consciousness of the ordinary man left to himself is a creature of desires rather than of intellectual study, inquiry or speculation. Man ceases to be primarily actuated by hopes and fears, loves and hates, only when he is subjected to a discipline which is foreign to human nature, which is, from the standpoint of natural man, artificial. Naturally our books, our scientific and philosophical books, are written by men who have subjected themselves in a superior degree to intellectual discipline and culture. Their thoughts are habitually reasonable. They have learned to check their fancies by facts, and to organize their ideas logically rather than emotionally and dramatically. When they do indulge in reverie and day-dreaming—which is probably more of the time than is conventionally acknowledged—they are aware of what they are doing. They label these excursions, and do not confuse their results with objective experiences. We tend to judge others by ourselves, and because scientific and philosophic books are composed by men in whom the reasonable, logical and objective habit of mind predominates, a similar rationality has been attributed by them to the average and ordinary man. It is then overlooked that both rationality and irrationality are largely irrelevant and episodical in undisciplined human nature; that men are governed by memory rather than by thought, and that memory is not a remembering of actual facts, but is association, suggestion, dramatic fancy. The standard used to measure the value of the suggestions that spring up in the mind is not congruity with fact but emotional congeniality. Do they stimulate and reinforce feeling, and fit into the dramatic tale? Are they consonant with the prevailing mood, and can they be rendered into the traditional hopes and fears of the community? If we are willing to take the word dreams with a certain liberality, it is hardly too much to say that man, save in his occasional times of actual work and struggle, lives in a world of dreams, rather than of facts, and a world of dreams that is organized about desires whose success and frustration form its stuff.

To treat the early beliefs and traditions of mankind as if they were attempts at scientific explanation of the world, only erroneous and absurd attempts, is thus to be guilty of a great mistake. The material out of which philosophy finally emerges is irrelevant to science and to explanation. It is figurative, symbolic of fears and hopes, made of imaginations and suggestions, not significant of a world of objective fact intellectually confronted. It is poetry and drama, rather than science, and is apart from scientific truth and falsity, rationality or absurdity of fact in the same way in which poetry is independent of these things.

This original material has, however, to pass through at least two stages before it becomes philosophy proper. One is the stage in which stories and legends and their accompanying dramatizations are consolidated. At first the emotionalized records of experiences are largely casual and transitory. Events that excite the emotions of an individual are seized upon and lived over in tale and pantomime. But some experiences are so frequent and recurrent that they concern the group as a whole. They are socially generalized. The piecemeal adventure of the single individual is built out till it becomes representative and typical of the emotional life of the tribe. Certain incidents affect the weal and woe of the group in its entirety and thereby get an exceptional emphasis and elevation. A certain texture of tradition is built up; the story becomes a social heritage and possession; the pantomime develops into the stated rite. Tradition thus formed becomes a kind of norm to which individual fancy and suggestion conform. An abiding framework of imagination is constructed. A communal way of conceiving life grows up into which individuals are inducted by education. Both unconsciously and by definite social requirement individual memories are assimilated to group memory or tradition, and individual fancies are accommodated to the body of beliefs characteristic of a community. Poetry becomes fixated and systematized. The story becomes a social norm. The original drama which re-enacts an emotionally important experience is institutionalized into a cult. Suggestions previously free are hardened into doctrines.

The systematic and obligatory nature of such doctrines is hastened and confirmed through conquests and political consolidation. As the area of a government is extended, there is a definite motive for systematizing and unifying beliefs once free and floating. Aside from natural accommodation and assimilation springing from the fact of intercourse and the needs of common understanding, there is often political necessity which leads the ruler to centralize traditions and beliefs in order to extend and strengthen his prestige and authority. Judea, Greece, Rome, and I presume all other countries having a long history, present records of a continual working over of earlier local rites and doctrines in the interests of a wider social unity and a more extensive political power. I shall ask you to assume with me that in this way the larger cosmogonies and cosmologies of the race as well as the larger ethical traditions have arisen. Whether this is literally so or not, it is not necessary to inquire, much less to demonstrate. It is enough for our purposes that under social influences there took place a fixing and organizing of doctrines and cults which gave general traits to the imagination and general rules to conduct, and that such a consolidation was a necessary antecedent to the formation of any philosophy as we understand that term.

Although a necessary antecedent, this organization and generalization of ideas and principles of belief is not the sole and sufficient generator of philosophy. There is still lacking the motive for logical system and intellectual proof. This we may suppose to be furnished by the need of reconciling the moral rules and ideals embodied in the traditional code with the matter-of-fact positivistic knowledge which gradually grows up. For man can never be wholly the creature of suggestion and fancy. The requirements of continued existence make indispensable some attention to the actual facts of the world. Although it is surprising how little check the environment actually puts upon the formation of ideas, since no notions are too absurd not to have been accepted by some people, yet the environment does enforce a certain minimum of correctness under penalty of extinction. That certain things are foods, that they are to be found in certain places, that water drowns, fire burns, that sharp points penetrate and cut, that heavy things fall unless supported, that there is a certain regularity in the changes of day and night and the alternation of hot and cold, wet and dry:—such prosaic facts force themselves upon even primitive attention. Some of them are so obvious and so important that they have next to no fanciful context. Auguste Comte says somewhere that he knows of no savage people who had a God of weight although every other natural quality or force may have been deified. Gradually there grows up a body of homely generalizations preserving and transmitting the wisdom of the race about the observed facts and sequences of nature. This knowledge is especially connected with industries, arts and crafts where observation of materials and processes is required for successful action, and where action is so continuous and regular that spasmodic magic will not suffice. Extravagantly fantastic notions are eliminated because they are brought into juxtaposition with what actually happens.

The sailor is more likely to be given to what we now term superstitions than say the weaver, because his activity is more at the mercy of sudden change and unforeseen occurrence. But even the sailor while he may regard the wind as the uncontrollable expression of the caprice of a great spirit, will still have to become acquainted with some purely mechanical principles of adjustment of boat, sails and oar to the wind. Fire may be conceived as a supernatural dragon because some time or other a swift, bright and devouring flame called before the mind's eye the quick-moving and dangerous serpent. But the housewife who tends the fire and the pots wherein food cooks will still be compelled to observe certain mechanical facts of draft and replenishment, and passage from wood to ash. Still more will the worker in metals accumulate verifiable details about the conditions and consequences of the operation of heat. He may retain for special and ceremonial occasions traditional beliefs, but everyday familiar use will expel these conceptions for the greater part of the time, when fire will be to him of uniform and prosaic behavior, controllable by practical relations of cause and effect. As the arts and crafts develop and become more elaborate, the body of positive and tested knowledge enlarges, and the sequences observed become more complex and of greater scope. Technologies of this kind give that common-sense knowledge of nature out of which science takes its origin. They provide not merely a collection of positive facts, but they give expertness in dealing with materials and tools, and promote the development of the experimental habit of mind, as soon as an art can be taken away from the rule of sheer custom.

For a long time the imaginative body of beliefs closely connected with the moral habits of a community group and with its emotional indulgences and consolations persists side by side with the growing body of matter-of-fact knowledge. Wherever possible they are interlaced. At other points, their inconsistencies forbid their interweaving, but the two things are kept apart as if in different compartments. Since one is merely superimposed upon the other their incompatibility is not felt, and there is no need of reconciliation. In most cases, the two kinds of mental products are kept apart because they become the possession of separate social classes. The religious and poetic beliefs having acquired a definite social and political value and function are in the keeping of a higher class directly associated with the ruling elements in the society. The workers and craftsmen who possess the prosaic matter-of-fact knowledge are likely to occupy a low social status, and their kind of knowledge is affected by the social disesteem entertained for the manual worker who engages in activities useful to the body. It doubtless was this fact in Greece which in spite of the keenness of observation, the extraordinary power of logical reasoning and the great freedom of speculation attained by the Athenian, postponed the general and systematic employment of the experimental method. Since the industrial craftsman was only just above the slave in social rank, his type of knowledge and the method upon which it depended lacked prestige and authority.

Nevertheless, the time came when matter-of-fact knowledge increased to such bulk and scope that it came into conflict with not merely the detail but with the spirit and temper of traditional and imaginative beliefs. Without going into the vexed question of how and why, there is no doubt that this is just what happened in what we term the sophistic movement in Greece, within which originated philosophy proper in the sense in which the western world understands that term. The fact that the sophists had a bad name given them by Plato and Aristotle, a name they have never been able to shake off, is evidence that with the sophists the strife between the two types of belief was the emphatic thing, and that the conflict had a disconcerting effect upon the traditional system of religious beliefs and the moral code of conduct bound up with it. Although Socrates was doubtless sincerely interested in the reconciliation of the two sides, yet the fact that he approached the matter from the side of matter-of-fact method, giving its canons and criteria primacy, was enough to bring him to the condemnation of death as a contemner of the gods and a corrupter of youth.

The fate of Socrates and the ill-fame of the sophists may be used to suggest some of the striking contrasts between traditional emotionalized belief on one hand and prosaic matter-of-fact knowledge on the other:—the purpose of the comparison being to bring out the point that while all the advantages of what we call science were on the side of the latter, the advantages of social esteem and authority, and of intimate contact with what gives life its deeper-lying values were on the side of traditional belief. To all appearances, the specific and verified knowledge of the environment had only a limited and technical scope. It had to do with the arts, and the purpose and good of the artisan after all did not extend very far. They were subordinate and almost servile. Who would put the art of the shoemaker on the same plane as the art of ruling the state? Who would put even the higher art of the physician in healing the body, upon the level of the art of the priest in healing the soul? Thus Plato constantly draws the contrast in his dialogues. The shoemaker is a judge of a good pair of shoes, but he is no judge at all of the more important question whether and when it is good to wear shoes; the physician is a good judge of health, but whether it is a good thing or not to be well or better to die, he knows not. While the artisan is expert as long as purely limited technical questions arise, he is helpless when it comes to the only really important questions, the moral questions as to values. Consequently, his type of knowledge is inherently inferior and needs to be controlled by a higher kind of knowledge which will reveal ultimate ends and purposes, and thus put and keep technical and mechanical knowledge in its proper place. Moreover, in Plato's pages we find, because of Plato's adequate dramatic sense, a lively depicting of the impact in particular men of the conflict between tradition and the new claims of purely intellectual knowledge. The conservative is shocked beyond measure at the idea of teaching the military art by abstract rules, by science. One does not just fight, one fights for one's country. Abstract science cannot convey love and loyalty, nor can it be a substitute, even upon the more technical side, for those ways and means of fighting in which devotion to the country has been traditionally embodied.

The way to learn the fighting art is through association with those who have themselves learned to defend the country, by becoming saturated with its ideals and customs; by becoming in short a practical adept in the Greek tradition as to fighting. To attempt to derive abstract rules from a comparison of native ways of fighting with the enemies' ways is to begin to go over to the enemies' traditions and gods: it is to begin to be false to one's own country.

Such a point of view vividly realized enables us to appreciate the antagonism aroused by the positivistic point of view when it came into conflict with the traditional. The latter was deeply rooted in social habits and loyalties; it was surcharged with the moral aims for which men lived and the moral rules by which they lived. Hence it was as basic and as comprehensive as life itself, and palpitated with the warm glowing colors of the community life in which men realized their own being. In contrast, the positivistic knowledge was concerned with merely physical utilities, and lacked the ardent associations of belief hallowed by sacrifices of ancestors and worship of contemporaries. Because of its limited and concrete character it was dry, hard, cold.

Yet the more acute and active minds, like that of Plato himself, could no longer be content to accept, along with the conservative citizen of the time, the old beliefs in the old way. The growth of positive knowledge and of the critical, inquiring spirit undermined these in their old form. The advantages in definiteness, in accuracy, in verifiability were all on the side of the new knowledge. Tradition was noble in aim and scope, but uncertain in foundation. The unquestioned life, said Socrates, was not one fit to be lived by man, who is a questioning being because he is a rational being. Hence he must search out the reason of things, and not accept them from custom and political authority. What was to be done? Develop a method of rational investigation and proof which should place the essential elements of traditional belief upon an unshakable basis; develop a method of thought and knowledge which while purifying tradition should preserve its moral and social values unimpaired; nay, by purifying them, add to their power and authority. To put it in a word, that which had rested upon custom was to be restored, resting no longer upon the habits of the past, but upon the very metaphysics of Being and the Universe. Metaphysics is a substitute for custom as the source and guarantor of higher moral and social values—that is the leading theme of the classic philosophy of Europe, as evolved by Plato and Aristotle—a philosophy, let us always recall, renewed and restated by the Christian philosophy of Medieval Europe.

Out of this situation emerged, if I mistake not, the entire tradition regarding the function and office of philosophy which till very recently has controlled the systematic and constructive philosophies of the western world. If I am right in my main thesis that the origin of philosophy lay in an attempt to reconcile the two different types of mental product, then the key is in our hands as to the main traits of subsequent philosophy so far as that was not of a negative and heterodox kind. In the first place, philosophy did not develop in an unbiased way from an open and unprejudiced origin. It had its task cut out for it from the start. It had a mission to perform, and it was sworn in advance to that mission. It had to extract the essential moral kernel out of the threatened traditional beliefs of the past. So far so good; the work was critical and in the interests of the only true conservatism—that which will conserve and not waste the values wrought out by humanity. But it was also precommitted to extracting this moral essence in a spirit congenial to the spirit of past beliefs. The association with imagination and with social authority was too intimate to be deeply disturbed. It was not possible to conceive of the content of social institutions in any form radically different from that in which they had existed in the past. It became the work of philosophy to justify on rational grounds the spirit, though not the form, of accepted beliefs and traditional customs.

The resulting philosophy seemed radical enough and even dangerous to the average Athenian because of the difference of form and method. In the sense of pruning away excrescences and eliminating factors which to the average citizen were all one with the basic beliefs, it was radical. But looked at in the perspective of history and in contrast with different types of thought which developed later in different social environments, it is now easy to see how profoundly, after all, Plato and Aristotle reflected the meaning of Greek tradition and habit, so that their writings remain, with the writings of the great dramatists, the best introduction of a student into the innermost ideals and aspirations of distinctively Greek life. Without Greek religion, Greek art, Greek civic life, their philosophy would have been impossible; while the effect of that science upon which the philosophers most prided themselves turns out to have been superficial and negligible. This apologetic spirit of philosophy is even more apparent when Medieval Christianity about the twelfth century sought for a systematic rational presentation of itself and made use of classic philosophy, especially that of Aristotle, to justify itself to reason. A not unsimilar occurrence characterizes the chief philosophic systems of Germany in the early nineteenth century, when Hegel assumed the task of justifying in the name of rational idealism the doctrines and institutions which were menaced by the new spirit of science and popular government. The result has been that the great systems have not been free from party spirit exercised in behalf of preconceived beliefs. Since they have at the same time professed complete intellectual independence and rationality, the result has been too often to impart to philosophy an element of insincerity, all the more insidious because wholly unconscious on the part of those who sustained philosophy.

And this brings us to a second trait of philosophy springing from its origin. Since it aimed at a rational justification of things that had been previously accepted because of their emotional congeniality and social prestige, it had to make much of the apparatus of reason and proof. Because of the lack of intrinsic rationality in the matters with which it dealt, it leaned over backward, so to speak, in parade of logical form. In dealing with matters of fact, simpler and rougher ways of demonstration may be resorted to. It is enough, so to say, to produce the fact in question and point to it—the fundamental form of all demonstration. But when it comes to convincing men of the truth of doctrines which are no longer to be accepted upon the say-so of custom and social authority, but which also are not capable of empirical verification, there is no recourse save to magnify the signs of rigorous thought and rigid demonstration. Thus arises that appearance of abstract definition and ultra-scientific argumentation which repels so many from philosophy but which has been one of its chief attractions to its devotees.

At the worst, this has reduced philosophy to a show of elaborate terminology, a hair-splitting logic, and a fictitious devotion to the mere external forms of comprehensive and minute demonstration. Even at the best, it has tended to produce an overdeveloped attachment to system for its own sake, and an over-pretentious claim to certainty. Bishop Butler declared that probability is the guide of life; but few philosophers have been courageous enough to avow that philosophy can be satisfied with anything that is merely probable. The customs dictated by tradition and desire had claimed finality and immutability. They had claimed to give certain and unvarying laws of conduct. Very early in its history philosophy made pretension to a similar conclusiveness, and something of this temper has clung to classic philosophies ever since. They have insisted that they were more scientific than the sciences—that, indeed, philosophy was necessary because after all the special sciences fail in attaining final and complete truth. There have been a few dissenters who have ventured to assert, as did William James, that "philosophy is vision" and that its chief function is to free men's minds from bias and prejudice and to enlarge their perceptions of the world about them. But in the main philosophy has set up much more ambitious pretensions. To say frankly that philosophy can proffer nothing but hypotheses, and that these hypotheses are of value only as they render men's minds more sensitive to life about them, would seem like a negation of philosophy itself.

In the third place, the body of beliefs dictated by desire and imagination and developed under the influence of communal authority into an authoritative tradition, was pervasive and comprehensive. It was, so to speak, omnipresent in all the details of the group life. Its pressure was unremitting and its influence universal. It was then probably inevitable that the rival principle, reflective thought, should aim at a similar universality and comprehensiveness. It would be as inclusive and far-reaching metaphysically as tradition had been socially. Now there was just one way in which this pretension could be accomplished in conjunction with a claim of complete logical system and certainty.

All philosophies of the classic type have made a fixed and fundamental distinction between two realms of existence. One of these corresponds to the religious and supernatural world of popular tradition, which in its metaphysical rendering became the world of highest and ultimate reality. Since the final source and sanction of all important truths and rules of conduct in community life had been found in superior and unquestioned religious beliefs, so the absolute and supreme reality of philosophy afforded the only sure guarantee of truth about empirical matters, and the sole rational guide to proper social institutions and individual behavior. Over against this absolute and noumenal reality which could be apprehended only by the systematic discipline of philosophy itself stood the ordinary empirical, relatively real, phenomenal world of everyday experience. It was with this world that the practical affairs and utilities of men were connected. It was to this imperfect and perishing world that matter-of-fact, positivistic science referred.

This is the trait which, in my opinion, has affected most deeply the classic notion about the nature of philosophy. Philosophy has arrogated to itself the office of demonstrating the existence of a transcendent, absolute or inner reality and of revealing to man the nature and features of this ultimate and higher reality. It has therefore claimed that it was in possession of a higher organ of knowledge than is employed by positive science and ordinary practical experience, and that it is marked by a superior dignity and importance—a claim which is undeniable *if* philosophy leads man to proof and intuition of a Reality beyond that open to day-by-day life and the special sciences.

This claim has, of course, been denied by various philosophers from time to time. But for the most part these denials have been agnostic and sceptical. They have contented themselves with asserting that absolute and ultimate reality is beyond human ken. But they have not ventured to deny that such Reality would be the appropriate sphere for the exercise of philosophic knowledge provided only it were within the reach of human intelligence. Only comparatively recently has another conception of the proper office of philosophy arisen. This course of lectures will be devoted to setting forth this different conception of philosophy in some of its main contrasts to what this lecture has termed the classic conception. At this point, it can be referred to only by anticipation and in cursory fashion. It is implied in the account which has been given of the origin of philosophy out of the background of an authoritative tradition; a tradition originally dictated by man's imagination working under the influence of love and hate and in the interest of emotional excitement and satisfaction. Common frankness requires that it be stated that this account of the origin of philosophies claiming to deal with absolute Being in a systematic way has been given with malice prepense. It seems to me that this genetic method of approach is a more effective way of undermining this type of philosophic theorizing than any attempt at logical refutation could be.

If this lecture succeeds in leaving in your minds as a reasonable hypothesis the idea that philosophy originated not out of intellectual material, but out of social and emotional material, it will also succeed in leaving with you a changed attitude toward traditional philosophies. They will be viewed from a new angle and placed in a new light. New questions about them will be aroused and new standards for judging them will be suggested.

If any one will commence without mental reservations to study the history of philosophy not as an isolated thing but as a chapter in the development of civilization and culture; if one will connect the story of philosophy with a study of anthropology, primitive life, the history of religion, literature and social institutions, it is confidently asserted that he will reach his own independent judgment as to the worth of the account which has been presented today. Considered in this way, the history of philosophy will take on a new significance. What is lost from the standpoint of would-be science is regained from the standpoint of humanity. Instead of the disputes of rivals about the nature of reality, we have the scene of human clash of social purpose and aspirations. Instead of impossible attempts to transcend experience, we have the significant record of the efforts of men to formulate the things of experience to which they are most deeply and passionately attached. Instead of impersonal and purely speculative endeavors to contemplate as remote beholders the nature of absolute things-in-themselves, we have a living picture of the choice of thoughtful men about what they would have life to be, and to what ends they would have men shape their intelligent activities.

Any one of you who arrives at such a view of past philosophy will of necessity be led to entertain a quite definite conception of the scope and aim of future philosophizing. He will inevitably be committed to the notion that what philosophy has been unconsciously, without knowing or intending it, and, so to speak, under cover, it must henceforth be openly and deliberately. When it is acknowledged that under disguise of dealing with ultimate reality, philosophy has been occupied with the precious values embedded in social traditions, that it has sprung from a clash of social ends and from a conflict of inherited institutions with incompatible contemporary tendencies, it will be seen that the task of future philosophy is to clarify men's ideas as to the social and moral strifes of their own day. Its aim is to become so far as is humanly possible an organ for dealing with these conflicts. That which may be pretentiously unreal when it is formulated in metaphysical distinctions becomes intensely significant when connected with the drama of the struggle of social beliefs and ideals. Philosophy which surrenders its somewhat barren monopoly of dealings with Ultimate and Absolute Reality will find a compensation in enlightening the moral forces which move mankind and in contributing to the aspirations of men to attain to a more ordered and intelligent happiness.

SOME HISTORICAL FACTORS IN
PHILOSOPHICAL RECONSTRUCTION

Francis Bacon of the Elizabethan age is the great forerunner of the spirit of modern life. Though slight in accomplishment, as a prophet of new tendencies he is an outstanding figure of the world's intellectual life. Like many another prophet he suffers from confused intermingling of old and new. What is most significant in him has been rendered more or less familiar by the later course of events. But page after page is filled with matter which belongs to the past from which Bacon thought he had escaped. Caught between these two sources of easy disparagement, Bacon hardly receives his due as the real founder of modern thought, while he is praised for merits which scarcely belong to him, such as an alleged authorship of the specific methods of induction pursued by science. What makes Bacon memorable is that breezes blowing from a new world caught and filled his sails and stirred him to adventure in new seas. He never himself discovered the land of promise, but he proclaimed the new goal and by faith he descried its features from afar.

The main traits of his thought put before our mind the larger features of a new spirit which was at work in causing intellectual reconstruction. They may suggest the social and historical forces out of which the new spirit was born. The best known aphorism of Bacon is that Knowledge is Power. Judged by this pragmatic criterion, he condemned the great body of learning then extant as *not*-knowledge, as pseudo- and pretentious-knowledge. For it did not give power. It was otiose, not operative. In his most extensive discussion he classified the learning of his day under three heads, delicate, fantastic and contentious. Under delicate learning, he included the literary learning which through the influence of the revival of ancient languages and literatures occupied so important a place in the intellectual life of the Renaissance. Bacon's condemnation is the more effective because he himself was a master of the classics and of all the graces and refinements which this literary study was intended to convey. In substance he anticipated most of the attacks which educational reformers since his time have made upon one-sided literary culture. It contributed not to power but to ornament and decoration. It was ostentatious and luxurious. By fantastic learning he meant the quasi-magical science that was so rife all over Europe in the sixteenth century—wild developments of alchemy, astrology, etc. Upon this he poured his greatest vials of wrath because the corruption of the good is the worst of evils. Delicate learning was idle and vain, but fantastic learning aped the form of true knowledge. It laid hold of the true principle and aim of knowledge—control of natural forces. But it neglected the conditions and methods by which alone such knowledge could be obtained, and thus deliberately led men astray.

For our purposes, however, what he says about contentious learning is the most important. For by this, he means the traditional science which had come down, in scanty and distorted measure to be sure, from antiquity through scholasticism. It is called contentious both because of the logical method used and the end to which it was put. In a certain sense it aimed at power, but power over other men in the interest of some class or sect or person, not power over natural forces in the common interest of all. Bacon's conviction of the quarrelsome, self-displaying character of the scholarship which had come down from antiquity was of course not so much due to Greek science itself as to the degenerate heritage of scholasticism in the fourteenth century, when philosophy had fallen into the hands of disputatious theologians, full of hair-splitting argumentativeness and quirks and tricks by which to win victory over somebody else.

But Bacon also brought his charge against the Aristotelian method itself. In its rigorous forms it aimed at demonstration, and in its milder forms at persuasion. But both demonstration and persuasion aim at conquest of mind rather than of nature. Moreover they both assume that some one is already in possession of a truth or a belief, and that the only problem is to convince some one else, or to teach. In contrast, his new method had an exceedingly slight opinion of the amount of truth already existent, and a lively sense of the extent and importance of truths still to be attained. It would be a logic of discovery, not a logic of argumentation, proof and persuasion. To Bacon, the old logic even at its best was a logic for teaching the already known, and teaching meant indoctrination, discipling. It was an axiom of Aristotle that only that which was already known could be learned, that growth in knowledge consisted simply in bringing together a universal truth of reason and a particular truth of sense which had previously been noted separately. In any case, learning meant *growth* of knowledge, and growth belongs in the region of becoming, change, and hence is inferior to *possession* of knowledge in the syllogistic self-revolving manipulation of what was already known—demonstration.

In contrast with this point of view, Bacon eloquently proclaimed the superiority of discovery of new facts and truths to demonstration of the old. Now there is only one road to discovery, and that is penetrating inquiry into the secrets of nature. Scientific principles and laws do not lie on the surface of nature. They are hidden, and must be wrested from nature by an active and elaborate technique of inquiry. Neither logical reasoning nor the passive accumulation of any number of observations—which the ancients called experience—suffices to lay hold of them. Active experimentation must force the apparent facts of nature into forms different to those in which they familiarly present themselves; and thus make them tell the truth about themselves, as torture may compel an unwilling witness to reveal what he has been concealing. Pure reasoning as a means of arriving at truth is like the spider who spins a web out of himself. The web is orderly and elaborate, but it is only a trap. The passive accumulation of experiences—the traditional empirical method—is like the ant who busily runs about and collects and piles up heaps of raw materials. True method, that which Bacon would usher in, is comparable to the operations of the bee who, like the ant, collects material from the external world, but unlike that industrious creature attacks and modifies the collected stuff in order to make it yield its hidden treasure.

Along with this contrast between subjugation of nature and subjection of other minds and the elevation of a method of discovery above a method of demonstration, went Bacon's sense of progress as the aim and test of genuine knowledge. According to his criticisms, the classic logic, even in its Aristotelian form, inevitably played into the hands of inert conservatism. For in accustoming the mind to think of truth as already known, it habituated men to fall back on the intellectual attainments of the past, and to accept them without critical scrutiny. Not merely the medieval but the renaissance mind tended to look back to antiquity as a Golden Age of Knowledge, the former relying upon sacred scriptures, the latter upon secular literatures. And while this attitude could not fairly be charged up against the classic logic, yet Bacon felt, and with justice, that any logic which identified the technique of knowing with demonstration of truths already possessed by the mind, blunts the spirit of investigation and confines the mind within the circle of traditional learning.

Such a logic could not avoid having for its salient features definition of what is already known (or thought to be known), and its systematization according to recognized canons of orthodoxy. A logic of discovery on the other hand looks to the future. Received truth it regards critically as something to be tested by new experiences rather than as something to be dogmatically taught and obediently received. Its chief interest in even the most carefully tested ready-made knowledge is the use which may be made of it in further inquiries and discoveries. Old truth has its chief value in assisting the detection of new truth. Bacon's own appreciation of the nature of induction was highly defective. But his acute sense that science means invasion of the unknown, rather than repetition in logical form of the already known, makes him nevertheless the father of induction. Endless and persistent uncovering of facts and principles not known—such is the true spirit of induction. Continued progress in knowledge is the only sure way of protecting old knowledge from degeneration into dogmatic doctrines received on authority, or from imperceptible decay into susperstition and old wives' tales.

Ever-renewed progress is to Bacon the test as well as the aim of genuine logic. Where, Bacon constantly demands, where are the works, the fruits, of the older logic? What has it done to ameliorate the evils of life, to rectify defects, to improve conditions? Where are the inventions that justify its claim to be in possession of truth? Beyond the victory of man over man in law courts, diplomacy and political administration, they are nil. One had to turn from admired "sciences" to despised arts to find works, fruits, consequences of value to human kind through power over natural forces. And progress in the arts was as yet intermittent, fitful, accidental. A true logic or technique of inquiry would make advance in the industrial, agricultural and medical arts continuous, cumulative and deliberately systematic.

If we take into account the supposed body of ready-made knowledge upon which learned men rested in supine acquiescence and which they recited in parrot-like chorus, we find it consists of two parts. One of these parts is made up of the errors of our ancestors, musty with antiquity and organized into pseudo-science through the use of the classic logic. Such "truths" are in fact only the systematized mistakes and prejudices of our ancestors. Many of them originated in accident; many in class interest and bias, perpetuated by authority for this very reason—a consideration which later actuated Locke's attack upon the doctrine of innate ideas. The other portion of accepted beliefs comes from instinctive tendencies of the human mind that give it a dangerous bias until counteracted by a conscious and critical logic.

The mind of man spontaneously assumes greater simplicity, uniformity and unity among phenomena than actually exists. It follows superficial analogies and jumps to conclusions; it overlooks the variety of details and the existence of exceptions. Thus it weaves a web of purely internal origin which it imposes upon nature. What had been termed science in the past consisted of this humanly constructed and imposed web. Men looked at the work of their own minds and thought they were seeing realities in nature. They were worshipping, under the name of science, the idols of their own making. So-called science and philosophy consisted of these "anticipations" of nature. And the worst thing that could be said about traditional logic was that instead of saving man from this natural source of error, it had, through attributing to nature a false rationality of unity, simplicity and generality, sanctioned these sources of delusion. The office of the new logic would be to protect the mind against itself: to teach it to undergo a patient and prolonged apprenticeship to fact in its infinite variety and particularity: to obey nature intellectually in order to command it practically. Such was the significance of the new logic—the new tool or organon of learning, so named in express opposition to the organon of Aristotle.

Certain other important oppositions are implied. Aristotle thought of reason as capable of solitary communion with rational truth. The counterpart of his celebrated saying that man is a po-

litical animal, is that Intelligence, *Nous*, is neither animal, human
nor political. It is divinely unique and self-enclosed. To Bacon,
error had been produced and perpetuated by social influences,
and truth must be discovered by social agencies organized for
that purpose. Left to himself, the individual can do little or nothing; he is likely to become involved in his own self-spun web of
misconceptions. The great need is the organization of cooperative
research, whereby men attack nature collectively and the work of
inquiry is carried on continuously from generation to generation.
Bacon even aspired to the rather absurd notion of a method so
perfected that differences in natural human ability might be dis-
counted, and all be put on the same level in production of new
facts and new truths. Yet this absurdity was only the negative side
of his great positive prophecy of a combined and cooperative pursuit of science such as characterizes our own day. In view of the
picture he draws in his *New Atlantis* of a State organized for collective inquiry, we readily forgive him his exaggerations.

Power over nature was not to be individual but collective; the
Empire, as he says, of Man over Nature, substituted for the Empire of Man over Man. Let us employ Bacon's own words with
their variety of picturesque metaphor:

Men have entered into the desire of learning and knowledge, . . . seldom
sincerely to give a true account of their gift of reason, to the benefit and
use of men, but as if they sought in knowledge a couch whereon to rest
a searching and wandering spirit; or a terrace for a wandering and vari-
able mind to walk up and down with a fair prospect; or a tower for a proud
mind to raise itself upon; or a fort or commanding ground for strife and
contention; or a shop for profit and sale; and not a rich storehouse for the
glory of the Creator and the relief of man's estate.

When William James called Pragmatism a New Name for an Old
Way of Thinking, I do not know that he was thinking expressly of
Francis Bacon, but so far as concerns the spirit and atmosphere
of the pursuit of knowledge, Bacon may be taken as the prophet
of a pragmatic conception of knowledge. Many misconceptions of
its spirit would be avoided if his emphasis upon the social factor
in both the pursuit and the end of knowledge were carefully observed.

This somewhat over-long résumé of Bacon's ideas has not
been gone into as a matter of historic retrospect. The summary is
rather meant to put before our minds an authentic document of

the new philosophy which may bring into relief the social causes of intellectual revolution. Only a sketchy account can be here attempted, but it may be of some assistance even barely to remind you of the direction of that industrial, political and religious change upon which Europe was entering.

Upon the industrial side, it is impossible, I think, to exaggerate the influence of travel, exploration and new commerce which fostered a romantic sense of adventure into novelty; loosened the hold of traditional beliefs; created a lively sense of new worlds to be investigated and subdued; produced new methods of manufacture, commerce, banking and finance; and then reacted everywhere to stimulate invention, and to introduce positive observation and active experimentation into science. The Crusades, the revival of the profane learning of antiquity and even more perhaps, the contact with the advanced learning of the Mohammedans, the increase of commerce with Asia and Africa, the introduction of the lens, compass and gunpowder, the finding and opening up of North and South America—most significantly called The New World—these are some of the obvious external facts. Contrast between peoples and races previously isolated is always, I think, most fruitful and influential for change when psychological and industrial changes coincide with and reinforce each other. Sometimes people undergo emotional change, what might almost be called a metaphysical change, through intercourse. The inner set of the mind, especially in religious matters, is altered. At other times, there is a lively exchange of goods, an adoption of foreign tools and devices, an imitation of alien habits of clothing, habitation and production of commodities. One of these changes is, so to speak, too internal and the other too external to bring about a profound intellectual development. But when the creation of a new mental attitude falls together with extensive material and economic changes, something significant happens.

This coincidence of two kinds of change was, I take it, characteristic of the new contacts of the sixteenth and seventeenth centuries. Clash of customs and traditional beliefs dispelled mental inertia and sluggishness; it aroused a lively curiosity as to different and new ideas. The actual adventure of travel and exploration purged the mind of fear of the strange and unknown: as new territories geographically and commercially speaking were opened up, the mind was opened up. New contacts promoted the desire for still more contacts; the appetite for novelty and discovery grew by what it fed upon. Conservative adherence to old beliefs and methods underwent a steady attrition with every new voyage into new parts and every new report of foreign ways. The mind became used to exploration and discovery. It found a delight and interest in the revelations of the novel and the unusual which it no longer took in what was old and customary. Moreover, the very act of exploration, of expedition, the process of enterprising adventure into the remote, yielded a peculiar joy and thrill.

This psychological change was essential to the birth of the new point of view in science and philosophy. Yet alone it could hardly have produced the new method of knowing. But positive changes in the habits and purposes of life gave objective conformation and support to the mental change. They also determined the channels in which the new spirit found exercise. New-found wealth, the gold from the Americas and new articles of consumption and enjoyment, tended to wean men from preoccupation with the metaphysical and theological, and to turn their minds with newly awakened interest to the joys of nature and this life. New material resources and new markets in America and India undermined the old dependence upon household and manual production for a local and limited market, and generated quantitative, large scale production by means of steam for foreign and expanding markets. Capitalism, rapid transit, and production for exchange against money and for profit, instead of against goods and for consumption, followed.

This cursory and superficial reminder of vast and complicated events may suggest the mutual interdependence of the scientific revolution and the industrial revolution. Upon the one hand, modern industry *is* so much applied science. No amount of desire to make money, or to enjoy new commodities, no amount of mere practical energy and enterprise, would have effected the economic transformation of the last few centuries and generations. Improvements in mathematical, physical, chemical and biological science were prerequisites. Business men through engineers of different sorts, have laid hold of the new insights gained by scientific men into the hidden energies of nature, and have turned them to account. The modern mine, factory, railway, steamship, telegraph, all of the appliances and equipment of production, and transportation, express scientific knowledge. They would continue unimpaired even if the ordinary pecuniary accompaniments of economic activity were radically altered. In short, through the intermediary of invention, Bacon's watchword that knowledge is power and his dream of continuous empire over natural forces by means of natural science have been actualized. The industrial revolution by steam and electricity is the reply to Bacon's prophecy.

On the other hand, it is equally true that the needs of modern industry have been tremendous stimuli to scientific investigation. The demands of progressive production and transportation have set new problems to inquiry; the processes used in industry have suggested new experimental appliances and operations in science; the wealth rolled up in business has to some extent been diverted to endowment of research. The uninterrupted and pervasive interaction of scientific discovery and industrial application has fructified both science and industry, and has brought home to the contemporary mind the fact that the gist of scientific knowledge is control of natural energies. These four facts, natural science, experimentation, control and progress have been inextricably bound up together. That up to the present the application of the newer methods and results has influenced the means of life rather than its ends; or, better put, that human aims have so far been affected in an accidental rather than in an intelligently directed way, signifies that so far the change has been technical rather than human and moral, that it has been economic rather than adequately social. Put in the language of Bacon, this means that while we have been reasonably successful in obtaining command of nature by means of science, our science is not yet such that this command is systematically and preeminently applied to the relief of human estate. Such applications occur and in great numbers, but they are incidental, sporadic and external. And this limitation defines the specific problem of philosophical reconstruction at the present time. For it emphasizes the larger social deficiencies that require intelligent diagnosis, and projection of aims and methods.

It is hardly necessary to remind you however that marked political changes have already followed upon the new science and its industrial applications, and that in so far some directions of social development have at least been marked out. The growth of the new technique of industry has everywhere been followed by the fall of feudal institutions, in which the social pattern was formed in agricultural occupations and military pursuits. Wherever business in the modern sense has gone, the tendency has been to transfer power from land to financial capital, from the country to the city, from the farm to factory, from social titles based on personal allegiance, service and protection, to those based on control of labor and exchange of goods. The change in the political centre of gravity has resulted in emancipating the individual from bonds of class and custom and in producing a political organization which depends less upon superior authority and more upon voluntary choice. Modern states, in other words, are regarded less as divine, and more as human works than they used to be; less as necessary manifestations of some supreme and over-ruling principles, and more as contrivances of men and women to realize their own desires.

The contract theory of the origin of the state is a theory whose falsity may easily be demonstrated both philosophically and historically. Nevertheless this theory has had great currency and influence. In form, it stated that some time in the past men voluntarily got together and made a compact with one another to observe certain laws and to submit to certain authority and in that way brought the state and the relation of ruler and subject into existence. Like many things in philosophy, the theory, though worthless as a record of fact, is of great worth as a symptom of the direction of human desire. It testified to a growing belief that the state existed to satisfy human needs and could be shaped by human intention and volition. Aristotle's theory that the state exists by nature failed to satisfy the thought of the seventeenth century because it seemed by making the state a product of nature to remove its constitution beyond human choice. Equally significant was the assumption of the contract theory that individuals by their personal decisions expressing their personal wishes bring the state into existence. The rapidity with which the theory gained a hold all over western Europe showed the extent to which the bonds of customary institutions had relaxed their grip. It proved that men had been so liberated from absorption in larger groups that they were conscious of themselves as individuals having rights and claims on their own account, not simply as members of a class, guild or social grade.

Side by side with this political individualism went a religious and moral individualism. The metaphysical doctrine of the superiority of the species to the individual, of the permanent universal to the changing particular, was the philosophic support of political and ecclesiastical institutionalism. The universal church was the ground, end and limit of the individual's beliefs and acts in spiritual matters, just as the feudal hierarchical organization was the basis, law and fixed limit of his behavior in secular affairs. The northern barbarians had never completely come under the sway of classic ideas and customs. That which was indigenous where life was primarily derived from Latin sources was borrowed and more or less externally imposed in Germanic Europe. Protestantism marked the formal breaking away from the domination of Roman ideas. It effected liberation of individual conscience and worship from control by an organized institution claiming to be permanent and universal. It cannot truly be said that at the outset the new religious movement went far in promoting freedom of thought and criticism, or in denying the notion of some supreme authority to which individual intelligence was absolutely in bonds. Nor at first did it go far in furthering tolerance or respect for divergency of moral and religious convictions. But practically it did tend to disintegration of established institutions. By multiplying sects and churches it encouraged at least a negative toleration of the right of individuals to judge ultimate matters for themselves. In time, there developed a formulated belief in the sacredness of individual conscience and in the right to freedom of opinion, belief and worship.

It is unnecessary to point out how the spread of this conviction increased political individualism, or how it accelerated the willingness of men to question received ideas in science and philosophy—to think and observe and experiment for themselves. Religious individualism served to supply a much needed sanction to initiative and independence of thought in all spheres, even when religious movements officially were opposed to such freedom when carried beyond a limited point. The greatest influence of Protestantism was, however, in developing the idea of the personality of every human being as an end in himself. When human beings were regarded as capable of direct relationship with God, without the intermediary of any organization like the Church, and the drama of sin, redemption and salvation was something enacted within the innermost soul of individuals rather than in the species of which the individual was a subordinate part, a fatal blow was struck at all doctrines which taught the subordination of personality—a blow which had many political reverberations in promoting democracy. For when in religion the idea of the intrinsic worth of every soul as such was proclaimed, it was difficult to keep the idea from spilling over, so to say, into secular relationships.

The absurdity is obvious of trying in a few paragraphs to summarize movements in industry, politics and religion whose influence is still far from exhausted and about which hundreds and thousands of volumes have been written. But I shall count upon your forbearance to recall that these matters are alluded to only in order to suggest some of the forces that operated to mark out the channels in which new ideas ran. First, there is the transfer of interest from the eternal and universal to what is changing and specific, concrete—a movement that showed itself practically in carrying over of attention and thought from another world to this, from the supernaturalism characteristic of the Middle Ages to delight in natural science, natural activity and natural intercourse. Secondly, there is the gradual decay of the authority of fixed institutions and class distinctions and relations, and a growing belief in the power of individual minds, guided by methods of observation, experiment and reflection, to attain the truths needed for the guidance of life. The operations and results of natural inquiry gained in prestige and power at the expense of principles dictated from high authority.

Consequently principles and alleged truths are judged more and more by criteria of their origin in experience and their consequences of weal and woe in experience, and less by criteria of sublime origin from beyond everyday experience and independent of fruits in experience. It is no longer enough for a principle to be elevated, noble, universal and hallowed by time. It must present its birth certificate, it must show under just what conditions of human experience it was generated, and it must justify itself by its works, present and potential. Such is the inner meaning of the modern appeal to experience as an ultimate criterion of value and validity. In the third place, great store is set upon the idea of progress. The future rather than the past dominates the imagination. The Golden Age lies ahead of us not behind us. Everywhere new possibilities beckon and arouse courage and effort. The great French thinkers of the later eighteenth century borrowed this idea from Bacon and developed it into the doctrine of the indefinite perfectibility of mankind on earth. Man is capable, if he will but exercise the required courage, intelligence and effort, of shaping his own fate. Physical conditions offer no insurmountable barriers. In the fourth place, the patient and experimental study of nature, bearing fruit in inventions which control nature and subdue her forces to social uses, is the method by which progress is made. Knowledge is power and knowledge is achieved by sending the mind to school to nature to learn her processes of change.

In this lecture as in the previous one, I can hardly close better than by reference to the new responsibilities imposed upon philosophy and the new opportunities opened to it. Upon the whole, the greatest effect of these changes up to date has been to substitute an Idealism based on epistemology, or the theory of knowledge, for the Idealism based on the metaphysics of classic antiquity.

Earlier modern philosophy (even though unconsciously to itself) had the problem of reconciling the traditional theory of the rational and ideal basis, stuff and end of the universe with the new interest in individual mind and the new confidence in its capacities. It was in a dilemma. On the one hand, it had no intention of losing itself in a materialism which subordinated man to physical existence and mind to matter—especially just at the moment when in actual affairs man and mind were beginning to achieve genuine rule over nature. On the other hand, the conception that the world as it stood was an embodiment of a fixed and comprehensive Mind or Reason was uncongenial to those whose main concern was with the deficiencies of the world and with an attempt to remedy them. The effect of the objective theological idealism that had developed out of classic metaphysical idealism was to make the mind submissive and acquiescent. The new individualism chafed under the restrictions imposed upon it by the notion of a universal reason which had once and for all shaped nature and destiny.

In breaking away from antique and medieval thought, accordingly, early modern thought continued the older tradition of a Reason that creates and constitutes the world, but combined it with the notion that this Reason operates through the human

mind, individual or collective. This is the common note of idealism sounded by all the philosophies of the seventeenth and eighteenth centuries, whether belonging to the British school of
Locke, Berkeley and Hume or the Continental school of Descartes. In Kant as everybody knows the two strains came together; and the theme of the formation of the knowable world by
means of a thought that operated exclusively through the human
knower became explicit. Idealism ceased to be metaphysical and
cosmic in order to become epistemological and personal.

It is evident that this development represents merely a transitional stage. It tried, after all, to put the new wine in the old
bottles. It did not achieve a free and unbiased formulation of the
meaning of the power to direct nature's forces through knowledge—that is, purposeful, experimental action acting to reshape
beliefs and institutions. The ancient tradition was still strong
enough to project itself unconsciously into men's ways of thinking, and to hamper and compromise the expression of the really
modern forces and aims. Essential philosophic reconstruction
represents an attempt to state these causes and results in a way
freed from incompatible inherited factors. It will regard intelligence not as the original shaper and final cause of things, but as
the purposeful energetic re-shaper of those phases of nature and
life that obstruct social well-being. It esteems the individual not
as an exaggeratedly self-sufficient Ego which by some magic creates the world, but as the agent who is responsible through initiative, inventiveness and intelligently directed labor for re-creating
the world, transforming it into an instrument and possession of
intelligence.

The train of ideas represented by the Baconian Knowledge is
Power thus failed in getting an emancipated and independent
expression. These become hopelessly entangled in standpoints
and prepossessions that embodied a social, political and scientific
tradition with which they were completely incompatible. The ob-
scurity, the confusion of modern philosophy is the product of this
attempt to combine two things which cannot possibly be combined either logically or morally. Philosophic reconstruction for
the present is thus the endeavor to undo the entanglement and to
permit the Baconian aspirations to come to a free and unhindered
expression. In succeeding lectures we shall consider the needed
reconstruction as it affects certain classic philosophic antitheses,

like those of experience and reason, the real and the ideal. But first we shall have to consider the modifying effect exercised upon philosophy by that changed conception of nature, animate and inanimate, which we owe to the progress of science.

3. THE SCIENTIFIC FACTOR IN RECONSTRUCTION OF PHILOSOPHY

Philosophy starts from some deep and wide way of responding to the difficulties life presents, but it grows only when material is at hand for making this practical response conscious, articulate and communicable. Accompanying the economic, political and ecclesiastical changes which were alluded to in an earlier lecture, was a scientific revolution enormous in scope and leaving unchanged almost no detail of belief about nature, physical and human. In part this scientific transformation was produced by just the change in practical attitude and temper. But as it progressed, it furnished that change an appropriate vocabulary, congenial to its needs, and made it articulate. The advance of science in its larger generalizations and in its specific detail of fact supplied precisely that intellectual equipment of ideas and concrete fact that was needed in order to formulate, precipitate, communicate and propagate the new disposition. Today, accordingly, we shall deal with those contrasting conceptions of the structure and constitution of Nature, which when they are accepted on the authority of science (alleged or real), form the intellectual framework of philosophy.

Contrasting conceptions of ancient and modern science have been selected. For I see no way in which the truly philosophic import of the picture of the world painted by modern science can be appreciated except to exhibit it in contrast with that earlier picture which gave classic metaphysics its intellectual foundation and confirmation. The world in which philosophers once put their trust was a closed world, a world consisting internally of a limited number of fixed forms, and having definite boundaries externally. The world of modern science is an open world, a world varying indefinitely without the possibility of assignable limit in its internal make-up, a world stretching beyond any assignable bounds externally. Again, the world in which even the most intelligent men of olden times thought they lived was a fixed world, a realm where changes went on only within immutable limits of rest and permanence, and a world where the fixed and unmoving was, as we have already noted, higher in quality and authority than the moving and altering. And in the third place, the world which men once saw with their eyes, portrayed in their imaginations and repeated in their plans of conduct, was a world of a limited number of classes, kinds, forms, distinct in quality (as kinds and species must be distinct) and arranged in a graded order of superiority and inferiority.

It is not easy to recall the image of the universe which was taken for granted in the world tradition. In spite of its dramatic rendering (as in Dante), of the dialectical elaborations of Aristotle and St. Thomas, in spite of the fact that it held men's minds captive until the last three hundred years, and that its overthrow involved a religious upheaval, it is already dim, faded and remote. Even as a separate and abstract thing of theory it is not easy to recover.

As something pervasive, interwoven with all the details of reflection and observation, with the plans and rules of behavior, it is impossible to call it back again. Yet, as best we can, we need to put before our minds a definitely enclosed universe, something which can be called a universe in a literal and visible sense, having the earth at its fixed and unchanging centre and at a fixed circumference the heavenly arch of fixed stars moving in an eternal round of divine ether, hemming in all things and keeping them forever at one and in order. The earth, though at the centre, is the coarsest, grossest, most material, least significant and good (or perfect) of the parts of this closed world. It is the scene of maximum fluctuation and vicissitude. It is the least rational, and therefore the least notable, or knowable; it offers the least to reward contemplation, provoke admiration and govern conduct. Between this grossly material centre and the immaterial, spiritual and eternal heavens lie a definite series of regions of moon, planets, sun, etc., each of which gains in rank, value, rationality and true being as it is farther from earth and nearer the heavens. Each of these regions is composed of its own appropriate stuff of earth, water, air, fire in its own dominant degree, until we reach the heavenly firmament which transcends all these principles, being constituted, as was just said, of that immaterial, inalterable energy called ether.

Within this tight and pent-in universe, changes take place of course. But they are only of a small number of fixed kinds; and they operate only within fixed limits. Each kind of stuff has its own appropriate motion. It is the nature of earthly things to be heavy, since they are gross, and hence to move downward. Fire and superior things are light and hence move upward to their proper place; air rises only to the plane of the planets, where it then takes its back and forth motion which naturally belongs to it, as is evident in the winds and in respiration. Ether being the highest of all physical things has a purely circular movement. The daily return of the fixed stars is the closest possible approximation to eternity, and to the self-involved revolution of mind upon its own ideal axis of reason. Upon the earth in virtue of its earthly nature—or rather its lack of virtue—is a scene of mere change. Mere flux, aimless and meaningless, starts at no definite point and arrives at nothing, amounts to nothing. Mere changes of quantity, all purely mechanical changes, are of this kind. They are like the shiftings of the sands by the sea. They may be sensed, but they cannot be "noted" or understood; they lack fixed limits which govern them. They are contemptible. They are casual, the sport of accident.

Only changes which lead to some defined or fixed outcome of form are of any account and can have any account—any *logos* or reason—made of them. The growth of plants and animals illustrates the highest kind of change which is possible in the sublunary or mundane sphere. They go from one definite fixed form to another. Oaks generate only oaks, oysters only oysters, man only man. The material factor of mechanical production enters in, but enters in as accident to prevent the full consummation of the type of the species, and to bring about the meaningless variations which diversify various oaks or oysters from one another; or in extreme cases to produce freaks, sports, monsters, three-handed or four-toed men. Aside from accidental and undesirable variations, each individual has a fixed career to pursue, a fixed path in which to travel. Terms which sound modern, words like potentiality and development abound in Aristotelian thought, and have misled some into reading into his thought modern meanings. But the significance of these words in classic and medieval thought is rigidly determined by their context. Development holds merely of the course of changes which takes place within a particular member of the species. It is only a name for the predetermined movement from the acorn to the oak tree. It takes place not in things generally but only in some one of the numerically insignificant members of the oak species. Development, evolution, never means, as in modern science, origin of new forms, a mutation from an old species, but only the monotonous traversing of a previously plotted cycle of change. So potentiality never means, as in modern life, the possibility of novelty, of invention, of radical deviation, but only that principle in virtue of which the acorn becomes the oak. Technically, it is the capacity for movement between opposites. Only the cold can become hot; only the dry can become wet; only the babe can become a man; the seed the full-grown wheat and so on. Potentiality instead of implying the emergence of anything novel means merely the facility with which a particular thing repeats the recurrent processes of its kind, and thus becomes a specific case of the eternal forms in and through which all things are constituted.

In spite of the almost infinite numerical diversity of individuals, there are only a limited number of species, kinds or sorts. And the world is essentially a world which falls into sorts; it is prearranged into distinct classes. Moreover, just as we naturally arrange plants and animals into series, ranks and grades, from the lower to the highest, so with all things in the universe. The distinct classes to which things belong by their very nature form a hierarchical order. There are castes in nature. The universe is constituted on an aristocratic, one can truly say a feudal, plan. Species, classes do not mix or overlap—except in cases of accident, and to the result of chaos. Otherwise, everything belongs in advance to a certain class, and the class has its own fixed place in the hierarchy of Being. The universe is indeed a tidy spot whose purity is interfered with only by those irregular changes in individuals which are due to the presence of an obdurate matter that refuses to yield itself wholly to rule and form. Otherwise it is a universe with a fixed place for everything and where everything knows its place, its station and class, and keeps it. Hence what are known technically as final and formal causes are supreme, and efficient causes are relegated to an inferior place. The so-called final cause is just a name for the fact that there is some fixed form characteristic of a class or sort of things which governs the changes going on, so that they tend toward it as their end and goal, the fulfilment of their true nature. The supralunar region is the end or final cause of the proper movements of air and fire; the earth of the motions of crass, heavy things; the oak of the acorn; the mature form in general of the germinal.

The "efficient cause," that which produces and instigates a movement is only some external change as it accidentally gives a kind of push to an immature, imperfect being and starts it moving toward its perfected or fulfilled form. The final cause is the perfected form regarded as the *explanation or reason* of prior changes. When it is not taken in reference to the changes completed and brought to rest in it, but in itself, it is the "formal cause": The inherent *nature* or character which "makes" or constitutes a thing *what it is* so far as it truly *is*, namely, what it is so far as it does not change. Logically and practically all of the traits which have been enumerated cohere. Attack one and you attack all. When any one is undermined, all go. This is the reason why the intellectual modification of the last few centuries may truly be called a revolution. It has substituted a conception of the world differing at every point. It makes little matter at what point you commence to trace the difference, you find yourself carried into all other points.

Instead of a closed universe, science now presents us with one infinite in space and time, having no limits here or there, at this end, so to speak, or at that, and as infinitely complex in internal structure as it is infinite in extent. Hence it is also an open world, an infinitely variegated one, a world which in the old sense can hardly be called a universe at all; so multiplex and far-reaching that it cannot be summed up and grasped in any one formula. And change rather than fixity is now a measure of "reality" or energy of being; change is omnipresent. The laws in which the modern man of science is interested are laws of motion, of generation and consequence. He speaks of law where the ancients spoke of kind and essence, because what he wants is a correlation of changes, an ability to detect one change occurring in correspondence with another. He does not try to define and delimit something remaining constant *in* change. He tries to describe a constant order *of* change. And while the word "constant" appears in both statements, the meaning of the word is not the same. In one case, we are dealing with something constant in *existence*, physical or metaphysical; in the other case, with something constant in *function* and operation. One is a form of independent being; the other is a formula of description and calculation of interdependent changes.

In short, classic thought accepted a feudally arranged order of classes or kinds, each "holding" from a superior and in turn giving the rule of conduct and service to an inferior. This trait reflects and parallels most closely the social situation we were considering at the last hour. We have a fairly definite notion of society as organized upon the feudal basis. The family principle, the principle of kinship is strong, and especially is this true as we ascend in the social scale. At the lower end, individuals may be lost more or less in the mass. Since all are parts of the common herd, there is nothing especial to distinguish their birth. But among the privileged and ruling class the case is quite different. The tie of kinship at once marks a group off externally and gives it distinction, and internally holds all its members together. Kinship, kind, class, genus are synonymous terms, starting from social and concrete facts and going to the technical and abstract. For kinship is a sign of a common nature, of something universal and permanent running through all particular individuals, and giving them a real and objective unity. Because such and such persons are kin they are *really*, and not merely conventionally, marked off into a class having something unique about it. All contemporary members are bound into an objective unity which includes ancestors and descendants and excludes all who belong to another kin or kind. Assuredly this parcelling out of the world into separate kinds, each having its qualitatively distinct nature in contrast with other species, binding numerically distinct individuals together, and preventing their diversities from exceeding fixed bounds, may without exaggeration be called a projection of the family principle into the world at large.

In a feudally organized society, moreover, each kinship group or species occupies a definite place. It is marked by the possession of a specific *rank* higher or lower with respect to other grades. This position confers upon it certain privileges, enabling it to enforce certain claims upon those lower in the scale and entailing upon it certain services and homage to be rendered to superiors. The relationship of causation, so to speak, is up and down. Influence, power, proceeds from above to below; the activities of the inferior are performed with respect, quite literally, to what is above. Action and reaction are far from being equal and in opposite directions. All action is of one sort, of the nature of lordship, and proceeds from the higher to the lower. Reaction is of the nature of subjection and deference and proceeds from lower to higher. The classic theory of the constitution of the world corresponds point by point to this ordering of classes in a scale of dignity and power.

A third trait assigned by historians to feudalism is that the ordering of ranks centres about armed service and the relationship of armed defense and protection. I am afraid that what has already been said about the parallelism of ancient cosmology with social organization may seem a fanciful analogy; and if a comparison is also drawn in this last regard, there will be no doubt in your minds that a metaphor is being forced. Such is truly the case if we take the comparison too literally. But not so, if we confine our attention to the notion of rule and command implied in both. Attention has already been called to the meaning that is now given the term law—a constant relationship among changes. Nevertheless, we often hear about laws which "govern" events, and it often seems to be thought that phenomena would be utterly disorderly were there not laws to keep them in order. This way of thinking is a survival of reading social relationships into nature— not necessarily a feudal relationship, but the relation of ruler and ruled, sovereign and subject. Law is assimilated to a command or order. If the factor of personal will is eliminated (as it was in the best Greek thought) still the idea of law or universal is impregnated with the sense of a guiding and ruling influence exerted from above on what is naturally inferior to it. The universal governs, as the end and model which the artisan has in mind "governs" his movements. The Middle Ages added to this Greek idea of control the idea of a command proceeding from a superior will; and hence thought of the operations of nature as if they were a fulfilment of a task set by one who had authority to direct action.

The traits of the picture of nature drawn by modern science fairly spring by contrast into high relief. Modern science took its first step when daring astronomers abolished the distinction of high, sublime and ideal forces operating in the heavens from lower and material forces actuating terrestrial events. The supposed heterogeneity of substances and forces between heaven and earth was denied. It was asserted that the same laws hold everywhere, that there is homogeneity of material and process everywhere throughout nature. The remote and esthetically sublime is to be scientifically described and explained in terms of homely familiar events and forces. The material of direct handling and observation is that of which we are surest; it is the better known. Until we can convert the grosser and more superficial observations of far-away things in the heavens into elements identical with those of things directly at hand, they remain blind and not understood. Instead of presenting superior worth, they present only problems. They are not means of enlightenment but challenges. The earth is not superior in rank to sun, moon and stars, but it is equal in dignity, and its occurrences give the key to the understanding of celestial existences. Being *at* hand, they are also capable of being brought *under* our hand; they can be manipulated, broken up, resolved into elements which can be managed, combined at will in old and new forms. The net result may be termed, I think, without any great forcing, the substitution of a democracy of individual facts equal in rank for the feudal system of an ordered gradation of general classes of unequal rank.

One important incident of the new science was the destruction of the idea that the earth is the centre of the universe. When the idea of a fixed centre went, there went with it the idea of a closed universe and a circumscribing heavenly boundary. To the Greek sense, just because its theory of knowing was dominated by esthetic considerations, the finite was the perfect. Literally, the finite was the finished, the ended, the completed, that with no ragged edges and unaccountable operations. The infinite or limitless was lacking in character just because it was in-finite. Being everything, it was nothing. It was unformed and chaotic, uncontrolled and unruly, the source of incalculable deviations and accidents. Our present feeling that associates infinity with boundless power, with capacity for expansion that knows no end, with the delight in a progress that has no external limit, would be incomprehensible were it not that interest has shifted from the esthetic to the practical; from interest in beholding a harmonious and complete scene to interest in transforming an inharmonious one. One has only to read the authors of the transition period, say Giordano Bruno, to realize what a pent-in, suffocating sensation they associated with a closed, finite world, and what a feeling of exhilaration, expansion and boundless possibility was aroused in them by the thought of a world infinite in stretch of space and

time, and composed internally of infinitesimal infinitely numerous elements. That which the Greeks withdrew from with repulsion they welcomed with an intoxicated sense of adventure. The
infinite meant, it was true, something forever untraversed even
by thought, and hence something forever unknown—no matter
how great attainment in learning. But this "forever unknown" instead of being chilling and repelling was now an inspiring challenge to ever-renewed inquiry, and an assurance of inexhaustible
possibilities of progress.

The student of history knows well that the Greeks made great
progress in the science of mechanics as well as of geometry. At
first sight, it appears strange that with this advance in mechanics
so little advance was made in the direction of modern science.
The seeming paradox impels us to ask why it was that mechanics
remained a separate science, why it was not used in description
and explanation of natural phenomena after the manner of Gali-
leo and Newton. The answer is found in the social parallelism
already mentioned. Socially speaking, machines, tools, were devices employed by artisans. The science of mechanics had to do
with the kind of things employed by human mechanics, and mechanics were base fellows. They were at the lower end of the social scale, and how could light on the heavens, the highest, be
derived from them? The application of considerations of mechanics to natural phenomena would moreover have implied an interest in the practical control and utilization of phenomena which
was totally incompatible with the importance attached to final
causes as fixed determiners of nature. All the scientific reformers
of the sixteenth and seventeenth centuries strikingly agree in regarding the doctrine of final causes as *the* cause of the failure of
science. Why? Because this doctrine taught that the processes of
nature are held in bondage to certain fixed ends which they must
tend to realize. Nature was kept in leading strings; it was
cramped down to production of a limited number of stereotyped
results. Only a comparatively small number of things could be
brought into being, and these few must be similar to the ends
which similar cycles of change had effected in the past. The scope
of inquiry and understanding was limited to the narrow round of
processes eventuating in the fixed ends which the observed world
offered to view. At best, invention and production of new results

by use of machines and tools must be restricted to articles of transient dignity and bodily, not intellectual, use.

When the rigid clamp of fixed ends was taken off from nature, observation and imagination were emancipated, and experimental control for scientific and practical purposes enormously stimulated. Because natural processes were no longer restricted to a fixed number of immovable ends or results, anything might conceivably happen. It was only a question of what elements could be brought into juxtaposition so that they would work upon one another. Immediately, mechanics ceased to be a separate science and became an organ for attacking nature. The mechanics of the lever, wheel, pulley and inclined plane told accurately what happens when things in space are used to move one another during definite periods of time. The whole of nature became a scene of pushes and pulls, of cogs and levers, of motions of parts or elements to which the formulae of movements produced by well-known machines were directly applicable.

The banishing of ends and forms from the universe has seemed to many an ideal and spiritual impoverishment. When nature was regarded as a set of mechanical interactions, it apparently lost all meaning and purpose. Its glory departed. Elimination of differences of quality deprived it of beauty. Denial to nature of all inherent longings and aspiring tendencies toward ideal ends removed nature and natural science from contact with poetry, religion and divine things. There seemed to be left only a harsh, brutal despiritualized exhibition of mechanical forces. As a consequence, it has seemed to many philosophers that one of their chief problems was to reconcile the existence of this purely mechanical world with belief in objective rationality and purpose— to save life from a degrading materialism. Hence many sought to re-attain by way of an analysis of the process of knowing, or epistemology, that belief in the superiority of Ideal Being which had anciently been maintained on the basis of cosmology. But when it is recognized that the mechanical view is determined by the requirements of an experimental control of natural energies, this problem of reconciliation no longer vexes us. Fixed forms and ends, let us recall, mark fixed limits to change. Hence they make futile all human efforts to produce and regulate change except within narrow and unimportant limits. They paralyze constructive human inventions by a theory which condemns them in advance to failure. Human activity can conform only to ends already set by nature. It was not till ends were banished from nature that purposes became important as factors in human minds capable of reshaping existence. A natural world that does not subsist for the sake of realizing a fixed set of ends is relatively malleable and plastic; it may be used for this end *or* that. That nature can be known through the application of mechanical formulae is the prime condition of turning it to human account. Tools, machines are means to be utilized. Only when nature is regarded as mechanical, is systematic invention and construction of machines relevant to nature's activities. Nature is subdued to human purpose because it is no longer the slave of metaphysical and theological purpose.

Bergson has pointed out that man might well be called *Homo Faber*. He is distinguished as the tool-making animal. This has held good since man was man; but till nature was construed in mechanical terms, the making of tools with which to attack and transform nature was sporadic and accidental. Under such circumstances it would not have occurred even to a Bergson that man's tool-making capacity was so important and fundamental that it could be used to define him. The very things that make the nature of the mechanical-physical scientist esthetically blank and dull are the things which render nature amenable to human control. When qualities were subordinated to quantitative and mathematical relationships, color, music and form disappeared from the object of the scientist's inquiry as such. But the remaining properties of weight, extension, numerable velocity of movement and so on were just the qualities which lent themselves to the substitution of one thing for another, to the conversion of one form of energy into another; to the effecting of transformations. When chemical fertilizers can be used in place of animal manures, when improved grain and cattle can be purposefully bred from inferior animals and grasses, when mechanical energy can be converted into heat and electricity into mechanical energy, man gains power to manipulate nature. Most of all he gains power to frame *new* ends and aims and to proceed in regular system to their actualization. Only indefinite substitution and convertibility regardless of quality render nature manageable. The mechanization of nature is the condition of a practical and progressive idealism in action.

It thus turns out that the old, old dread and dislike of matter as something opposed to mind and threatening it, to be kept within the narrowest bounds of recognition; something to be denied so far as possible lest it encroach upon ideal purposes and finally exclude them from the real world, is as absurd practically as it was impotent intellectually. Judged from the only scientific standpoint, what it does and how it functions, matter means conditions. To respect matter means to respect the conditions of achievement; conditions which hinder and obstruct and which have to be changed, conditions which help and further and which can be used to modify obstructions and attain ends. Only as men have learned to pay sincere and persistent regard to matter, to the conditions upon which depends negatively and positively the success of all endeavor, have they shown sincere and fruitful respect for ends and purposes. To profess to have an aim and then neglect the means of its execution is self-delusion of the most dangerous sort. Education and morals will begin to find themselves on the same road of advance that say chemical industry and medicine have found for themselves when they too learn fully the lesson of wholehearted and unremitting attention to means and conditions—that is, to what mankind so long despised as material and mechanical. When we take means for ends we indeed fall into moral materialism. But when we take ends without regard to means we degenerate into sentimentalism. In the name of the ideal we fall back upon mere luck and chance and magic or exhortation and preaching; or else upon a fanaticism that will force the realization of preconceived ends at any cost.

I have touched in this lecture upon many things in a cursory way. Yet there has been but one point in mind. The revolution in our conceptions of nature and in our methods of knowing it has bred a new temper of imagination and aspiration. It has confirmed the new attitude generated by economic and political changes. It has supplied this attitude with definite intellectual material with which to formulate and justify itself.

In the first lecture it was noted that in Greek life prosaic matter-of-fact or empirical knowledge was at a great disadvantage as compared with the imaginative beliefs that were bound up with special institutions and moral habitudes. Now this empirical knowledge has grown till it has broken its low and limited sphere of application and esteem. It has itself become an organ of inspiring imagination through introducing ideas of boundless possibility, indefinite progress, free movement, equal opportunity irrespective of fixed limits. It has reshaped social institutions, and in so far developed a new morale. It has achieved ideal values. It is convertible into creative and constructive philosophy.

Convertible, however, rather than already converted. When we consider how deeply embedded in customs of thought and action the classic philosophy came to be and how congenial it is to man's more spontaneous beliefs, the throes that attended its birth are not to be wondered at. We should rather wonder that a view so upsetting, so undermining, made its way without more persecutions, martyrdoms and disturbances. It certainly is not surprising that its complete and consistent formulation in philosophy has been long delayed. The main efforts of thinkers were inevitably directed to minimizing the shock of change, easing the strains of transition, mediating and reconciling. When we look back upon almost all of the thinkers of the seventeenth and eighteenth centuries, upon all excepting those who were avowedly sceptical and revolutionary, what strikes us is the amount of traditional subject-matter and method that is to be found even among those who were regarded as most advanced. Men cannot easily throw off their old habits of thinking, and never can throw off all of them at once. In developing, teaching and receiving new ideas we are compelled to use some of the old ones as tools of understanding and communication. Only piecemeal, step-by-step, could the full import of the new science be grasped. Roughly speaking, the seventeenth century witnessed its application in astronomy and general cosmology; the eighteenth century in physics and chemistry; the nineteenth century undertook an application in geology and the biological sciences.

It was said that it has now become extremely difficult to recover the view of the world which universally obtained in Europe till the seventeenth century. Yet after all we need only recur to the science of plants and animals as it was before Darwin and to the ideas which even now are dominant in moral and political matters to find the older order of conceptions in full possession of the popular mind. Until the dogma of fixed unchangeable types and species, of arrangement in classes of higher and lower, of subordination of the transitory individual to the universal or kind had been shaken in its hold upon the science of life, it was impossible that the new ideas and method should be made at home in social and moral life. Does it not seem to be the intellectual task of the twentieth century to take this last step? When this step is taken the circle of scientific development will be rounded out and the reconstruction of philosophy be made an accomplished fact.

4. CHANGED CONCEPTIONS OF EXPERIENCE AND REASON

What is experience and what is Reason, Mind? What is the scope of experience and what are its limits? How far is it a sure ground of belief and a safe guide of conduct? Can we trust it in science and in behavior? Or is it a quagmire as soon as we pass beyond a few low material interests? Is it so shaky, shifting, and shallow that instead of affording sure footing, safe paths to fertile fields, it misleads, betrays, and engulfs? Is a Reason outside experience and above it needed to supply assured principles to science and conduct? In one sense, these questions suggest technical problems of abstruse philosophy; in another sense, they contain the deepest possible questionings regarding the career of man. They concern the criteria he is to employ in forming his beliefs; the principles *by* which he is to direct his life and the ends *to* which he is to direct it. Must man transcend experience by some organ of unique character that carries him into the super-empirical? Failing this, must he wander sceptical and disillusioned? Or is human experience itself worth while in its purposes and its methods of guidance? Can it organize itself into stable courses or must it be sustained from without?

We know the answers of traditional philosophy. They do not thoroughly agree among themselves, but they agree that experience never rises above the level of the particular, the contingent, and the probable. Only a power transcending in origin and content any and all conceivable experience can attain to universal, necessary and certain authority and direction. The empiricists themselves admitted the correctness of these assertions. They only said that since there is no faculty of Pure Reason in the possession of mankind, we must put up with what we have, experience, and make the most possible out of it. They contented themselves with sceptical attacks upon the transcendentalist, with indications of the ways in which we might best seize the meaning and good of the passing moment; or like Locke, asserted that in spite of the limitation of experience, it affords the light needed to guide men's footsteps modestly in conduct. They affirmed that the alleged authoritative guidance by a higher faculty had practically hampered men.

It is the function of this lecture to show how and why it is now possible to make claims for experience as a guide in science and moral life which the older empiricists did not and could not make for it.

Curiously enough, the key to the matter may be found in the fact that the old notion of experience was itself a product of experience—the only kind of experience which was then open to men. If another conception of experience is now possible, it is precisely because the quality of experience as it may now be lived has undergone a profound social and intellectual change from that of earlier times. The account of experience which we find in Plato and Aristotle is an account of what Greek experience actually was. It agrees very closely with what the modern psychologist knows as the method of learning by trial and error as distinct from the method of learning by ideas. Men tried certain acts, they underwent certain sufferings and affections. Each of these in the time of its occurrence is isolated, particular—its counterpart is transient appetite and transient sensation. But memory preserves and accumulates these separate incidents. As they pile up, irregular variations get cancelled, common features are selected, reinforced and combined. Gradually a habit of action is built up, and corresponding to this habit there forms a certain generalized picture of an object or situation. We come to know or note not merely this particular which as a particular cannot strictly be known at all (for not being classed it cannot be characterized and identified) but to recognize it as man, tree, stone, leather—an individual of a certain kind, marked by a certain universal form characteristic of a whole species of thing. Along with the development of this common-sense knowledge, there grows up a certain regularity of conduct. The particular incidents fuse, and a *way* of acting which is general, as far as it goes, builds up. The skill develops which is shown by the artisan, the shoemaker, the carpenter, the gymnast, the physician, who have regular ways of handling cases. This regularity signifies, of course, that the particular case is not treated as an isolated particular, but as one of a kind, which therefore demands a *kind* of action. From the multitude of particular illnesses encountered, the physician in learning to class some of them as indigestion learns also to treat the cases of the class in a common or general way. He forms the rule of recommending a certain diet, and prescribing a certain remedy. All this forms what we call experience. It results, as the illustration shows, in a certain general insight and a certain organized ability in action.

But needless to insist, the generality and the organization are restricted and fallible. They hold, as Aristotle was fond of pointing out, usually, in most cases, as a rule, but not universally, of necessity, or as a principle. The physician is bound to make mistakes, because individual cases are bound to vary unaccountably: such is their very nature. The difficulty does not arise in *a* defective experience which is capable of remedy in some better experience. Experience itself, as such, is defective, and hence default is inevitable and irremediable. The only universality and certainty is in a region above experience, that of the rational and conceptual. As the particular was a stepping-stone to image and habit, so the latter may become a stepping-stone to conceptions and principles. But the latter leave experience behind, untouched; they do not react to rectify it. Such is the notion which still lingers in the contrast of "empirical" and "rational" as when we say that a certain architect or physician is empirical, not scientific in his procedures. But the difference between the classic and the modern notion of experience is revealed in the fact that such a statement is now a charge, a disparaging accusation, brought against *a* particular architect or physician. With Plato, Aristotle and the Scholastic, it was a charge against the callings, since they were modes of experience. It was an indictment of all practical action in contrast with conceptual contemplation.

The modern philosopher who has professed himself an empiricist has usually had a critical purpose in mind. Like Bacon, Locke, Condillac and Helvétius, he stood face to face with a body of beliefs and a set of institutions in which he profoundly disbelieved. His problem was the problem of attack upon so much dead weight carried uselessly by humanity, crushing and distorting it. His readiest way of undermining and disintegrating was by appealing to experience as a final test and criterion. In every case, active reformers were "empiricists" in the philosophical sense. They made it their business to show that some current belief or institution that claimed the sanction of innate ideas or necessary conceptions, or an origin in an authoritative revelation of reason, had in fact proceeded from a lowly origin in experience, and had been confirmed by accident, by class interest or by biased authority.

The philosophic empiricism initiated by Locke was thus disintegrative in intent. It optimistically took it for granted that when the burden of blind custom, imposed authority, and accidental associations was removed, progress in science and social organization would spontaneously take place. Its part was to help in removing the burden. The best way to liberate men from the burden was through a natural history of the origin and growth in the mind of the ideas connected with objectionable beliefs and customs. Santayana justly calls the psychology of this school a malicious psychology. It tended to identify the history of the formation of certain ideas with an account of the things to which the ideas refer—an identification which naturally had an unfavorable effect on the things. But Mr. Santayana neglects to notice the social zeal and aim latent in the malice. He fails to point out that this "malice" was aimed at institutions and traditions which had lost their usefulness; he fails to point out that to a large extent it was true of them that an account of their psychological origin was equivalent to a destructive account of the things themselves. But after Hume with debonair clarity pointed out that the analysis of beliefs into sensations and associations left "natural" ideas and institutions in the same position in which the reformers had placed "artificial" ones, the situation changed. The rationalists employed the logic of sensationalistic-empiricism to show that experience, giving only a heap of chaotic and isolated particulars, is as fatal to science and to moral laws and obligations as to obnoxious institutions; and concluded that "Reason" must be resorted to if experience was to be furnished with any binding and connecting principles. The new rationalistic idealism of Kant and his successors seemed to be necessitated by the totally destructive results of the new empirical philosophy.

Two things have rendered possible a new conception of experience and a new conception of the relation of reason to experience, or, more accurately, of the place of reason *in* experience. The primary factor is the change that has taken place in the actual nature of experience, its contents and methods, as it is actually lived. The other is the development of a psychology based upon biology which makes possible a new scientific formulation of the nature of experience.

Let us begin with the technical side—the change in psychology. We are only just now commencing to appreciate how completely exploded is the psychology that dominated philosophy throughout the eighteenth and nineteenth centuries. According to this theory, mental life originated in sensations which are separately and passively received, and which are formed, through laws of retention and association, into a mosaic of images, perceptions, and conceptions. The senses were regarded as gateways or avenues of knowledge. Except in combining atomic sensations, the mind was wholly passive and acquiescent in knowing. Volition, action, emotion, and desire follow in the wake of sensations and images. The intellectual or cognitive factor comes first and emotional and volitional life is only a consequent conjunction of ideas with sensations of pleasure and pain.

The effect of the development of biology has been to reverse the picture. Wherever there is life, there is behavior, activity. In order that life may persist, this activity has to be both continuous and adapted to the environment. This adaptive adjustment, moreover, is not wholly passive; is not a mere matter of the moulding of the organism by the environment. Even a clam acts upon the environment and modifies it to some extent. It selects materials for food and for the shell that protects it. It does something to the environment as well as has something done to itself. There is no such thing in a living creature as mere conformity to conditions, though parasitic forms may approach this limit. In the interests of the maintenance of life there is transformation of some elements in the surrounding medium. The higher the form of life, the more important is the active reconstruction of the medium. This increased control may be illustrated by the contrast of savage with civilized man. Suppose the two are living in a wilderness. With the savage there is the maximum of accommodation to given conditions; the minimum of what we may call hitting back. The savage takes things "as they are," and by using caves and roots and occasional pools leads a meagre and precarious existence. The civilized man goes to distant mountains and dams streams. He builds reservoirs, digs channels, and conducts the waters to what had been a desert. He searches the world to find plants and animals that will thrive. He takes native plants and by selection and cross-fertilization improves them. He introduces machinery to till the soil and care for the harvest. By such means he may succeed in making the wilderness blossom like the rose.

Such transformation scenes are so familiar that we overlook their meaning. We forget that the inherent power of life is illustrated in them. Note what a change this point of view entails in the traditional notions of experience. Experience becomes an affair primarily of doing. The organism does not stand about, Micawber-like, waiting for something to turn up. It does not wait passive and inert for something to impress itself upon it from without. The organism acts in accordance with its own structure, simple or complex, upon its surroundings. As a consequence the changes produced in the environment react upon the organism and its activities. The living creature undergoes, suffers, the consequences of its own behavior. This close connection between doing and suffering or undergoing forms what we call experience. Disconnected doing and disconnected suffering are neither of them experiences. Suppose fire encroaches upon a man when he is asleep. Part of his body is burned away. The burn does not perceptibly result from what he has done. There is nothing which in any instructive way can be named experience. Or again there is a series of mere activities, like twitchings of muscles in a spasm. The movements amount to nothing; they have no consequences for life. Or, if they have, these consequences are not connected with prior doing. There is no experience, no learning, no cumulative process. But suppose a busy infant puts his finger in the fire; the doing is random, aimless, without intention or reflection. But something happens in consequence. The child undergoes heat, he suffers pain. The doing and undergoing, the reaching and the burn, are connected. One comes to suggest and mean the other. Then there is experience in a vital and significant sense.

Certain important implications for philosophy follow. In the first place, the interaction of organism and environment, resulting in some adaptation which secures utilization of the latter, is the primary fact, the basic category. Knowledge is relegated to a derived position, secondary in origin, even if its importance, when once it is established, is overshadowing. Knowledge is not something separate and self-sufficing, but is involved in the process by which life is sustained and evolved. The senses lose their place as gateways of knowing to take their rightful place as stimuli to action. To an animal an affection of the eye or ear is not an idle piece of information about something indifferently going on in the world. It is an invitation and inducement to act in a needed way. It is a clue in behavior, a directive factor in adaptation of life in its surroundings. It is urgent not cognitive in quality. The whole controversy between empiricism and rationalism as to the intellectual worth of sensations is rendered strangely obsolete. The discussion of sensations belongs under the head of immediate stimulus and response, not under the head of knowledge.

As a *conscious* element, a sensation marks an interruption in a course of action previously entered upon. Many psychologists since the time of Hobbes have dwelt upon what they call the relativity of sensations. We *feel* or sense cold in transition from warmth rather than absolutely; hardness is sensed upon a background of less resistance; a color in contrast with pure light or pure dark or in contrast with some other hue. A continuously unchanged tone or color cannot be attended to or sensed. What we take to be such monotonously prolonged sensations are in truth constantly interrupted by incursions of other elements, and represent a series of excursions back and forth. This fact was, however, misconstrued into a doctrine about the nature of knowledge. Rationalists used it to discredit sense as a valid or high mode of knowing things, since according to it we never get hold of anything *in itself* or intrinsically. Sensationalists used it to disparage all pretence at absolute knowledge.

Properly speaking, however, this fact of the relativity of sensation does not in the least belong in the sphere of knowing. Sensations of this sort are emotional and practical rather than cognitive and intellectual. They are shocks of change, due to interruption of a prior adjustment. They are signals to redirections of action. Let me take a trivial illustration. The person who is taking notes has no sensation of the pressure of his pencil on the paper or on his hand as long as it functions properly. It operates merely as stimulus to ready and effective adjustment. The sensory activity incites automatically and unconsciously its proper motor response. There is a preformed physiological connection, acquired from habit but ultimately going back to an original connection in the nervous system. If the pencil-point gets broken or too blunt and the habit of writing does not operate smoothly, there is a conscious shock:—the feeling of something the matter, something gone wrong. This emotional change operates as a stimulus to a needed change in operation. One looks at his pencil, sharpens it or takes another pencil from one's pocket. The sensation operates as a pivot of readjusting behavior. It marks a break in the prior routine of writing and the beginning of some other mode of action. Sensations are "relative" in the sense of marking transitions in habits of behavior from one course to another way of behaving.

The rationalist was thus right in denying that sensations as such are true elements of knowledge. But the reasons he gave for this conclusion and the consequences he drew from it were all wrong. Sensations are not parts of *any* knowledge, good or bad, superior or inferior, imperfect or complete. They are rather provocations, incitements, challenges to an act of inquiry which is to *terminate* in knowledge. They are not ways of knowing things inferior in value to reflective ways, to the ways that require thought and inference, because they are not ways of knowing at all. They are stimuli to reflection and inference. As interruptions, they raise the questions: What does this shock mean? What is happening? What is the matter? How is my relation to the environment disturbed? What should be done about it? How shall I alter my course of action to meet the change that has taken place in the surroundings? How shall I readjust my behavior in response? Sensation is thus, as the sensationalist claimed, the beginning of knowledge, but only in the sense that the experienced shock of change is the necessary stimulus to the investigating and comparing which eventually produce knowledge.

When experience is aligned with the life-process and sensations are seen to be points of readjustment, the alleged atomism of sensations totally disappears. With this disappearance is abolished the need for a synthetic faculty of super-empirical reason to connect them. Philosophy is not any longer confronted with the hopeless problem of finding a way in which separate grains of sand may be woven into a strong and coherent rope—or into the illusion and pretence of one. When the isolated and simple existences of Locke and Hume are seen not to be truly empirical at all but to answer to certain demands of their theory of mind, the necessity ceases for the elaborate Kantian and Post-Kantian machinery of *a priori* concepts and categories to synthesize the alleged stuff of experience. The true "stuff" of experience is recognized to be adaptive courses of action, habits, active functions,

connections of doing and undergoing; sensori-motor coordina-
tions. Experience carries principles of connection and organization within itself. These principles are none the worse because
they are vital and practical rather than epistemological. Some degree of organization is indispensable to even the lowest grade of
life. Even an amoeba must have some continuity in time in its
activity and some adaptation to its environment in space. Its life
and experience cannot possibly consist in momentary, atomic,
and self-enclosed sensations. Its activity has reference to its surroundings and to what goes before and what comes after. This
organization intrinsic to life renders unnecessary a super-natural
and super-empirical synthesis. It affords the basis and material
for a positive evolution of intelligence as an organizing factor
within experience.

Nor is it entirely aside from the subject to point out the extent
in which social as well as biological organization enters into the
formation of human experience. Probably one thing that
strengthened the idea that the mind is passive and receptive in
knowing was the observation of the helplessness of the human
infant. But the observation points in quite another direction. Because of his physical dependence and impotency, the contacts of
the little child with nature are mediated by other persons. Mother
and nurse, father and older children, determine what experiences
the child shall have; they constantly instruct him as to the meaning of what he does and undergoes. The conceptions that are socially current and important become the child's principles of
interpretation and estimation long before he attains to personal
and deliberate control of conduct. Things come to him clothed in
language, not in physical nakedness, and this garb of communication makes him a sharer in the beliefs of those about him.
These beliefs coming to him as so many facts form his mind; they
furnish the centres about which his own personal expeditions
and perceptions are ordered. Here we have "categories" of connection and unification as important as those of Kant, but empirical not mythological.

From these elementary, if somewhat technical considerations, we turn to the change which experience itself has undergone in the passage from ancient and medieval to modern life. To
Plato, experience meant enslavement to the past, to custom. Experience was almost equivalent to established customs formed

not by reason or under intelligent control but by repetition and blind rule of thumb. Only reason can lift us above subjection to the accidents of the past. When we come to Bacon and his successors, we discover a curious reversal. Reason and its bodyguard of general notions is now the conservative, mind-enslaving factor. Experience is the liberating power. Experience means the new, that which calls us away from adherence to the past, that which reveals novel facts and truths. Faith in experience produces not devotion to custom but endeavor for progress. This difference in temper is the more significant because it was so unconsciously taken for granted. Some concrete and vital change must have occurred in actual experience as that is lived. For, after all, the thought of experience follows after and is modelled upon the experience actually undergone.

When mathematics and other rational sciences developed among the Greeks, scientific truths did not react back into daily experience. They remained isolated, apart and super-imposed. Medicine was the art in which perhaps the greatest amount of positive knowledge was obtained, but it did not reach the dignity of science. It remained an art. In practical arts, moreover, there was no conscious invention or purposeful improvement. Workers followed patterns that were handed down to them, while departure from established standards and models usually resulted in degenerate productions. Improvements came either from a slow, gradual, and unacknowledged accumulation of changes or else from some sudden inspiration, which at once set a new standard. Being the result of no conscious method, it was fittingly attributed to the gods. In the social arts, such a radical reformer as Plato felt that existing evils were due to the absence of such fixed patterns as controlled the productions of artisans. The ethical purport of philosophy was to furnish them, and when once they were instituted, they were to be consecrated by religion, adorned by art, inculcated by education and enforced by magistrates so that alteration of them would be impossible.

It is unnecessary to repeat what has been so often dwelt upon as to the effect of experimental science in enabling man to effect a deliberate control of his environment. But since the impact of this control upon the traditional notion of experience is often overlooked, we must point out that when experience ceased to be empirical and became experimental, something of radical impor-

tance occurred. Aforetime man employed the results of his prior
experience only to form customs that henceforth had to be blindly
followed or blindly broken. Now, old experience is used to suggest
aims and methods for developing a new and improved experience. Consequently experience becomes in so far constructively
self-regulative. What Shakespeare so pregnantly said of nature, it
is "made better by no mean, but nature makes that mean," becomes true of experience. We do not merely have to repeat the
past, or wait for accidents to force change upon us. We *use* our
past experiences to construct new and better ones in the future.
The very fact of experience thus includes the process by which it
directs itself in its own betterment.

Science, "reason" is not therefore something laid from above
upon experience. Suggested and tested in experience, it is also
employed through inventions in a thousand ways to expand and
enrich experience. Although, as has been so often repeated, this
self-creation and self-regulation of experience is still largely technological rather than truly artistic or human, yet what has been
achieved contains the guarantee of the possibility of an intelligent
administering of experience. The limits are moral and intellectual, due to defects in our good will and knowledge. They are not
inherent metaphysically in the very nature of experience. "Reason" as a faculty separate from experience, introducing us to a
superior region of universal truths begins now to strike us as remote, uninteresting and unimportant. Reason, as a Kantian faculty that introduces generality and regularity into experience,
strikes us more and more as superfluous—the unnecessary creation of men addicted to traditional formalism and to elaborate terminology. Concrete suggestions arising from past experiences,
developed and matured in the light of the needs and deficiencies
of the present, employed as aims and methods of specific reconstruction, and tested by success or failure in accomplishing this
task of readjustment, suffice. To such empirical suggestions used
in constructive fashion for new ends the name intelligence is
given.

This recognition of the place of active and planning thought
within the very processes of experience radically alters the traditional status of the technical problems of particular and universal,
sense and reason, perceptual and conceptual. But the alteration
is of much more than technical significance. For reason is ex-

perimental intelligence, conceived after the pattern of science, and used in the creation of social arts; it has something to do. It liberates man from the bondage of the past, due to ignorance and accident hardened into custom. It projects a better future and assists man in its realization. And its operation is always subject to test in experience. The plans which are formed, the principles which man projects as guides of reconstructive action, are not dogmas. They are hypotheses to be worked out in practice, and to be rejected, corrected and expanded as they fail or succeed in giving our present experience the guidance it requires. We may call them programs of action, but since they are to be used in making our future acts less blind, more directed, they are flexible. Intelligence is not something possessed once for all. It is in constant process of forming, and its retention requires constant alertness in observing consequences, an open-minded will to learn and courage in re-adjustment.

In contrast with this experimental and re-adjusting intelligence, it must be said that Reason as employed by historic rationalism has tended to carelessness, conceit, irresponsibility, and rigidity—in short absolutism. A certain school of contemporary psychology uses the term "rationalization" to denote those mental mechanisms by which we unconsciously put a better face on our conduct or experience than facts justify. We excuse ourselves to ourselves by introducing a purpose and order into that of which we are secretly ashamed. In like fashion, historic rationalism has often tended to use Reason as an agency of justification and apologetics. It has taught that the defects and evils of actual experience disappear in the "rational whole" of things; that things *appear* evil merely because of the partial, incomplete nature of experience. Or, as was noted by Bacon, "reason" assumes a false simplicity, uniformity and universality, and opens for science a path of fictitious ease. This course results in intellectual irresponsibility and neglect:—irresponsibility because rationalism assumes that the concepts of reason are so self-sufficient and so far above experience that they need and can secure no confirmation in experience. Neglect, because this same assumption makes men careless about concrete observations and experiments. Contempt for experience has had a tragic revenge *in* experience; it has cultivated disregard for fact and this disregard has been paid for in failure, sorrow and war.

The dogmatic rigidity of Rationalism is best seen in the consequences of Kant's attempt to buttress an otherwise chaotic experience with pure concepts. He set out with a laudable attempt at restricting the extravagant pretensions of Reason apart from experience. He called his philosophy critical. But because he taught that the understanding employs fixed, *a priori*, concepts, in order to introduce connection into experience and thereby make known *objects* possible (stable, regular relationships of qualities), he developed in German thought a curious contempt for the living variety of experience and a curious overestimate of the value of system, order, regularity for their own sakes. More practical causes were at work in producing the peculiarly German regard for drill, discipline, "order" and docility.

But Kant's philosophy served to provide an intellectual justification or "rationalization" of subordination of individuals to fixed and ready-made universals, "principles," laws. Reason and law were held to be synonyms. And as reason came into experience from without and above, so law had to come into life from some external and superior authority. The practical correlate to absolutism is rigidity, stiffness, inflexibility of disposition. When Kant taught that some conceptions, and these the important ones, are *a priori*, that they do not arise in experience and cannot be verified or tested in experience, that without such ready-made injections into experience the latter is anarchic and chaotic, he fostered the spirit of absolutism, even though technically he denied the possibility of absolutes. His successors were true to his spirit rather than his letter, and so they taught absolutism systematically. That the Germans with all their scientific competency and technological proficiency should have fallen into their tragically rigid and "superior" style of thought and action (tragic because involving them in inability to understand the world in which they lived) is a sufficient lesson of what may be involved in a systematical denial of the experimental character of intelligence and its conceptions.

By common consent, the effect of English empiricism was sceptical where that of German rationalism was apologetic; it undermined where the latter justified. It detected accidental associations formed into customs under the influence of self- or class-interest where German rational-idealism discovered profound meanings due to the necessary evolution of absolute reason. The modern world has suffered because in so many matters philosophy has offered it only an arbitrary choice between hard and fast opposites: Disintegrating analysis *or* rigid synthesis; complete radicalism neglecting and attacking the historic past as trivial and harmful, *or* complete conservatism idealizing institutions as embodiments of eternal reason; a resolution of experience into atomic elements that afford no support to stable organization *or* a clamping down of all experience by fixed categories and necessary concepts—these are the alternatives that conflicting schools have presented.

They are the logical consequences of the traditional opposition of Sense and Thought, Experience and Reason. Common sense has refused to follow both theories to their ultimate logic, and has fallen back on faith, intuition or the exigencies of practical compromise. But common sense too often has been confused and hampered instead of enlightened and directed by the philosophies proffered it by professional intellectuals. Men who are thrown back upon "common sense" when they appeal to philosophy for some general guidance are likely to fall back on routine, the force of some personality, strong leadership or on the pressure of momentary circumstances. It would be difficult to estimate the harm that has resulted because the liberal and progressive movement of the eighteenth and earlier nineteenth centuries had no method of intellectual articulation commensurate with its practical aspirations. Its heart was in the right place. It was humane and social in intention. But it had no theoretical instrumentalities of constructive power. Its head was sadly deficient. Too often the logical import of its professed doctrines was almost anti-social in its atomistic individualism, anti-human in devotion to brute sensation. This deficiency played into the hands of the reactionary and obscurantist. The strong point of the appeal to fixed principles transcending experience, to dogmas incapable of experimental verification, the strong point of reliance upon *a priori* canons of truth and standards of morals in opposition to dependence upon fruits and consequences in experience, has been the unimaginative conception of experience which professed philosophic empiricists have entertained and taught.

A philosophic reconstruction which should relieve men of having to choose between an impoverished and truncated experience on one hand and an artificial and impotent reason on the other would relieve human effort from the heaviest intellectual burden it has to carry. It would destroy the division of men of good will into two hostile camps. It would permit the cooperation of those who respect the past and the institutionally established with those who are interested in establishing a freer and happier future. For it would determine the conditions under which the funded experience of the past and the contriving intelligence which looks to the future can effectually interact with each other. It would enable men to glorify the claims of reason without at the same time falling into a paralyzing worship of super-empirical authority or into an offensive "rationalization" of things as they are.

5. CHANGED CONCEPTIONS OF THE IDEAL AND THE REAL

It has been noted that human experience is made human through the existence of associations and recollections, which are strained through the mesh of imagination so as to suit the demands of the emotions. A life that is humanly interesting is, short of the results of discipline, a life in which the tedium of vacant leisure is filled with images that excite and satisfy. It is in this sense that poetry preceded prose in human experience, religion antedated science, and ornamental and decorative art while it could not take the place of utility early reached a development out of proportion to the practical arts. In order to give contentment and delight, in order to feed present emotion and give the stream of conscious life intensity and color, the suggestions which spring from past experiences are worked over so as to smooth out their unpleasantnesses and enhance their enjoyableness. Some psychologists claim that there is what they call a natural tendency to obliviscence of the disagreeable—that men turn from the unpleasant in thought and recollection as they do from the obnoxious in action. Every serious-minded person knows that a large part of the effort required in moral discipline consists in the courage needed to acknowledge the unpleasant consequences of one's past and present acts. We squirm, dodge, evade, disguise, cover up, find excuses and palliations—anything to render the mental scene less uncongenial. In short, the tendency of spontaneous suggestion is to idealize experience, to give it in consciousness qualities which it does not have in actuality. Time and memory are true artists; they remould reality nearer to the heart's desire.

As imagination becomes freer and less controlled by concrete actualities, the idealizing tendency takes further flights unrestrained by the rein of the prosaic world. The things most emphasized in imagination as it reshapes experience are things which are absent in reality. In the degree in which life is placid and easy, imagination is sluggish and bovine. In the degree in which life is uneasy and troubled, fancy is stirred to frame pictures of a contrary state of things. By reading the characteristic features of any man's castles in the air you can make a shrewd guess as to his underlying desires which are frustrated. What is difficulty and disappointment in real life becomes conspicuous achievement and triumph in revery; what is negative in fact will be positive in the image drawn by fancy; what is vexation in conduct will be compensated for in high relief in idealizing imagination.

These considerations apply beyond mere personal psychology. They are decisive for one of the most marked traits of classic philosophy:—its conception of an ultimate supreme Reality which is essentially ideal in nature. Historians have more than once drawn an instructive parallel between the developed Olympian Pantheon of Greek religion and the Ideal Realm of Platonic philosophy. The gods, whatever their origin and original traits, became idealized projections of the selected and matured achievements which the Greeks admired among their mortal selves. The gods were like mortals, but mortals living only the lives which men would wish to live, with power intensified, beauty perfected, and wisdom ripened. When Aristotle criticized the theory of Ideas of his master, Plato, by saying that the Ideas were after all only things of sense eternalized, he pointed out in effect the parallelism of philosophy with religion and art to which allusion has just been made. And save for matters of merely technical import, is it not possible to say of Aristotle's Forms just what he said of Plato's Ideas? What are they, these Forms and Essences which so profoundly influenced for centuries the course of science and theology, save the objects of ordinary experience with their blemishes removed, their imperfections eliminated, their lacks rounded out, their suggestions and hints fulfilled? What are they in short but the objects of familiar life divinized because reshaped by the idealizing imagination to meet the demands of desire in just those respects in which actual experience is disappointing?

That Plato, and Aristotle in somewhat different fashion, and Plotinus and Marcus Aurelius and Saint Thomas Aquinas, and Spinoza and Hegel all taught that Ultimate Reality is either perfectly Ideal and Rational in nature, or else has absolute ideality and rationality as its necessary attribute, are facts well known to the student of philosophy. They need no exposition here. But it is worth pointing out that these great systematic philosophies de-

fined perfect Ideality in conceptions that express the opposite of
those things which make life unsatisfactory and troublesome.
What is the chief source of the complaint of poet and moralist
with the goods, the values and satisfactions of experience? Rarely
is the complaint that such things do not exist; it is that although
existing they are momentary, transient, fleeting. They do not stay;
at worst they come only to annoy and tease with their hurried and
disappearing taste of what might be; at best they come only to
inspire and instruct with a passing hint of truer reality. This commonplace of the poet and moralist as to the impermanence not
only of sensuous enjoyment, but of fame and civic achievements
was profoundly reflected upon by philosophers, especially by
Plato and Aristotle. The results of their thinking have been
wrought into the very fabric of western ideas. Time, change,
movement are signs that what the Greeks called Non-Being
somehow infects true Being. The phraseology is now strange, but
many a modern who ridicules the conception of Non-Being repeats the same thought under the name of the Finite or Imperfect.

Wherever there is change, there is instability, and instability
is proof of something the matter, of absence, deficiency, incompleteness. These are the ideas common to the connection between change, becoming and perishing, and Non-Being, finitude
and imperfection. Hence complete and true Reality must be
changeless, unalterable, so full of Being that it always and forever
maintains itself in fixed rest and repose. As Bradley, the most dialectically ingenious Absolutist of our own day, expresses the doctrine, "Nothing that is perfectly real moves." And while Plato took,
comparatively speaking, a pessimistic view of change as mere
lapse and Aristotle a complacent view of it as tendency to realization, yet Aristotle doubted no more than Plato that the fully realized reality, the divine and ultimate, is changeless. Though it is
called Activity or Energy, the Activity knew no change, the energy
did nothing. It was the activity of an army forever marking time
and never going anywhere.

From this contrast of the permanent with the transient arise
other features which mark off the Ultimate Reality from the imperfect realities of practical life. Where there is change, there is
of necessity numerical plurality, multiplicity, and from variety
comes opposition, strife. Change is alteration, or "othering" and

this means diversity. Diversity means division, and division means two sides and their conflict. The world which is transient *must* be a world of discord, for in lacking stability it lacks the government of unity. Did unity completely rule, these would remain an unchanging totality. What alters has parts and partialities which, not recognizing the rule of unity, assert themselves independently and make life a scene of contention and discord. Ultimate and true Being on the other hand, since it is changeless, is Total, All-Comprehensive and One. Since it is One, it knows only harmony, and therefore enjoys complete and eternal Good. It *is* Perfection.

Degrees of knowledge and truth correspond with degrees of reality point by point. The higher and more complete the Reality the truer and more important the knowledge that refers to it. Since the world of becoming, of origins and perishings, is deficient in true Being, it cannot be known in the best sense. To know it means to neglect its flux and alteration and discover some permanent form which limits the processes that alter in time. The acorn undergoes a series of changes; these are knowable only in reference to the fixed form of the oak which is the same in the entire oak species in spite of the numerical diversity of trees. Moreover, this form limits the flux of growth at both ends, the acorn coming from the oak as well as passing into it. Where such unifying and limiting eternal forms cannot be detected, there is mere aimless variation and fluctuation, and knowledge is out of the question. On the other hand, as objects are approached in which there is no movement at all, knowledge becomes really demonstrative, certain, perfect—truth pure and unalloyed. The heavens can be more truly known than the earth, God the unmoved mover than the heavens.

From this fact follows the superiority of contemplative to practical knowledge, of pure theoretical speculation to experimentation, and to any kind of knowing that depends upon changes in things or that induces change in them. Pure knowing is pure beholding, viewing, noting. It is complete in itself. It looks for nothing beyond itself; it lacks nothing and hence has no aim or purpose. It is most emphatically its own excuse for being. Indeed, pure contemplative knowing is so much the most truly self-enclosed and self-sufficient thing in the universe that it is the highest and indeed the only attribute that can be ascribed to God, the Highest Being in the scale of Being. Man himself is divine in the rare moments when he attains to purely self-sufficient theoretical insight.

In contrast with such knowing, the so-called knowing of the artisan is base. He has to bring about changes in things, in wood and stone, and this fact is of itself evidence that his material is deficient in Being. What condemns his knowledge even more is the fact that it is not disinterestedly for its own sake. It has reference to results to be attained, food, clothing, shelter, etc. It is concerned with things that perish, the body and its needs. It thus has an ulterior aim, and one which itself testifies to imperfection. For want, desire, affection of every sort, indicate lack. Where there is need and desire—as in the case of all practical knowledge and activity—there is incompleteness and insufficiency. While civic or political and moral knowledge rank higher than do the conceptions of the artisan, yet intrinsically considered they are a low and untrue type. Moral and political action is practical; that is, it implies needs and effort to satisfy them. It has an end beyond itself. Moreover, the very fact of association shows lack of self-sufficiency; it shows dependence upon others. Pure knowing is alone solitary, and capable of being carried on in complete, self-sufficing independence.

In short, the measure of the worth of knowledge according to Aristotle, whose views are here summarized, is the degree in which it is purely contemplative. The highest degree is attained in knowing ultimate Ideal Being, pure Mind. This is Ideal, the Form of Forms, because it has no lacks, no needs, and experiences no change or variety. It has no desires because in it all desires are consummated. Since it is perfect Being, it is perfect Mind and perfect Bliss;—the acme of rationality and ideality. One point more and the argument is completed. The kind of knowing that concerns itself with this ultimate reality (which is also ultimate ideality) is philosophy. Philosophy is therefore the last and highest term in pure contemplation. Whatever may be said for any other kind of knowledge, philosophy is self-enclosed. It has nothing to do beyond itself; it has no aim or purpose or function—except to be philosophy—that is, pure, self-sufficing beholding of ultimate reality. There is of course such a thing as philosophic *study* which falls short of this perfection. Where there is learning, there is change and becoming. But the function of study and

learning of philosophy is, as Plato put it, to convert the eye of the
soul from dwelling contentedly upon the images of things, upon
the inferior realities that are born and that decay, and to lead it to
the intuition of supernal and eternal Being. Thus the mind of the
knower is transformed. It becomes assimilated to what it knows.

Through a variety of channels, especially Neo-Platonism and
St. Augustine, these ideas found their way into Christian theology; and great scholastic thinkers taught that the end of man is
to know True Being, that knowledge is contemplative, that True
Being is pure Immaterial Mind, and to know it is Bliss and Salvation. While this knowledge cannot be achieved in this stage of
life nor without supernatural aid, yet so far as it is accomplished
it assimilates the human mind to the divine essence and so constitutes salvation. Through this taking over of the conception of
knowledge as Contemplative into the dominant religion of Europe, multitudes were affected who were totally innocent of theoretical philosophy. There was bequeathed to generations of thinkers as an unquestioned axiom the idea that knowledge is
intrinsically a mere beholding or viewing of reality—the spectator
conception of knowledge. So deeply engrained was this idea that
it prevailed for centuries after the actual progress of science had
demonstrated that knowledge is power to transform the world,
and centuries after the practice of effective knowledge had
adopted the method of experimentation.

Let us turn abruptly from this conception of the measure of
true knowledge and the nature of true philosophy to the existing
practice of knowledge. Nowadays if a man, say a physicist or
chemist, wants to know something, the last thing he does is
merely to contemplate. He does not look in however earnest and
prolonged way upon the object expecting that thereby he will detect its fixed and characteristic form. He does not expect any
amount of such aloof scrutiny to reveal to him any secrets. He
proceeds to *do* something, to bring some energy to bear upon the
substance to see how it reacts; he places it under unusual conditions in order to induce some change. While the astronomer cannot change the remote stars, even he no longer merely gazes. If
he cannot change the stars themselves, he can at least by lens
and prism change their light as it reaches the earth; he can lay
traps for discovering changes which would otherwise escape notice. Instead of taking an antagonistic attitude toward change and

denying it to the stars because of their divinity and perfection, he is on constant and alert watch to find some change through which he can form an inference as to the formation of stars and systems of stars.

Change in short is no longer looked upon as a fall from grace, as a lapse from reality or a sign of imperfection of Being. Modern science no longer tries to find some fixed form or essence behind each process of change. Rather, the experimental method tries to break down apparent fixities and to induce changes. The form that remains unchanged to sense, the form of seed or tree, is regarded not as the key to knowledge of the thing, but as a wall, an obstruction to be broken down. Consequently the scientific man experiments with this and that agency applied to this and that condition until something begins to happen; until there is, as we say, something doing. He assumes that there is change going on all the time, that there is movement within each thing in seeming repose; and that since the process is veiled from perception the way to know it is to bring the thing into novel circumstances until change becomes evident. In short, the thing which is to be accepted and paid heed to is not what is originally given but that which emerges after the thing has been set under a great variety of circumstances in order to see how it behaves.

Now this marks a much more general change in the human attitude than perhaps appears at first sight. It signifies nothing less than that the world or any part of it as it presents itself at a given time is accepted or acquiesced in only as *material* for change. It is accepted precisely as the carpenter, say, accepts things as he finds them. If he took them as things to be observed and noted for their own sake, he never would be a carpenter. He would observe, describe, record the structures, forms and changes which things exhibit to him, and leave the matter there. If perchance some of the changes going on should present him with a shelter, so much the better. But what makes the carpenter a *builder* is the fact that he notes things not just as objects in themselves, but with reference to what he wants to do to them and with them; to the end he has in mind. Fitness to effect certain special changes that he wishes to see accomplished is what concerns him in the wood and stones and iron which he observes. His attention is directed to the changes they undergo and the changes they make other things undergo so that he may select that combination of changes which will yield him his desired result. It is only by these processes of active manipulation of things in order to realize his purpose that he discovers what the properties of things are. If he foregoes his own purpose and in the name of a meek and humble subscription to things as they "really are" refuses to bend things as they "are" to his own purpose, he not only never achieves his purpose but he never learns what the things themselves are. They *are* what they can do and what can be done with them,—things that can be found by deliberate trying.

The outcome of this idea of the right way to know is a profound modification in man's attitude toward the natural world. Under differing social conditions, the older or classic conception sometimes bred resignation and submission; sometimes contempt and desire to escape; sometimes, notably in the case of the Greeks, a keen esthetic curiosity which showed itself in acute noting of all the traits of given objects. In fact, the whole conception of knowledge as beholding and noting is fundamentally an idea connected with esthetic enjoyment and appreciation where the environment is beautiful and life is serene, and with esthetic repulsion and depreciation where life is troubled, nature morose and hard. But in the degree in which the active conception of knowledge prevails, and the environment is regarded as something that has to be changed in order to be truly known, men are imbued with courage, with what may almost be termed an aggressive attitude toward nature. The latter becomes plastic, something to be subjected to human uses. The moral disposition toward change is deeply modified. This loses its pathos, it ceases to be haunted with melancholy through suggesting only decay and loss. Change becomes significant of new possibilities and ends to be attained; it becomes prophetic of a better future. Change is associated with progress rather than with lapse and fall. Since changes are going on anyway, the great thing is to learn enough about them so that we be able to lay hold of them and turn them in the direction of our desires. Conditions and events are neither to be fled from nor passively acquiesced in; they are to be utilized and directed. They are either obstacles to our ends or else means for their accomplishment. In a profound sense knowing ceases to be contemplative and becomes practical.

Unfortunately men, educated men, cultivated men in particular, are still so dominated by the older conception of an aloof and self-sufficing reason and knowledge that they refuse to perceive the import of this doctrine. They think they are sustaining the cause of impartial, thorough-going and disinterested reflection when they maintain the traditional philosophy of intellectualism—that is, of knowing as something self-sufficing and self-enclosed. But in truth, historic intellectualism, the spectator view of knowledge, is a purely compensatory doctrine which men of an intellectual turn have built up to console themselves for the actual and social impotency of the calling of thought to which they are devoted. Forbidden by conditions and held back by lack of courage from making their knowledge a factor in the determination of the course of events, they have sought a refuge of complacency in the notion that knowing is something too sublime to be contaminated by contact with things of change and practice. They have transformed knowing into a morally irresponsible estheticism. The true import of the doctrine of the operative or practical character of knowing, of intelligence, is objective. It means that the structures and objects which science and philosophy set up in contrast to the things and events of concrete daily experience do not constitute a realm apart in which rational contemplation may rest satisfied; it means that they represent the selected obstacles, material means and ideal methods of giving direction to that change which is bound to occur anyway.

This change of human disposition toward the world does not mean that man ceases to have ideals, or ceases to be primarily a creature of the imagination. But it does signify a radical change in the character and function of the ideal realm which man shapes for himself. In the classic philosophy, the ideal world is essentially a haven in which man finds rest from the storms of life; it is an asylum in which he takes refuge from the troubles of existence with the calm assurance that it alone is supremely real. When the belief that knowledge is active and operative takes hold of men, the ideal realm is no longer something aloof and separate; it is rather that collection of imagined possibilities that stimulates men to new efforts and realizations. It still remains true that the troubles which men undergo are the forces that lead them to project pictures of a better state of things. But the picture of the better is shaped so that it may become an instrumentality of action, while in the classic view the Idea belongs ready-made in a noumenal world. Hence, it is only an object of personal aspiration or consolation, while to the modern, an idea is a suggestion of something to be done or of a way of doing.

An illustration will, perhaps, make the difference clear. Distance is an obstacle, a source of trouble. It separates friends and prevents intercourse. It isolates, and makes contact and mutual understanding difficult. This state of affairs provokes discontent and restlessness; it excites the imagination to construct pictures of a state of things where human intercourse is not injuriously affected by space. Now there are two ways out. One way is to pass from a mere dream of some heavenly realm in which distance is abolished and by some magic all friends are in perpetual transparent communication, to pass, I say, from some idle castle-building to philosophic reflection. Space, distance, it will then be argued, is merely phenomenal; or, in a more modern version, subjective. It is not, metaphysically speaking, real. Hence the obstruction and trouble it gives is not after all "real" in the metaphysical sense of reality. Pure minds, pure spirits, do not live in a space world; for them distance is not. Their relationships in the true world are not in any way affected by special considerations. Their intercommunication is direct, fluent, unobstructed.

Does the illustration involve a caricature of ways of philosophizing with which we are all familiar? But if it is not an absurd caricature, does it not suggest that much of what philosophies have taught about the ideal and noumenal or superiorly real world, is after all, only casting a dream into an elaborate dialectic form through the use of a speciously scientific terminology? Practically, the difficulty, the trouble, remains. Practically, however it may be "metaphysically," space is still real:—it acts in a definite objectionable way. Again, man dreams of some better state of things. From troublesome fact he takes refuge in fantasy. But this time, the refuge does not remain a permanent and remote asylum.

The idea becomes a standpoint from which to examine existing occurrences and to see if there is not among them something which gives a hint of how communication at a distance can be effected, something to be utilized as a medium of speech at long range. The suggestion or fancy though still ideal is treated as a possibility capable of realization *in* the concrete natural world, not as a superior reality apart from that world. As such, it becomes a platform from which to scrutinize natural events. Observed from the point of view of this possibility, things disclose properties hitherto undetected. In the light of these ascertainments, the idea of some agency for speech at a distance becomes less vague and floating: it takes on positive form. This action and reaction goes on. The possibility or idea is employed as a method for observing actual existence; and in the light of what is discovered the possibility takes on concrete existence. It becomes less of a mere idea, a fancy, a wished-for possibility, and more of an actual fact. Invention proceeds, and at last we have the telegraph, the telephone, first through wires, and then with no artificial medium. The concrete environment is transformed in the desired direction; it is idealized in fact and not merely in fancy. The ideal is realized through its own use as a tool or method of inspection, experimentation, selection and combination of concrete natural operations.

Let us pause to take stock of results. The division of the world into two kinds of Being, one superior, accessible only to reason and ideal in nature, the other inferior, material, changeable, empirical, accessible to sense-observation, turns inevitably into the idea that knowledge is contemplative in nature. It assumes a contrast between theory and practice which was all to the disadvantage of the latter. But in the actual course of the development of science, a tremendous change has come about. When the practice of knowledge ceased to be dialectical and became experimental, knowing became preoccupied with changes and the test of knowledge became the ability to bring about certain changes. Knowing, for the experimental sciences, means a certain kind of intelligently conducted doing; it ceases to be contemplative and becomes in a true sense practical. Now this implies that philosophy, unless it is to undergo a complete break with the authorized spirit of science, must also alter its nature. It must assume a practical nature; it must become operative and experimental. And we have pointed out what an enormous change this transformation of philosophy entails in the two conceptions which have played the greatest role in historic philosophizing—the conceptions of the "real" and "ideal" respectively. The former ceases to be something ready-made and final; it becomes that which has to be accepted as the material of change, as the obstructions and the means of certain specific desired changes. The ideal and rational also ceased to be a separate ready-made world incapable of being used as a lever to transform the actual empirical world, a mere asylum from empirical deficiencies. They represent intelligently thought-out possibilities *of* the existent world which may be used as methods for making over and improving it.

Philosophically speaking, this is the great difference involved in the change from knowledge and philosophy as contemplative to operative. The change does not mean the lowering in dignity of philosophy from a lofty plane to one of gross utilitarianism. It signifies that the prime function of philosophy is that of rationalizing the *possibilities* of experience, especially collective human experience. The scope of this change may be realized by considering how far we are from accomplishing it. In spite of inventions which enable men to use the energies of nature for their purposes, we are still far from habitually treating knowledge as the method of active control of nature and of experience. We tend to think of it after the model of a spectator viewing a finished picture rather than after that of the artist producing the painting. Thus there arise all the questions of epistemology with which the technical student of philosophy is so familiar, and which have made modern philosophy in especial so remote from the understanding of the everyday person and from the results and processes of science. For these questions all spring from the assumption of a merely beholding mind on one side and a foreign and remote object to be viewed and noted on the other. They ask how a mind and world, subject and object, so separate and independent can by any possibility come into such relationship to each other as to make true knowledge possible. If knowing were habitually conceived of as active and operative, after the analogy of experiment guided by hypothesis, or of invention guided by the imagination of some possibility, it is not too much to say that the first effect would be to emancipate philosophy from all the epistemological puzzles which now perplex it. For these all arise from a conception of the relation of mind and world, subject and object, in knowing, which assumes that to know is to seize upon what is already in existence.

Modern philosophic thought has been so preoccupied with these puzzles of epistemology and the disputes between realist and idealist, between phenomenalist and absolutist, that many students are at a loss to know what would be left for philosophy if there were removed both the metaphysical task of distinguishing between the noumenal and phenomenal worlds and the epistemological task of telling how a separate subject can know an independent object. But would not the elimination of these traditional problems permit philosophy to devote itself to a more fruitful and more needed task? Would it not encourage philosophy to face the great social and moral defects and troubles from which humanity suffers, to concentrate its attention upon clearing up the causes and exact nature of these evils and upon developing a clear idea of better social possibilities; in short upon projecting an idea or ideal which, instead of expressing the notion of another world or some far-away unrealizable goal, would be used as a method of understanding and rectifying specific social ills?

This is a vague statement. But note in the first place that such a conception of the proper province of philosophy where it is released from vain metaphysics and idle epistemology is in line with the origin of philosophy sketched in the first hour. And in the second place, note how contemporary society, the world over, is in need of more general and fundamental enlightenment and guidance than it now possesses. I have tried to show that a radical change of the conception of knowledge from contemplative to active is the inevitable result of the way in which inquiry and invention are now conducted. But in claiming this, it must also be conceded, or rather asserted, that so far the change has influenced for the most part only the more technical side of human life. The sciences have created new industrial arts. Man's physical command of natural energies has been indefinitely multiplied. There is control of the sources of material wealth and prosperity. What would once have been miracles are now daily performed with steam and coal and electricity and air, and with the human body. But there are few persons optimistic enough to declare that any similar command of the forces which control man's social and moral welfare has been achieved.

Where is the moral progress that corresponds to our economic accomplishments? The latter is the direct fruit of the revolution that has been wrought in physical science. But where is there a corresponding human science and art? Not only has the improvement in the method of knowing remained so far mainly limited to technical and economic matters, but this progress has brought with it serious new moral disturbances. I need only cite the late war, the problem of capital and labor, the relation of economic classes, the fact that while the new science has achieved wonders in medicine and surgery, it has also produced and spread occasions for diseases and weaknesses. These considerations indicate to us how undeveloped are our politics, how crude and primitive our education, how passive and inert our morals. The causes remain which brought philosophy into existence as an attempt to find an intelligent substitute for blind custom and blind impulse as guides to life and conduct. The attempt has not been successfully accomplished. Is there not reason for believing that the release of philosophy from its burden of sterile metaphysics and sterile epistemology instead of depriving philosophy of problems and subject-matter would open a way to questions of the most perplexing and the most significant sort?

Let me specify one problem quite directly suggested by certain points in this lecture. It has been pointed out that the really fruitful application of the contemplative idea was not in science but in the esthetic field. It is difficult to imagine any high development of the fine arts except where there is curious and loving interest in forms and motions of the world quite irrespective of any use to which they may be put. And it is not too much to say that every people that has attained a high esthetic development has been a people in which the contemplative attitude has flourished—as the Greek, the Hindoo, the medieval Christian. On the other hand, the scientific attitude that has actually proved itself in scientific progress is, as has been pointed out, a practical attitude. It takes forms as disguises for hidden processes. Its interest in change is in what it leads to, what can be done with it, to what use it can be put. While it has brought nature under control, there is something hard and aggressive in its attitude toward nature unfavorable to the esthetic enjoyment of the world. Surely there is no more significant question before the world than this question of the possibility and method of reconciliation of the attitudes of practical science and contemplative esthetic appreciation. Without the former, man will be the sport and victim of natural forces which he cannot use or control. Without the latter, mankind might become a race of economic monsters, restlessly driving hard bargains with nature and with one another, bored with leisure or capable of putting it to use only in ostentatious display and extravagant dissipation.

Like other moral questions, this matter is social and even political. The western peoples advanced earlier on the path of experimental science and its applications in control of nature than the oriental. It is not, I suppose, wholly fanciful to believe that the latter have embodied in their habits of life more of the contemplative, esthetic and speculatively religious temper, and the former more of the scientific, industrial and practical. This difference and others which have grown up around it is one barrier to easy mutual understanding, and one source of misunderstanding. The philosophy which, then, makes a serious effort to comprehend these respective attitudes in their relation and due balance, could hardly fail to promote the capacity of peoples to profit by one another's experience and to cooperate more effectually with one another in the tasks of fruitful culture.

Indeed, it is incredible that the question of the relation of the "real" and the "ideal" should ever have been thought to be a problem belonging distinctively to philosophy. The very fact that this most serious of all human issues has been taken possession of by philosophy is only another proof of the disasters that follow in the wake of regarding knowledge and intellect as something self-sufficient. Never have the "real" and the "ideal" been so clamorous, so self-assertive, as at the present time. And never in the history of the world have they been so far apart. The world war was carried on for purely ideal ends:—for humanity, justice and equal liberty for strong and weak alike. And it was carried on by realistic means of applied science, by high explosives, and bombing airplanes and blockading marvels of mechanism that reduced the world well nigh to ruin, so that the serious-minded are concerned for the perpetuity of those choice values we call civilization. The peace settlement is loudly proclaimed in the name of the ideals that stir man's deepest emotions, but with the most realistic attention to details of economic advantage distributed in proportion to physical power to create future disturbances.

It is not surprising that some men are brought to regard all idealism as a mere smoke-screen behind which the search for material profit may be more effectually carried on, and are converted to the materialistic interpretation of history. "Reality" is then conceived as physical force and as sensations of power, profit and enjoyment; any politics that takes account of other factors, save as elements of clever propaganda and for control of those human beings who have not become realistically enlightened, is

based on illusions. But others are equally sure that the real lesson
of the war is that humanity took its first great wrong step when it
entered upon a cultivation of physical science and an application
of the fruits of science to the improvement of the instruments of
life—industry and commerce. They will sigh for the return of the
day when, while the great mass died as they were born in animal
fashion, the few elect devoted themselves not to science and the
material decencies and comforts of existence but to "ideal" things,
the things of the spirit.

Yet the most obvious conclusion would seem to be the impotency and the harmfulness of any and every ideal that is proclaimed wholesale and in the abstract, that is, as something in
itself apart from the detailed concrete existences whose moving
possibilities it embodies. The true moral would seem to lie in enforcing the tragedy of that idealism which believes in a spiritual
world which exists in and by itself, and the tragic need for the
most realistic study of forces and consequences, a study conducted in a more scientifically accurate and complete manner
than that of the professed *Real-politik*. For it is not truly realistic
or scientific to take short views, to sacrifice the future to immediate pressure, to ignore facts and forces that are disagreeable and
to magnify the enduring quality of whatever falls in with immediate desire. It is false that the evils of the situation arise from
absence of ideals; they spring from wrong ideals. And these
wrong ideals have in turn their foundation in the absence in social matters of that methodic, systematic, impartial, critical,
searching inquiry into "real" and operative conditions which we
call science and which has brought man in the technical realm to
the command of physical energies.

Philosophy, let it be repeated, cannot "solve" the problem of
the relation of the ideal and the real. That is the standing problem
of life. But it can at least lighten the burden of humanity in dealing with the problem by emancipating mankind from the errors
which philosophy has itself fostered—the existence of conditions
which are real apart from their movement into something new
and different, and the existence of ideals, spirit and reason independent of the possibilities of the material and physical. For as
long as humanity is committed to this radically false bias, it will
walk forward with blinded eyes and bound limbs. And philosophy
can effect, if it will, something more than this negative task. It

can make it easier for mankind to take the right steps in action by making it clear that a sympathetic and integral intelligence brought to bear upon the observation and understanding of concrete social events and forces, can form ideals, that is aims, which shall not be either illusions or mere emotional compensations.

6. THE SIGNIFICANCE OF LOGICAL RECONSTRUCTION

Logic—like philosophy itself—suffers from a curious oscillation. It is elevated into the supreme and legislative science only to fall into the trivial estate of keeper of such statements as A is A and the scholastic verses for the syllogistic rules. It claims power to state the laws of the ultimate structure of the universe, on the ground that it deals with the laws of thought which are the laws according to which Reason has formed the world. Then it limits its pretensions to laws of correct reasoning which is correct even though it leads to no matter of fact, or even to material falsity. It is regarded by the modern objective idealist as the adequate substitute for ancient ontological metaphysics; but others treat it as that branch of rhetoric which teaches proficiency in argumentation. For a time a superficial compromise equilibrium was maintained wherein the logic of formal demonstration which the Middle Ages extracted from Aristotle was supplemented by an inductive logic of discovery of truth that Mill extracted from the practice of scientific men. But students of German philosophy, of mathematics, and of psychology, no matter how much they attacked one another, have made common cause in attack upon the orthodox logics both of deductive proof and inductive discovery.

Logical theory presents a scene of chaos. There is little agreement as to its subject-matter, scope or purpose. This disagreement is not formal or nominal but affects the treatment of every topic. Take such a rudimentary matter as the nature of judgment. Reputable authority can be quoted in behalf of every possible permutation of doctrine. Judgment is the central thing in logic; and judgment is not logical at all, but personal and psychological. If logical, it is the primary function to which both conception and inference are subordinate; and it is an after-product from them. The distinction of subject and predicate is necessary, and it is totally irrelevant; or again, though it is found in some cases, it is not of great importance. Among those who hold that the subject-predicate relationship is essential, some hold that judgment is an analysis of something prior into them, and others assert that it is a synthesis of them into something else. Some hold that reality is always the subject of judgment, and others that "reality" is logically irrelevant. Among those who deny that judgment is the attribution of predicate to subject, who regard it as a relation of elements, some hold that the relation is "internal," some that it is "external," and others that it is sometimes one and sometimes the other.

Unless logic is a matter of some practical account, these contrarieties are so numerous, so extensive, and so irreconcilable that they are ludicrous. If logic is an affair of practical moment, then these inconsistencies are serious. They testify to some deep-lying cause of intellectual disagreement and incoherency. In fact, contemporary logical theory is the ground upon which all philosophical differences and disputes are gathered together and focussed. How does the modification in the traditional conception of the relation of experience and reason, the real and ideal affect logic?

It affects, in the first place, the nature of logic itself. If thought or intelligence is the means of intentional reconstruction of experience, then logic, as an account of the procedure of thought, is not purely formal. It is not confined to laws of formally correct reasoning apart from truth of subject-matter. Neither, on the contrary, is it concerned with the inherent thought structures of the universe, as Hegel's logic would have it; nor with the successive approaches of human thought to this objective thought structure as the logic of Lotze, Bosanquet, and other epistemological logicians would have it. If thinking is the way in which deliberate reorganization of experience is secured, then logic is such a clarified and systematized formulation of the procedures of thinking as will enable the desired reconstruction to go on more economically and efficiently. In language familiar to students, logic is both a science and an art; a science so far as it gives an organized and tested descriptive account of the way in which thought actually goes on; an art, so far as on the basis of this description it projects methods by which future thinking shall take advantage of the operations that lead to success and avoid those which result in failure.

Thus is answered the dispute whether logic is empirical or normative, psychological or regulative. It is both. Logic is based on a definite and executive supply of empirical material. Men have been thinking for ages. They have observed, inferred, and reasoned in all sorts of ways and to all kinds of results. Anthropology, the study of the origin of myth, legend and cult; linguistics and grammar; rhetoric and formal logical compositions all tell us how men have thought and what have been the purposes and consequences of different kinds of thinking. Psychology, experimental and pathological, makes important contributions to our knowledge of how thinking goes on and to what effect. Especially does the record of the growth of the various sciences afford instruction in those concrete ways of inquiry and testing which have led men astray and which have proved efficacious. Each science from mathematics to history exhibits typical fallacious methods and typical efficacious methods in special subject-matters. Logical theory has thus a large, almost inexhaustible field of empirical study.

The conventional statement that experience only tells us how men have thought or *do* think, while logic is concerned with norms, with how men *should* think, is ludicrously inept. Some sorts of thinking are shown *by* experience to have got nowhere, or worse than nowhere—into systematized delusion and mistake. Others have proved in manifest experience that they lead to fruitful and enduring discoveries. It is precisely in experience that the different consequences of different methods of investigation and ratiocination are convincingly shown. The parrot-like repetition of the distinction between an empirical description of what is and a normative account of what should be merely neglects the most striking fact about thinking as it empirically is—namely, its flagrant exhibition of cases of failure and success—that is, of good thinking and bad thinking. Any one who considers this empirical manifestation will not complain of lack of material from which to construct a *regulative* art. The more study that is given to empirical records of actual thought, the more apparent becomes the connection between the specific features of thinking which have produced failure and success. Out of this relationship of cause and effect as it is empirically ascertained grow the norms and regulations of an art of thinking.

Mathematics is often cited as an example of purely normative thinking dependent upon *a priori* canons and supra-empirical material. But it is hard to see how the student who approaches the matter historically can avoid the conclusion that the status of mathematics is as empirical as that of metallurgy. Men began with counting and measuring things just as they began with pounding and burning them. One thing, as common speech profoundly has it, led to another. Certain ways were successful—not merely in the immediately practical sense, but in the sense of being interesting, of arousing attention, of exciting attempts at improvement. The present-day mathematical logician may present the structure of mathematics as if it had sprung all at once from the brain of a Zeus whose anatomy is that of pure logic. But, nevertheless, this very structure is a product of long historic growth, in which all kinds of experiments have been tried, in which some men have struck out in this direction and some in that, and in which some exercises and operations have resulted in confusion and others in triumphant clarifications and fruitful growths; a history in which matter and methods have been constantly selected and worked over on the basis of empirical success and failure.

The structure of alleged normative *a priori* mathematics is in truth the crowned result of ages of toilsome experience. The metallurgist who should write on the most highly developed method of dealing with ores would not, in truth, proceed any differently. He too selects, refines, and organizes the methods which in the past have been found to yield the maximum of achievement. Logic is a matter of profound human importance precisely because it is empirically founded and experimentally applied. So considered, the problem of logical theory is none other than the problem of the possibility of the development and employment of intelligent method in inquiries concerned with deliberate reconstruction of experience. And it is only saying again in more specific form what has been said in general form to add that while such a logic has been developed in respect to mathematics and physical science, intelligent method, logic, is still far to seek in moral and political affairs.

Assuming, accordingly, this idea of logic without argument, let us proceed to discuss some of its chief features. First, light is thrown by the *origin* of thinking upon a logic which shall be a method of intelligent guidance of experience. In line with what has already been said about experience being a matter primarily of behavior, a sensori-motor matter, is the fact that thinking takes its departure from specific conflicts in experience that occasion

perplexity and trouble. Men do not, in their natural estate, think
when they have no troubles to cope with, no difficulties to overcome. A life of ease, of success without effort, would be a thought-
less life, and so also would a life of ready omnipotence. Beings
who think are beings whose life is so hemmed in and constricted
that they cannot directly carry through a course of action to victorious consummation. Men also do not tend to think when their
action, when they are amid difficulties, is dictated to them by authority. Soldiers have difficulties and restrictions in plenty, but
qua soldiers (as Aristotle would say) they are not notorious for
being thinkers. Thinking is done for them, higher up. The same
is too true of most workingmen under present economic conditions. Difficulties occasion thinking only when thinking is the imperative or urgent way out, only when it is the indicated road to a
solution. Wherever external authority reigns, thinking is sus-
pected and obnoxious.

Thinking, however, is not the only way in which a personal
solution of difficulties is sought. As we have seen, dreams, rever-
ies, emotional idealizations are roads which are taken to escape
the strain of perplexity and conflict. According to modern psychology, many systematized delusions and mental disorders,
probably hysteria itself, originate as devices for getting freedom
from troublesome conflicting factors. Such considerations throw
into relief some of the traits essential to thinking as a way of responding to difficulty. The short-cut "solutions" alluded to do not
get rid of the conflict and problems; they only get rid of the feeling
of it. They cover up consciousness of it. Because the conflict remains in fact and is evaded in thought, disorders arise.

The first distinguishing characteristic of thinking then is fac-
ing the facts—inquiry, minute and extensive scrutinizing, observation. Nothing has done greater harm to the successful conduct
of the enterprise of thinking (and to the logics which reflect and
formulate the undertaking) than the habit of treating observation
as something outside of and prior to thinking, and thinking as
something which can go on in the head without *including* observation of new facts as part of itself. Every approximation to such
"thinking" is really an approach to the method of escape and self-
delusion just referred to. It substitutes an emotionally agreeable
and rationally self-consistent train of meanings for inquiry into
the features of the situation which cause the trouble. It leads to

that type of Idealism which has well been termed intellectual somnambulism. It creates a class of "thinkers" who are remote from practice and hence from testing their thought by application—a socially superior and irresponsible class. This is the condition causing the tragic division of theory and practice, and leading to an unreasonable exaltation of theory on one side and an unreasonable contempt for it on the other. It confirms current practice in its hard brutalities and dead routines just because it has transferred thinking and theory to a separate and nobler region. Thus has the idealist conspired with the materialist to keep actual life impoverished and inequitable.

The isolation of thinking from confrontation with facts encourages that kind of observation which merely accumulates brute facts, which occupies itself laboriously with mere details, but never inquires into their meaning and consequences—a safe occupation, for it never contemplates any use to be made of the observed facts in determining a plan for changing the situation. Thinking which is a method of reconstructing experience treats observation of facts, on the other hand, as the indispensable step of defining the problem, of locating the trouble, of forcing home a definite, instead of a merely vague emotional, sense of what the difficulty is and where it lies. It is not aimless, random, miscellaneous, but purposeful, specific and limited by the character of the trouble undergone. The purpose is so to clarify the disturbed and confused situation that reasonable ways of dealing with it may be suggested. When the scientific man appears to observe aimlessly, it is merely that he is so in love with problems as sources and guides of inquiry, that he is striving to turn up a problem where none appears on the surface: he is, as we say, hunting for trouble because of the satisfaction to be had in coping with it.

Specific and wide observation of concrete fact always, then, corresponds not only with a sense of a problem or difficulty, but with some vague sense of the *meaning* of the difficulty, that is, of what it imports or signifies in subsequent experience. It is a kind of anticipation or prediction of what is coming. We speak, very truly, of *impending* trouble, and in observing the signs of what the trouble is, we are at the same time expecting, forecasting—in short, framing an *idea*, becoming aware of meaning. When the trouble is not only impending but completely actual and present, we are overwhelmed. We do not think, but give way to depression.

The kind of trouble that occasions thinking is that which is incomplete and developing, and where what is found already in existence can be employed as a sign from which to infer what is likely to come. When we intelligently observe, we are, as we say apprehensive, as well as apprehending. We are on the alert for something still to come. Curiosity, inquiry, investigation, are directed quite as truly into what is going to happen next as into what has happened. An intelligent interest in the latter is an interest in getting evidence, indications, symptoms for inferring the former. Observation is diagnosis and diagnosis implies an interest in anticipation and preparation. It makes ready in advance an attitude of response so that we shall not be caught unawares.

That which is not already in existence, that which is only anticipated and inferred, cannot be observed. It does not have the status of fact, of something given, a datum, but of a meaning, an idea. So far as ideas are not fancies, framed by emotionalized memory for escape and refuge, they are precisely anticipations of something still to come aroused by looking into the facts of a developing situation. The blacksmith watches his iron, its color and texture, to get evidence of what it is getting ready to pass into; the physician observes his patient to detect symptoms of change in some definite direction; the scientific man keeps his attention upon his laboratory material to get a clue as to what *will* happen under certain conditions. The very fact that observation is not an end in itself but a search for evidence and signs shows that along with observation goes inference, anticipatory forecast—in short an idea, thought or conception.

In a more technical context, it would be worth while to see what light this logical correspondence of observed fact and projected idea or meaning throws upon certain traditional philosophical problems and puzzles, including that of subject and predicate in judgment, object and subject in knowledge, "real" and "ideal" generally. But at this time, we must confine ourselves to pointing out that this view of the correlative origin and function of observed fact and projected idea in experience, commits us to some very important consequences concerning the nature of ideas, meanings, conceptions, or whatever word may be employed to denote the specifically *mental* function. Because they are suggestions of something that may happen or eventuate, they are (as we saw in the case of ideals generally) platforms of response to what is going on. The man who detects that the cause of his difficulty is an automobile bearing down upon him is not guaranteed safety; he may have made his observation-forecast too late. But if his anticipation-perception comes in season, he has the basis for doing something which will avert threatening disaster. Because he foresees an impending result, he may do something that will lead to the situation eventuating in some other way. All intelligent thinking means an increment of freedom in action—an emancipation from chance and fatality. "Thought" represents the suggestion of a way of response that is different from that which would have been followed if intelligent observation had not effected an inference as to the future.

Now a method of action, a mode of response, intended to produce a certain result—that is, to enable the blacksmith to give a certain form to his hot iron, the physician to treat the patient so as to facilitate recovery, the scientific experimenter to draw a conclusion which will apply to other cases,—is by the nature of the case tentative, uncertain till tested by its results. The significance of this fact for the theory of truth will be discussed below. Here it is enough to note that notions, theories, systems, no matter how elaborate and self-consistent they are, must be regarded as hypotheses. They are to be accepted as bases of actions which test them, not as finalities. To perceive this fact is to abolish rigid dogmas from the world. It is to recognize that conceptions, theories and systems of thought are always open to development through use. It is to enforce the lesson that we must be on the lookout quite as much for indications to alter them as for opportunities to assert them. They are tools. As in the case of all tools, their value resides not in themselves but in their capacity to work shown in the consequences of their use.

Nevertheless, inquiry is free only when the interest in knowing is so developed that thinking carries with it something worth while for itself, something having its own esthetic and moral interest. Just because knowing is not self-enclosed and final but is instrumental to reconstruction of situations, there is always danger that it will be subordinated to maintaining some preconceived purpose or prejudice. Then reflection ceases to be complete; it falls short. Being precommitted to arriving at some special result, it is not sincere. It is one thing to say that all knowing has an end beyond itself, and another thing, a thing of a contrary kind, to say that an act of knowing has a particular end which it is bound, in advance, to reach. Much less is it true that the instrumental nature of thinking means that it exists for the sake of attaining some private, one-sided advantage upon which one has set one's heart. Any limitation whatever of the end means limitation in the thinking process itself. It signifies that it does not attain its full growth and movement, but is cramped, impeded, interfered with. The only situation in which knowing is fully stimulated is one in which the end is developed in the process of inquiry and testing.

Disinterested and impartial inquiry is then far from meaning that knowing is self-enclosed and irresponsible. It means that there is no particular end set up in advance so as to shut in the activities of observation, forming of ideas, and application. Inquiry is emancipated. It is encouraged to attend to every fact that is relevant to defining the problem or need, and to follow up every suggestion that promises a clue. The barriers to free inquiry are so many and so solid that mankind is to be congratulated that the very act of investigation is capable of itself becoming a delightful and absorbing pursuit, capable of enlisting on its side man's sporting instincts.

Just in the degree in which thought ceases to be held down to ends fixed by social custom, a social division of labor grows up. Investigation has become a dominant life occupation for some persons. Only superficially, however, does this confirm the idea that theory and knowledge are ends in themselves. They are, relatively speaking, ends in themselves for some persons. But these persons represent a social division of labor; and their specialization can be trusted only when such persons are in unobstructed cooperation with other social occupations, sensitive to others' problems and transmitting results to them for wider application in action. When this social relationship of persons particularly engaged in carrying on the enterprise of knowing is forgotten and the class becomes isolated, inquiry loses stimulus and purpose. It degenerates into sterile specialization, a kind of intellectual busy work carried on by socially absent-minded men. Details are heaped up in the name of science, and abstruse dialectical developments of systems occur. Then the occupation is "rationalized" under the lofty name of devotion to truth for its own sake. But when the path of true science is retaken these things are brushed aside and forgotten. They turn out to have been the toyings of vain and irresponsible men. The only guarantee of impartial, disinterested inquiry is the social sensitiveness of the inquirer to the needs and problems of those with whom he is associated.

As the instrumental theory is favorable to high esteem for impartial and disinterested inquiry, so, contrary to the impressions of some critics, it sets much store upon the apparatus of deduction. It is a strange notion that because one says that the cognitive value of conceptions, definitions, generalizations, classifications and the development of consecutive implications is not self-resident, that therefore one makes light of the deductive function, or denies its fruitfulness and necessity. The instrumental theory only attempts to state with some scrupulousness *where* the value is found and to prevent its being sought in the wrong place. It says that knowing begins with specific observations that define the problem and ends with specific observations that test a hypothesis for its solution. But that the idea, the meaning, which the original observations suggest and the final ones test, itself requires careful scrutiny and prolonged development, the theory would be the last to deny. To say that a locomotive is an agency, that it is intermediate between a need in experience and its satisfaction, is not to depreciate the worth of careful and elaborate construction of the locomotive, or the need of subsidiary tools and processes that are devoted to introducing improvements into its structure. One would rather say that *because* the locomotive is intermediary in experience, not primary and not final, it is impossible to devote too much care to its constructive development.

Such a deductive science as mathematics represents the perfecting of method. That a method to those concerned with it should present itself as an end on its own account is no more surprising than that there should be a distinct business for making any tool. Rarely are those who invent and perfect a tool those who employ it. There is, indeed, one marked difference between the physical and the intellectual instrumentality. The development of the latter runs far beyond any immediately visible use. The artistic interest in perfecting the method by itself is strong—as the utensils of civilization may themselves become works of finest art. But from the practical standpoint this difference shows that the advantage as an instrumentality is on the side of the intellectual tool. Just because it is not formed with a special application in mind, because it is a highly generalized tool, it is the more flexible in adaptation to unforeseen uses. It can be employed in dealing with problems that were not anticipated. The mind is prepared in advance for all sorts of intellectual emergencies, and when the new problem occurs it does not have to wait till it can get a special instrument ready.

More definitely, abstraction is indispensable if one experience is to be applicable in other experiences. Every concrete experience in its totality is unique; it is itself, non-reduplicable. Taken in its full concreteness, it yields no instruction, it throws no light. What is called abstraction means that some phase of it is selected for the sake of the aid it gives in grasping something else. Taken by itself, it is a mangled fragment, a poor substitute for the living whole from which it is extracted. But viewed teleologically or practically, it represents the only way in which one experience can be made of any value for another—the only way in which something enlightening can be secured. What is called false or vicious abstractionism signifies that the *function* of the detached fragment is forgotten and neglected, so that it is esteemed barely in itself as something of a higher order than the muddy and irregular concrete from which it was wrenched. Looked at functionally, not structurally and statically, abstraction means that something has been released from one experience for transfer to another. Abstraction is liberation. The more theoretical, the more abstract, an abstraction, or the farther away it is from anything experienced in its concreteness, the better fitted it is to deal with any one of the indefinite variety of things that may later present themselves. Ancient mathematics and physics were much nearer the gross concrete experience than are modern. For that very reason they were more impotent in affording any insight into and control over such concretes as present themselves in new and unexpected forms.

Abstraction and generalization have always been recognized as close kin. It may be said that they are the negative and positive sides of the same function. Abstraction sets free some factor so that it may be used. Generalization is the use. It carries over and extends. It is always in some sense a leap in the dark. It is an adventure. There can be no assurance in advance that what is extracted from one concrete can be fruitfully extended to another individual case. Since these other cases are individual and concrete they *must* be dissimilar. The trait of flying is detached from the concrete bird. This abstraction is then carried over to the bat, and it is expected in view of the application of the quality to have some of the other traits of the bird. This trivial instance indicates the essence of generalization, and also illustrates the riskiness of the proceeding. It transfers, extends, applies, a result of some former experience to the reception and interpretation of a new one. Deductive processes define, delimit, purify and set in order the conceptions through which this enriching and directive operation is carried on, but they cannot, however perfect, guarantee the outcome.

The pragmatic value of organization is so conspicuously enforced in contemporary life that it hardly seems necessary to dwell upon the instrumental significance of classification and systematization. When the existence of qualitative and fixed species was denied to be the supreme object of knowledge, classification was often regarded, especially by the empirical school, as merely a linguistic device. It was convenient for memory and communication to have words that sum up a number of particulars. Classes were supposed to exist only in speech. Later, ideas were recognized as a kind of *tertium quid* between things and words. Classes were allowed to exist in the mind as purely mental things. The critical disposition of empiricism is well exemplified here. To assign any objectivity to classes was to encourage a belief in eternal species and occult essences and to strengthen the arms of a decadent and obnoxious science—a point of view well illustrated in Locke. General *ideas* are useful in economizing effort, enabling us to condense particular experiences into simpler and more easily carried bunches and making it easier to identify new observations.

So far nominalism and conceptualism—the theory that kinds exist only in words or in ideas—was on the right track. It emphasized the teleological character of systems and classifications, that they exist for the sake of economy and efficiency in reaching ends. But this truth was perverted into a false notion, because the active and doing side of experience was denied or ignored. Concrete things have *ways* of acting, as many ways of acting as they have points of interaction with other things. One thing is callous, unresponsive, inert in the presence of some other things; it is alert, eager, and on the aggressive with respect to other things; in a third case, it is receptive, docile. Now different ways of behaving, in spite of their endless diversity, may be classed together in view of common relationship to an end. No sensible person tries to do everything. He has certain main interests and leading aims by which he makes his behavior coherent and effective. To have an aim is to limit, select, concentrate, group. Thus a basis is furnished for selecting and organizing things according as their ways of acting are related to carrying forward pursuit. Cherry trees will be differently grouped by woodworkers, orchardists, artists, scientists and merry-makers. To the execution of different purposes different ways of acting and reacting on the part of trees are important. Each classification may be equally sound when the difference of ends is borne in mind.

Nevertheless there is a genuine objective standard for the goodness of special classifications. One will further the cabinetmaker in reaching his end while another will hamper him. One classification will assist the botanist in carrying on fruitfully his work of inquiry, and another will retard and confuse him. The teleological theory of classification does not therefore commit us to the notion that classes are purely verbal or purely mental. Organization is no more merely nominal or mental in any art, including the art of inquiry, than it is in a department store or railway system. The necessity of execution supplies objective criteria. Things have to be sorted out and arranged so that their grouping will promote successful action for ends. Convenience, economy and efficiency are the bases of classification, but these things are not restricted to verbal communication with others nor to inner consciousness; they concern objective action. They must take effect in the world.

At the same time, a classification is not a bare transcript or duplicate of some finished and done-for arrangement pre-existing in nature. It is rather a repertory of weapons for attack upon the future and the unknown. For success, the details of past knowledge must be reduced from bare facts to meanings, the fewer, simpler and more extensive the better. They must be broad enough in scope to prepare inquiry to cope with any phenomenon however unexpected. They must be arranged so as not to overlap, for otherwise when they are applied to new events they interfere and produce confusion. In order that there may be ease and economy of movement in dealing with the enormous diversity of occurrences that present themselves, we must be able to move promptly and definitely from one tool of attack to another. In other words, our various classes and kinds must be themselves classified in graded series from the larger to the more specific. There must not only be streets, but the streets must be laid out with reference to facilitating passage from any one to any other. Classification transforms a wilderness of by-ways in experience into a well-ordered system of roads, promoting transportation and communication in inquiry. As soon as men begin to take foresight for the future and to prepare themselves in advance to meet it effectively and prosperously, the deductive operations and their results gain in importance. In every practical enterprise there are goods to be produced, and whatever eliminates wasted material and promotes economy and efficiency of production is precious.

Little time is left to speak of the account of the nature of truth given by the experimental and functional type of logic. This is less to be regretted because this account is completely a corollary from the nature of thinking and ideas. If the view held as to the latter is understood, the conception of truth follows as a matter of course. If it be not understood, any attempt to present the theory of truth is bound to be confusing, and the theory itself to seem arbitrary and absurd. *If* ideas, meanings, conceptions, notions, theories, systems are instrumental to an active reorganization of the given environment, to a removal of some specific trouble and perplexity, then the test of their validity and value lies in accomplishing this work. If they succeed in their office, they are reliable, sound, valid, good, true. If they fail to clear up confusion, to eliminate defects, if they increase confusion, uncertainty and evil when they are acted upon, then are they false. Confirmation, corroboration, verification lie in works, consequences. Handsome is that handsome does. By their fruits shall ye *know* them. That which guides us truly is true—demonstrated capacity for such guidance is precisely what is meant by truth. The adverb "truly" is more fundamental than either the adjective, true, or the noun, truth. An adverb expresses a way, a mode of acting. Now an idea or conception is a claim or injunction or plan to *act* in a certain way as the way to arrive at the clearing up of a specific situation. When the claim or pretension or plan is acted upon *it guides us truly or falsely*; it leads us to our end or away from it. Its active, dynamic function is the all-important thing about it, and in the quality of activity induced by it lies all its truth and falsity. The hypothesis that works is the *true* one; and *truth* is an abstract noun applied to the collection of cases, actual, foreseen and desired, that receive confirmation in their works and consequences.

So wholly does the worth of this conception of truth depend upon the correctness of the prior account of thinking that it is more profitable to consider why the conception gives offence than to expound it on its own account. Part of the reason why it has been found so obnoxious is doubtless its novelty and defects in its statement. Too often, for example, when truth has been thought of as satisfaction, it has been thought of as merely emotional satisfaction, a private comfort, a meeting of purely personal need. But the satisfaction in question means a satisfaction of the needs and conditions of the problem out of which the idea, the purpose and method of action, arises. It includes public and objective conditions. It is not to be manipulated by whim or personal idiosyncrasy. Again when truth is defined as utility, it is often thought to mean utility for some purely personal end, some profit upon which a particular individual has set his heart. So repulsive is a conception of truth which makes it a mere tool of private ambition and aggrandizement, that the wonder is that critics have attributed such a notion to sane men. As matter of fact, truth as utility means service in making just that contribution to reorganization in experience that the idea or theory claims to be able to make. The usefulness of a road is not measured by the degree in which it lends itself to the purposes of a highwayman. It is measured by whether it actually functions *as* a road, as a means of easy and effective public transportation and communication. And so with the serviceableness of an idea or hypothesis as a measure of its truth.

Turning from such rather superficial misunderstandings, we find, I think, the chief obstacle to the reception of this notion of truth in an inheritance from the classic tradition that has become so deeply engrained in men's minds. In just the degree in which existence is divided into two realms, a higher one of perfect being and a lower one of seeming, phenomenal, deficient reality, truth and falsity are thought of as fixed, ready-made static properties of things themselves. Supreme Reality is true Being, inferior and imperfect Reality is false Being. It makes claims to Reality which it cannot substantiate. It is deceitful, fraudulent, inherently unworthy of trust and belief. Beliefs are false not because they mislead us; they are not mistaken ways of thinking. They are false because they admit and adhere to false existences or subsistences. Other notions are true because they do have to do with true Being—with full and ultimate Reality. Such a notion lies at the back of the head of every one who has, in however an indirect way, been a recipient of the ancient and medieval tradition. This view is radically challenged by the pragmatic conception of truth, and the impossibility of reconciliation or compromise is, I think, the cause of the shock occasioned by the newer theory.

This contrast, however, constitutes the importance of the new theory as well as the unconscious obstruction to its acceptance. The older conception worked out practically to identify truth with authoritative dogma. A society that chiefly esteems order, that finds growth painful and change disturbing, inevitably seeks for a fixed body of superior truths upon which it may depend. It looks backward, to something already in existence, for the source and sanction of truth. It falls back upon what is antecedent, prior, original, *a priori*, for assurance. The thought of looking ahead, toward the eventual, toward consequences, creates uneasiness and fear. It disturbs the sense of rest that is attached to the ideas of fixed Truth already in existence. It puts a heavy burden of responsibility upon us for search, unremitting observation, scrupulous development of hypotheses and thoroughgoing testing. In physical matters men have slowly grown accustomed in all specific beliefs to identifying the true with the verified. But they still hesitate to recognize the implication of this identification and to derive the definition of truth from it. For while it is nominally agreed upon as a commonplace that definitions ought to spring from concrete and specific cases rather than be invented in the empty air and imposed upon particulars, there is a strange unwillingness to act upon the maxim in defining truth. To generalize the recognition that the true means the verified and means nothing else places upon men the responsibility for surrendering political and moral dogmas, and subjecting to the test of consequences their most cherished prejudices. Such a change involves a great change in the seat of authority and the methods of decision in society. Some of them, as first fruits of the newer logic, will be considered in the following lectures.

The impact of the alteration in methods of scientific thinking upon moral ideas is, in general, obvious. Goods, ends are multiplied. Rules are softened into principles, and principles are modified into methods of understanding. Ethical theory began among the Greeks as an attempt to find a regulation for the conduct of life which should have a rational basis and purpose instead of being derived from custom. But reason as a substitute for custom was under the obligation of supplying objects and laws as fixed as those of custom had been. Ethical theory ever since has been singularly hypnotized by the notion that its business is to discover some final end or good or some ultimate and supreme law. This is the common element among the diversity of theories. Some have held that the end is loyalty or obedience to a higher power or authority; and they have variously found this higher principle in Divine Will, the will of the secular ruler, the maintenance of institutions in which the purpose of superiors is embodied, and the rational consciousness of duty. But they have differed from one another because there was one point in which they were agreed: a single and final source of law. Others have asserted that it is impossible to locate morality in conformity to law-giving power, and that it must be sought in ends that are goods. And some have sought the good in self-realization, some in holiness, some in happiness, some in the greatest possible aggregate of pleasures. And yet these schools have agreed in the assumption that there is a single, fixed and final good. They have been able to dispute with one another only because of their common premise.

The question arises whether the way out of the confusion and conflict is not to go to the root of the matter by questioning this common element. Is not the belief in the single, final and ultimate (whether conceived as good or as authoritative law) an intellectual product of that feudal organization which is disappearing historically and of that belief in a bounded, ordered cosmos, wherein rest is higher than motion, which has disappeared from natural science? It has been repeatedly suggested that the present limit of intellectual reconstruction lies in the fact that it has not as yet been seriously applied in the moral and social disciplines. Would not this further application demand precisely that we advance to a belief in a plurality of changing, moving, individualized goods and ends, and to a belief that principles, criteria, laws are intellectual instruments for analyzing individual or unique situations?

The blunt assertion that every moral situation is a unique situation having its own irreplaceable good may seem not merely blunt but preposterous. For the established tradition teaches that it is precisely the irregularity of special cases which makes necessary the guidance of conduct by universals, and that the essence of the virtuous disposition is willingness to subordinate every particular case to adjudication by a fixed principle. It would then follow that submission of a generic end and law to determination by the concrete situation entails complete confusion and unrestrained licentiousness. Let us, however, follow the pragmatic rule, and in order to discover the meaning of the idea ask for its consequences. Then it surprisingly turns out that the primary significance of the unique and morally ultimate character of the concrete situation is to transfer the weight and burden of morality to intelligence. It does not destroy responsibility; it only locates it. A moral situation is one in which judgment and choice are required antecedently to overt action. The practical meaning of the situation—that is to say the action needed to satisfy it—is not self-evident. It has to be searched for. There are conflicting desires and alternative apparent goods. What is needed is to find the right course of action, the right good. Hence, inquiry is exacted: observation of the detailed makeup of the situation; analysis into its diverse factors; clarification of what is obscure; discounting of the more insistent and vivid traits; tracing the consequences of the various modes of action that suggest themselves; regarding the decision reached as hypothetical and tentative until the anticipated or supposed consequences which led to its adoption have been squared with actual consequences. This inquiry is intelligence. Our moral failures go back to some weakness of disposition, some absence of sympathy, some one-sided bias that makes us perform the judgment of the concrete case carelessly or perversely. Wide sympathy, keen sensitiveness, persistence in the face of the disagreeable, balance of interests enabling us to undertake the work of analysis and decision intelligently are the distinctively moral traits—the virtues or moral excellencies.

It is worth noting once more that the underlying issue is, after all, only the same as that which has been already threshed out in physical inquiry. There too it long seemed as if rational assurance and demonstration could be attained only if we began with universal conceptions and subsumed particular cases under them. The men who initiated the methods of inquiry that are now everywhere adopted were denounced in their day (and sincerely) as subverters of truth and foes of science. If they have won in the end, it is because, as has already been pointed out, the method of universals confirmed prejudices and sanctioned ideas that had gained currency irrespective of evidence for them; while placing the initial and final weight upon the individual case, stimulated painstaking inquiry into facts and examination of principles. In the end, loss of eternal truths was more than compensated for in the accession of quotidian facts. The loss of the system of superior and fixed definitions and kinds was more than made up for by the growing system of hypotheses and laws used in classifying facts. After all, then, we are only pleading for the adoption in moral reflection of the logic that has been proved to make for security, stringency and fertility in passing judgments upon physical phenomena. And the reason is the same. The old method in spite of its nominal and esthetic worship of reason discouraged reason, because it hindered the operation of scrupulous and unremitting inquiry.

More definitely, the transfer of the burden of the moral life from following rules or pursuing fixed ends over to the detection of the ills that need remedy in a special case and the formation of plans and methods for dealing with them, eliminates the causes which have kept moral theory controversial, and which have also kept it remote from helpful contact with the exigencies of practice. The theory of fixed ends inevitably leads thought into the bog of disputes that cannot be settled. If there is one *summum bonum*, one supreme end, what is it? To consider this problem is to place ourselves in the midst of controversies that are as acute now as they were two thousand years ago. Suppose we take a seemingly more empirical view, and say that while there is not a single end, there also are not as many as there are specific situations that require amelioration; but there are a number of such natural goods as health, wealth, honor or good name, friendship, esthetic appreciation, learning and such moral goods as justice, temperance, benevolence, etc. What or who is to decide the right of way when these ends conflict with one another, as they are sure to do? Shall we resort to the method that once brought such disrepute upon the whole business of ethics: Casuistry? Or shall we have recourse to what Bentham well called the *ipse dixit* method: the arbitrary preference of this or that person for this or that end? Or shall we be forced to arrange them all in an order of degrees from the highest good down to the least precious? Again we find ourselves in the middle of unreconciled disputes with no indication of the way out.

Meantime, the special moral perplexities where the aid of intelligence is required go unenlightened. We cannot seek or attain health, wealth, learning, justice or kindness in general. Action is always specific, concrete, individualized, unique. And consequently judgments as to acts to be performed must be similarly specific. To say that a man seeks health or justice is only to say that he seeks to live healthily or justly. These things, like truth, are adverbial. They are modifiers of action in special cases. How to live healthily or justly is a matter which differs with every person. It varies with his past experience, his opportunities, his temperamental and acquired weaknesses and abilities. Not man in general but a particular man suffering from some particular disability aims to live healthily, and consequently health cannot mean for him exactly what it means for any other mortal. Healthy living is not something to be attained by itself apart from other ways of living. A man needs to be healthy *in* his life, not apart from it, and what does life mean except the aggregate of his pursuits and activities? A man who aims at health as a distinct end becomes a valetudinarian, or a fanatic, or a mechanical performer of exercises, or an athlete so one-sided that his pursuit of bodily development injures his heart. When the endeavor to realize a so-called end does not temper and color all other activities, life is portioned out into strips and fractions. Certain acts and times are devoted to getting health, others to cultivating religion, others to seeking learning, to being a good citizen, a devotee of fine art and so on. This is the only logical alternative to subordinating all aims to the accomplishment of one alone—fanaticism. This is out of fashion at present, but who can say how much of distraction and dissipation in life, and how much of its hard and narrow rigidity is the outcome of men's failure to realize that each situation has its own unique end and that the whole personality should be concerned with it? Surely, once more, what a man needs is to live healthily, and this result so affects all the activities of his life that it cannot be set up as a separate and independent good.

Nevertheless the general notions of health, disease, justice, artistic culture are of great importance: Not, however, because this or that case may be brought exhaustively under a single head and its specific traits shut out, but because generalized science provides a man as physician and artist and citizen, with questions to ask, investigations to make, and enables him to understand the meaning of what he sees. Just in the degree in which a physician is an artist in his work he uses his science, no matter how extensive and accurate, to furnish him with tools of inquiry into the individual case, and with methods of forecasting a method of dealing with it. Just in the degree in which, no matter how great his learning, he subordinates the individual case to some classification of diseases and some generic rule of treatment, he sinks to the level of the routine mechanic. His intelligence and his action become rigid, dogmatic, instead of free and flexible.

Moral goods and ends exist only when something has to be done. The fact that something has to be done proves that there are deficiencies, evils in the existent situation. This ill is just the specific ill that it is. It never is an exact duplicate of anything else. Consequently the good of the situation has to be discovered, projected and attained on the basis of the exact defect and trouble to be rectified. It cannot intelligently be injected into the situation from without. Yet it is the part of wisdom to compare different cases, to gather together the ills from which humanity suffers, and to generalize the corresponding goods into classes. Health, wealth, industry, temperance, amiability, courtesy, learning, esthetic capacity, initiative, courage, patience, enterprise, thoroughness and a multitude of other generalized ends are acknowledged as goods. But the *value* of this systematization is intellectual or analytic. Classifications *suggest* possible traits to be on the lookout for in studying a particular case; they suggest methods of action to be tried in removing the inferred causes of ill. They are tools of insight; their value is in promoting an individualized response in the individual situation.

Morals is not a catalogue of acts nor a set of rules to be applied like drugstore prescriptions or cook-book recipes. The need in morals is for specific methods of inquiry and of contrivance: Methods of inquiry to locate difficulties and evils; methods of contrivance to form plans to be used as working hypotheses in dealing with them. And the pragmatic import of the logic of individualized situations, each having its own irreplaceable good and principle, is to transfer the attention of theory from preoccupation with general conceptions to the problem of developing effective methods of inquiry.

Two ethical consequences of great moment should be remarked. The belief in fixed values has bred a division of ends into intrinsic and instrumental, of those that are really worth while in themselves and those that are of importance only as means to intrinsic goods. Indeed, it is often thought to be the very beginning of wisdom, of moral discrimination, to make this distinction. Dialectically, the distinction is interesting and seems harmless. But carried into practice it has an import that is tragic. Historically, it has been the source and justification of a hard and fast difference between ideal goods on one side and material goods on the other. At present those who would be liberal conceive intrinsic goods as esthetic in nature rather than as exclusively religious or as intellectually contemplative. But the effect is the same. So-called intrinsic goods, whether religious or esthetic, are divorced from those interests of daily life which because of their constancy and urgency form the preoccupation of the great mass. Aristotle used this distinction to declare that slaves and the working class though they are necessary *for* the state—the commonweal—are not constituents *of* it. That which is regarded as *merely* instrumental must approach drudgery; it cannot command either intellectual, artistic or moral attention and respect. Anything becomes *unworthy* whenever it is thought of as intrinsically lacking worth. So men of "ideal" interests have chosen for the most part the way of neglect and escape. The urgency and pressure of "lower" ends have been covered up by polite conventions. Or, they have been relegated to a baser class of mortals in order that the few might be free to attend to the goods that are really or intrinsically worth while. This withdrawal, in the name of higher ends, has left, for mankind at large and especially for energetic "practical" people the lower activities in complete command.

No one can possibly estimate how much of the obnoxious materialism and brutality of our economic life is due to the fact that economic ends have been regarded as *merely* instrumental. When they are recognized to be as intrinsic and final in their place as any others, then it will be seen that they are capable of idealization, and that if life is to be worth while, they must acquire ideal and intrinsic value. Esthetic, religious and other "ideal" ends are now thin and meagre or else idle and luxurious because of the separation from "instrumental" or economic ends. Only in connection with the latter can they be woven into the texture of daily life and made substantial and pervasive. The vanity and irresponsibility of values that are merely final and not also in turn means to the enrichment of other occupations of life ought to be obvious. But now the doctrine of "higher" ends gives aid, comfort and support to every socially isolated and socially irresponsible scholar, specialist, esthete and religionist. It protects the vanity and irresponsibility of his calling from observation by others and by himself. The moral deficiency of the calling is transformed into a cause of admiration and gratulation.

The other generic change lies in doing away once for all with the traditional distinction between moral goods, like the virtues, and natural goods like health, economic security, art, science and the like. The point of view under discussion is not the only one which has deplored this rigid distinction and endeavored to abolish it. Some schools have even gone so far as to regard moral excellencies, qualities of character as of value only because they promote natural goods. But the experimental logic when carried into morals makes every quality that is judged to be good according as it contributes to amelioration of existing ills. And in so doing, it enforces the moral meaning of natural science. When all is said and done in criticism of present social deficiencies, one may well wonder whether the root difficulty does not lie in the separation of natural and moral science. When physics, chemistry, biology, medicine, contribute to the detection of concrete human woes and to the development of plans for remedying them and relieving the human estate, they become moral; they become part of the apparatus of moral inquiry or science. The latter then loses its peculiar flavor of the didactic and pedantic; its ultra-moralistic and hortatory tone. It loses its thinness and shrillness as well as its vagueness. It gains agencies that are efficacious. But the gain is not confined to the side of moral science. Natural science loses its divorce from humanity; it becomes itself humanistic in quality. It is something to be pursued not in a technical and specialized way for what is called truth for its own sake, but with the sense of its social bearing, its intellectual indispensableness. It is technical only in the sense that it provides the technique of social and moral engineering.

When the consciousness of science is fully impregnated with the consciousness of human value, the greatest dualism which now weighs humanity down, the split between the material, the mechanical, the scientific and the moral and ideal will be destroyed. Human forces that now waver because of this division will be unified and reinforced. As long as ends are not thought of as individualized according to specific needs and opportunities, the mind will be content with abstractions, and the adequate stimulus to the moral or social use of natural science and historical data will be lacking. But when attention is concentrated upon the diversified concretes, recourse to all intellectual materials needed to clear up the special cases will be imperative. At the same time that morals are made to focus in intelligence, things intellectual are moralized. The vexatious and wasteful conflict between naturalism and humanism is terminated.

These general considerations may be amplified. First: Inquiry, discovery take the same place in morals that they have come to occupy in sciences of nature. Validation, demonstration become experimental, a matter of consequences. Reason, always an honorific term in ethics, becomes actualized in the methods by which the needs and conditions, the obstacles and resources, of situations are scrutinized in detail, and intelligent plans of improvement are worked out. Remote and abstract generalities promote jumping at conclusions, "anticipations of nature." Bad consequences are then deplored as due to natural perversity and untoward fate. But shifting the issue to analysis of a specific situation makes inquiry obligatory and alert observation of consequences imperative. No past decision nor old principle can ever be wholly relied upon to justify a course of action. No amount of pains taken in forming a purpose in a definite case is final; the consequences of its adoption must be carefully noted, and a purpose held only as a working hypothesis until results confirm its rightness. Mistakes are no longer either mere unavoidable accidents to be mourned or moral sins to be expiated and forgiven. They are lessons in wrong methods of using intelligence and instructions as to a better course in the future. They are indications of the need of revision, development, readjustment. Ends grow, standards of judgment are improved. Man is under just as much obligation to develop his most advanced standards and ideals as to use conscientiously those which he already possesses. Moral life is protected from falling into formalism and rigid repetition. It is rendered flexible, vital, growing.

In the second place, every case where moral action is required becomes of equal moral importance and urgency with every other. If the need and deficiencies of a specific situation indicate improvement of health as the end and good, then for that situation health is the ultimate and supreme good. It is no means to something else. It is a final and intrinsic value. The same thing is true of improvement of economic status, of making a living, of attending to business and family demands—all of the things which under the sanction of fixed ends have been rendered of secondary and merely instrumental value, and so relatively base and unimportant. Anything that in a given situation is an end and good at all is of equal worth, rank and dignity with every other good of any other situation, and deserves the same intelligent attention.

We note thirdly the effect in destroying the roots of Phariseeism. We are so accustomed to thinking of this as deliberate hypocrisy that we overlook its intellectual premises. The conception which looks for the end of action within the circumstances of the actual situation will not have the same measure of judgment for all cases. When one factor of the situation is a person of trained mind and large resources, more will be expected than with a person of backward mind and uncultured experience. The absurdity of applying the same standard of moral judgment to savage peoples that is used with civilized will be apparent. No individual or group will be judged by whether they come up to or fall short of some fixed result, but by the direction in which they are moving. The bad man is the man who no matter how good he *has* been is beginning to deteriorate, to grow less good. The good man is the man who no matter how morally unworthy he *has* been is moving to become better. Such a conception makes one severe in judging himself and humane in judging others. It excludes that arrogance which always accompanies judgment based on degree of approximation to fixed ends.

In the fourth place, the process of growth, of improvement and progress, rather than the static outcome and result, becomes the significant thing. Not health as an end fixed once and for all, but the needed improvement in health—a continual process—is the end and good. The end is no longer a terminus or limit to be reached. It is the active process of transforming the existent situation. Not perfection as a final goal, but the ever-enduring process of perfecting, maturing, refining is the aim in living. Honesty, industry, temperance, justice, like health, wealth and learning, are not goods to be possessed as they would be if they expressed fixed ends to be attained. They are directions of change in the quality of experience. Growth itself is the only moral "end."

Although the bearing of this idea upon the problem of evil and the controversy between optimism and pessimism is too vast to be here discussed, it may be worth while to touch upon it superficially. The problem of evil ceases to be a theological and metaphysical one, and is perceived to be the practical problem of reducing, alleviating, as far as may be removing, the evils of life. Philosophy is no longer under obligation to find ingenious methods for proving that evils are only apparent, not real, or to elaborate schemes for explaining them away or, worse yet, for justifying them. It assumes another obligation:—That of contributing in however humble a way to methods that will assist us in discovering the causes of humanity's ills. Pessimism is a paralyzing doctrine. In declaring that the world is evil wholesale, it makes futile all efforts to discover the remediable causes of specific evils and thereby destroys at the root every attempt to make the world better and happier. Wholesale optimism, which has been the consequence of the attempt to explain evil away, is, however, equally an incubus.

After all, the optimism that says that the world is already the best possible of all worlds might be regarded as the most cynical of pessimisms. If this is the best possible, what would a world which was fundamentally bad be like? Meliorism is the belief that the specific conditions which exist at one moment, be they comparatively bad or comparatively good, in any event may be bettered. It encourages intelligence to study the positive means of good and the obstructions to their realization, and to put forth endeavor for the improvement of conditions. It arouses confidence and a reasonable hopefulness as optimism does not. For the latter in declaring that good is already realized in ultimate reality tends to make us gloss over the evils that concretely exist. It becomes too readily the creed of those who live at ease, in comfort, of those who have been successful in obtaining this world's rewards. Too readily optimism makes the men who hold it callous and blind to the sufferings of the less fortunate, or ready to find the cause of troubles of others in their personal viciousness. It thus cooperates with pessimism, in spite of the extreme nominal differences between the two, in benumbing sympathetic insight and intelligent effort in reform. It beckons men away from the world of relativity and change into the calm of the absolute and eternal.

The import of many of these changes in moral attitude focusses in the idea of happiness. Happiness has often been made the object of the moralists' contempt. Yet the most ascetic moralist has usually restored the idea of happiness under some other name, such as bliss. Goodness without happiness, valor and virtue without satisfaction, ends without conscious enjoyment— these things are as intolerable practically as they are self-contradictory in conception. Happiness is not, however, a bare possession; it is not a fixed attainment. Such a happiness is either the unworthy selfishness which moralists have so bitterly condemned, or it is, even if labelled bliss, an insipid tedium, a millennium of ease in relief from all struggle and labor. It could satisfy only the most delicate of molly-coddles. Happiness is found only in success; but success means succeeding, getting forward, moving in advance. It is an active process, not a passive outcome. Accordingly it includes the overcoming of obstacles, the elimination of sources of defect and ill. Esthetic sensitiveness and enjoyment are a large constituent in any worthy happiness. But the esthetic appreciation which is totally separated from renewal of spirit, from re-creation of mind and purification of emotion is a weak and sickly thing, destined to speedy death from starvation. That the renewal and re-creation come unconsciously not by set intention but makes them the more genuine.

Upon the whole, utilitarianism has marked the best in the

transition from the classic theory of ends and goods to that which is now possible. It had definite merits. It insisted upon getting away from vague generalities, and down to the specific and concrete. It subordinated law to human achievement instead of subordinating humanity to external law. It taught that institutions are made for man and not man for institutions; it actively promoted all issues of reform. It made moral good natural, humane, in touch with the natural goods of life. It opposed unearthly and other-worldly morality. Above all, it acclimatized in human imagination the idea of social welfare as a supreme test. But it was still profoundly affected in fundamental points by old ways of thinking. It never questioned the idea of a fixed, final and supreme end. It only questioned the current notions as to the nature of this end; and then inserted pleasure and the greatest possible aggregate of pleasures in the position of the fixed end.

Such a point of view treats concrete activities and specific interests not as worth while in themselves, or as constituents of happiness, but as mere external means to getting pleasures. The upholders of the old tradition could therefore easily accuse utilitarianism of making not only virtue but art, poetry, religion and the state into mere servile means of attaining sensuous enjoyments. Since pleasure was an outcome, a result valuable on its own account independently of the active processes that achieve it, happiness was a thing to be possessed and held onto. The acquisitive instincts of man were exaggerated at the expense of the creative. Production was of importance not because of the intrinsic worth of invention and reshaping the world, but because its external results feed pleasure. Like every theory that sets up fixed and final aims, in making the end passive and possessive, it made all active operations *mere* tools. Labor was an unavoidable evil to be minimized. Security in possession was the chief thing practically. Material comfort and ease were magnified in contrast with the pains and risk of experimental creation.

These deficiencies, under certain conceivable conditions, might have remained merely theoretical. But the disposition of the times and the interests of those who propagated the utilitarian ideas, endowed them with power for social harm. In spite of the power of the new ideas in attacking old social abuses, there were elements in the teaching which operated or protected to sanction new social abuses. The reforming zeal was shown in criticism of

the evils inherited from the class system of feudalism, evils economic, legal and political. But the new economic order of capitalism that was superseding feudalism brought its own social evils
with it, and some of these ills utilitarianism tended to cover up or
defend. The emphasis upon acquisition and possession of enjoyments took on an untoward color in connection with the contemporary enormous desire for wealth and the enjoyments it makes
possible.

If utilitarianism did not actively promote the new economic
materialism, it had no means of combating it. Its general spirit of
subordinating productive activity to the bare product was indirectly favorable to the cause of an unadorned commercialism. In
spite of its interest in a thoroughly social aim, utilitarianism fostered a new class interest, that of the capitalistic property-owning
interests, provided only property was obtained through free competition and not by governmental favor. The stress that Bentham
put on security tended to consecrate the legal institution of private property provided only certain legal abuses in connection
with its acquisition and transfer were abolished. *Beati possi-
dentes*—provided possessions had been obtained in accord with
the rules of the competitive game—without, that is, extraneous
favors from government. Thus utilitarianism gave intellectual
confirmation to all those tendencies which make "business" not a
means of social service and an opportunity for personal growth in
creative power but a way of accumulating the means of private
enjoyments. Utilitarian ethics thus afford a remarkable example
of the need of philosophic reconstruction which these lectures
have been presenting. Up to a certain point, it reflected the meaning of modern thought and aspirations. But it was still tied down
by fundamental ideas of that very order which it thought it had
completely left behind: The idea of a fixed and single end lying
beyond the diversity of human needs and acts rendered utilitarianism incapable of being an adequate representative of the modern spirit. It has to be reconstructed through emancipation from
its inherited elements.

If a few words are added upon the topic of education, it is
only for the sake of suggesting that the educative process is all
one with the moral process, since the latter is a continuous passage of experience from worse to better. Education has been traditionally thought of as preparation: as learning, acquiring certain

things because they will later be useful. The end is remote, and education is getting ready, is a preliminary to something more important to happen later on. Childhood is only a preparation for adult life, and adult life for another life. Always the future, not the present, has been the significant thing in education: Acquisition of knowledge and skill for future use and enjoyment; formation of habits required later in life in business, good citizenship and pursuit of science. Education is thought of also as something needed by some human beings merely because of their dependence upon others. We are born ignorant, unversed, unskilled, immature, and consequently in a state of social dependence. Instruction, training, moral discipline are processes by which the mature, the adult, gradually raise the helpless to the point where they can look out for themselves. The business of childhood is to grow into the independence of adulthood by means of the guidance of those who have already attained it. Thus the process of education as the main business of life ends when the young have arrived at emancipation from social dependence.

These two ideas, generally assumed but rarely explicitly reasoned out, contravene the conception that growing, or the continuous reconstruction of experience, is the only end. If at whatever period we choose to take a person, he is still in process of growth, then education is not, save as a by-product, a preparation for something coming later. Getting from the present the degree and kind of growth there is in it is education. This is a constant function, independent of age. The best thing that can be said about any special process of education, like that of the formal school period, is that it renders its subject capable of further education: more sensitive to conditions of growth and more able to take advantage of them. Acquisition of skill, possession of knowledge, attainment of culture are not ends: they are marks of growth and means to its continuing.

The contrast usually assumed between the period of education as one of social dependence and of maturity as one of social independence does harm. We repeat over and over that man is a social animal, and then confine the significance of this statement to the sphere in which sociality usually seems least evident, politics. The heart of the sociality of man is in education. The idea of education as preparation and of adulthood as a fixed limit of growth are two sides of the same obnoxious untruth. If the moral business of the adult as well as the young is a growing and developing experience, then the instruction that comes from social dependencies and interdependencies are as important for the adult as for the child. Moral independence for the adult means arrest of growth, isolation means induration. We exaggerate the intellectual dependence of childhood so that children are too much kept in leading strings, and then we exaggerate the independence of adult life from intimacy of contacts and communication with others. When the identity of the moral process with the processes of specific growth is realized, the more conscious and formal education of childhood will be seen to be the most economical and efficient means of social advance and reorganization, and it will also be evident that the test of all the institutions of adult life is their effect in furthering continued education. Government, business, art, religion, all social institutions have a meaning, a purpose. That purpose is to set free and to develop the capacities of human individuals without respect to race, sex, class or economic status. And this is all one with saying that the test of their value is the extent to which they educate every individual into the full stature of his possibility. Democracy has many meanings, but if it has a moral meaning, it is found in resolving that the supreme test of all political institutions and industrial arrangements shall be the contribution they make to the all-around growth of every member of society.

8. RECONSTRUCTION AS AFFECTING SOCIAL PHILOSOPHY

How can philosophic change seriously affect social philosophy? As far as fundamentals are concerned, every view and combination appears to have been formulated already. Society is composed of individuals: this obvious and basic fact no philosophy, whatever its pretensions to novelty, can question or alter. Hence these three alternatives: Society must exist for the sake of individuals; or individuals must have their ends and ways of living set for them by society; or else society and individuals are correlative, organic, to one another, society requiring the service and subordination of individuals and at the same time existing to serve them. Beyond these three views, none seems to be logically conceivable. Moreover, while each of the three types includes many subspecies and variations within itself, yet the changes seem to have been so thoroughly rung that at most only minor variations are now possible.

Especially would it seem true that the "organic" conception meets all the objections to the extreme individualistic and extreme socialistic theories, avoiding the errors alike of Plato and Bentham. Just because society is composed of individuals, it would seem that individuals and the associative relations that hold them together must be of coequal importance. Without strong and competent individuals, the bonds and ties that form society have nothing to lay hold on. Apart from associations with one another, individuals are isolated from one another and fade and wither; or are opposed to one another and their conflicts injure individual development. Law, state, church, family, friendship, industrial association, these and other institutions and arrangements are necessary in order that individuals may grow and find their specific capacities and functions. Without their aid and support human life is, as Hobbes said, brutish, solitary, nasty.

We plunge into the heart of the matter, by asserting that these various theories suffer from a common defect. They are all committed to the logic of general notions under which specific

situations are to be brought. What we want light upon is this or
that group of individuals, this or that concrete human being, this
or that special institution or social arrangement. For such a logic
of inquiry, the traditionally accepted logic substitutes discussion
of the meaning of concepts and their dialectical relationship to
one another. The discussion goes on in terms of *the* state, *the*
individual; the nature of institutions as such, society in general.

We need guidance in dealing with particular perplexities in
domestic life, and are met by dissertations on the Family or by
assertions of the sacredness of individual Personality. We want to
know about the worth of the institution of private property as it
operates under given conditions of definite time and place. We
meet with the reply of Proudhon that property generally is theft,
or with that of Hegel that the realization of will is the end of all
institutions, and that private ownership as the expression of mas-
tery of personality over physical nature is a necessary element in
such realization. Both answers may have a certain suggestiveness
in connection with specific situations. But the conceptions are
not proffered for what they may be worth in connection with special historic phenomena. They are general answers supposed to
have a universal meaning that covers and dominates all particulars. Hence they do not assist inquiry. They close it. They are not
instrumentalities to be employed and tested in clarifying concrete
social difficulties. They are ready-made principles to be imposed
upon particulars in order to determine their nature. They tell us
about *the* state when we want to know about *some* state. But the
implication is that what is said about *the* state applies to any state
that we happen to wish to know about.

In transferring the issue from concrete situations to definitions and conceptual deductions, the effect, especially of the organic theory, is to supply the apparatus for intellectual justification of the established order. Those most interested in practical
social progress and the emancipation of groups from oppression
have turned a cold shoulder to the organic theory. The effect, if
not the intention, of German idealism as applied in social philosophy was to provide a bulwark for the maintenance of the political
status quo against the tide of radical ideas coming from revolutionary France. Although Hegel asserted in explicit form that the
end of states and institutions is to further the realization of the
freedom of all, his effect was to consecrate the Prussian State and

to enshrine bureaucratic absolutism. Was this apologetic tendency accidental, or did it spring from something in the logic of the notions that were employed?

Surely the latter. If we talk about *the* state and *the* individual, rather than about this or that political organization and this or that group of needy and suffering human beings, the tendency is to throw the glamor and prestige, the meaning and value attached to the general notion, over the concrete situation and thereby to cover up the defects of the latter and disguise the need of serious reforms. The meanings which are found in the general notions are injected into the particulars that come under them. Quite properly so if we once grant the logic of rigid universals under which the concrete cases have to be subsumed in order to be understood and explained.

Again, the tendency of the organic point of view is to minimize the significance of specific conflicts. Since the individual and the state or social institution are but two sides of the same reality, since they are already reconciled in principle and conception, the conflict in any particular case can be but apparent. Since in theory the individual and the state are reciprocally necessary and helpful to one another, why pay much attention to the fact that in *this* state a whole group of individuals are suffering from oppressive conditions? In "reality" their interests cannot be in conflict with those of the state to which they belong; the opposition is only superficial and casual. Capital and labor cannot "really" conflict because each is an organic necessity to the other, and both to the organized community as a whole. There cannot "really" be any sex-problem because men and women are indispensable both to one another and to the state. In his day, Aristotle could easily employ the logic of general concepts superior to individuals to show that the institution of slavery was in the interests both of the state and of the slave class. Even if the intention is not to justify the existing order the effect is to divert attention from special situations. Rationalistic logic formerly made men careless in observation of the concrete in physical philosophy. It now operates to depress and retard observation in specific social phenomena. The social philosopher, dwelling in the region of his concepts, "solves" problems by showing the relationship of ideas, instead of helping men solve problems in the concrete by supplying them hypotheses to be used and tested in projects of reform.

Meanwhile, of course, the concrete troubles and evils remain. They are not magically waived out of existence because in theory society is organic. The region of concrete difficulties, where the assistance of intelligent method for tentative plans for experimentation is urgently needed, is precisely where intelligence fails to operate. In this region of the specific and concrete, men are thrown back upon the crudest empiricism, upon short-sighted opportunism and the matching of brute forces. In theory, the particulars are all neatly disposed of; they come under their appropriate heading and category; they are labelled and go into an orderly pigeon-hole in a systematic filing cabinet, labelled political science or sociology. But in empirical fact they remain as perplexing, confused and unorganized as they were before. So they are dealt with not by even an endeavor at scientific method but by blind rule of thumb, citation of precedents, considerations of immediate advantage, smoothing things over, use of coercive force and the clash of personal ambitions. The world still survives; it has therefore got on somehow:—so much cannot be denied. The method of trial and error and competition of selfishnesses has somehow wrought out many improvements. But social theory nevertheless exists as an idle luxury rather than as a guiding method of inquiry and planning. In the question of methods concerned with reconstruction of special situations rather than in any refinements in the general concepts of institution, individuality, state, freedom, law, order, progress, etc., lies the true impact of philosophical reconstruction.

Consider the conception of the individual self. The individualistic school of England and France in the eighteenth and nineteenth centuries was empirical in intent. It based its individualism, philosophically speaking, upon the belief that individuals are alone real, that classes and organizations are secondary and derived. They are artificial, while individuals are natural. In what way then can individualism be said to come under the animadversions that have been passed? To say the defect was that this school overlooked those connections with other persons which are a part of the constitution of every individual is true as far as it goes; but unfortunately it rarely goes beyond the point of just that wholesale justification of institutions which has been criticized.

The real difficulty is that the individual is regarded as something *given*, something already there. Consequently, he can only be something to be catered to, something whose pleasures are to be magnified and possessions multiplied. When the individual is taken as something given already, anything that can be done to him or for him can only be by way of external impressions and belongings: sensations of pleasure and pain, comforts, securities. Now it is true that social arrangements, laws, institutions are made for man, rather than that man is made for them; that they are means and agencies of human welfare and progress. But they are not means for obtaining something for individuals, not even happiness. They are means of *creating* individuals. Only in the physical sense of physical bodies that to the senses are separate is individuality an original datum. Individuality in a social and moral sense is something to be wrought out. It means initiative, inventiveness, varied resourcefulness, assumption of responsibility in choice of belief and conduct. These are not gifts, but achievements. As achievements, they are not absolute but relative to the use that is to be made of them. And this use varies with the environment.

The import of this conception comes out in considering the fortunes of the idea of self-interest. All members of the empirical school emphasized this idea. It was the sole motive of mankind. Virtue was to be attained by making benevolent action profitable to the individual; social arrangements were to be reformed so that egoism and altruistic consideration of others would be identified. Moralists of the opposite school were not backward in pointing out the evils of any theory that reduced both morals and political science to means of calculating self-interest. Consequently they threw the whole idea of interest overboard as obnoxious to morals. The effect of this reaction was to strengthen the cause of authority and political obscurantism. When the play of interest is eliminated, what remains? What concrete moving forces can be found? Those who identified the self with something ready-made and its interest with acquisition of pleasure and profit took the most effective means possible to reinstate the logic of abstract conceptions of law, justice, sovereignty, freedom, etc.—all of those vague general ideas that for all their seeming rigidity can be manipulated by any clever politician to cover up his designs and to make the worse seem the better cause. Interests are specific and dynamic; they are the natural terms of any concrete social thinking. But they are damned beyond recovery when they are identified with the things of a petty selfishness. They can be employed as vital terms only when the self is seen to be in process, and interest to be a name for whatever is concerned in furthering its movement.

The same logic applies to the old dispute of whether reform should start with the individual or with institutions. When the self is regarded as something complete within itself, then it is readily argued that only internal moralistic changes are of importance in general reform. Institutional changes are said to be merely external. They may add conveniences and comforts to life, but they cannot effect moral improvements. The result is to throw the burden for social improvement upon free-will in its most impossible form. Moreover, social and economic passivity are encouraged. Individuals are led to concentrate in moral introspection upon their own vices and virtues, and to neglect the character of the environment. Morals withdraw from active concern with detailed economic and political conditions. Let us perfect ourselves within, and in due season changes in society will come of themselves is the teaching. And while saints are engaged in introspection, burly sinners run the world. But when self-hood is perceived to be an active process it is also seen that social modifications are the only means of the creation of changed personalities. Institutions are viewed in their educative effect:—with reference to the types of individuals they foster. The interest in individual moral improvement and the social interest in objective reform of economic and political conditions are identified. And inquiry into the meaning of social arrangements gets definite point and direction. We are led to ask what the specific stimulating, fostering and nurturing power of each specific social arrangement may be. The old-time separation between politics and morals is abolished at its root.

Consequently we cannot be satisfied with the general statement that society and the state is organic to the individual. The question is one of specific causations. Just what response does *this* social arrangement, political or economic, evoke, and what effect does it have upon the disposition of those who engage in it? Does it release capacity? If so, how widely? Among a few, with a corresponding depression in others, or in an extensive and equitable way? Is the capacity which is set free also directed in some coherent way, so that it becomes a power, or its manifestation spasmodic and capricious? Since responses are of an indefinite diversity of kind, these inquiries have to be detailed and specific. Are men's senses rendered more delicately sensitive and appreciative, or are they blunted and dulled by this and that form of social organization? Are their minds trained so that the hands are more deft and cunning? Is curiosity awakened or blunted? What is its quality: is it merely esthetic, dwelling on the forms and surfaces of things or is it also an intellectual searching into their meaning? Such questions as these (as well as the more obvious ones about the qualities conventionally labelled moral), become the starting-points of inquiries about every institution of the community when it is recognized that individuality is not originally given but is created under the influences of associated life. Like utilitarianism, the theory subjects every form of organization to continual scrutiny and criticism. But instead of leading us to ask what it does in the way of causing pains and pleasures to individuals already in existence, it inquires what is done to release specific capacities and coordinate them into working powers. What sort of individuals are created?

The waste of mental energy due to conducting discussion of social affairs in terms of conceptual generalities is astonishing. How far would the biologist and the physician progress if when the subject of respiration is under consideration, discussion confined itself to bandying back and forth the concepts of organ and organism:—If for example one school thought respiration could be known and understood by insisting upon the fact that it occurs in an individual body and therefore is an "individual" phenomenon, while an opposite school insisted that it is simply one function in organic interaction with others and can be known or understood therefore only by reference to other functions taken in an equally general or wholesale way? Each proposition is equally true and equally futile. What is needed is specific inquiries into a multitude of specific structures and interactions. Not only does the solemn reiteration of categories of individual and organic or social whole not further these definite and detailed inquiries, but it checks them. It detains thought within pompous and sonorous generalities wherein controversy is as inevitable as it is incapable of solution. It is true enough that if cells were not in vital interaction with one another, they could neither conflict nor cooperate. But the fact of the existence of an "organic" social group, instead of answering any questions merely marks the fact that questions exist: Just what conflicts and what cooperations occur, and what are their specific causes and consequences? But because of the persistence within social philosophy of the order of ideas that has been expelled from natural philosophy, even sociologists take conflict or cooperation as general categories upon which to base their science, and condescend to empirical facts only for illustrations. As a rule, their chief "problem" is a purely dialectical one, covered up by a thick quilt of empirical anthropological and historical citations: How do individuals unite to form society? How are individuals socially controlled? And the problem is justly called dialectical because it springs from antecedent conceptions of "individual" and "social."

Just as "individual" is not one thing, but is a blanket term for the immense variety of specific reactions, habits, dispositions and powers of human nature that are evoked, and confirmed under the influences of associated life, so with the term "social." Society is one word, but infinitely many things. It covers all the ways in which by associating together men share their experiences, and build up common interests and aims; street gangs, schools for burglary, clans, social cliques, trades unions, joint-stock corporations, villages and international alliances. The new method takes effect in substituting inquiry into these specific, changing and relative facts (relative to problems and purposes, not metaphysically relative) for solemn manipulation of general notions.

Strangely enough, the current conception of the state is a case in point. For one direct influence of the classic order of fixed species arranged in hierarchical order is the attempt of German political philosophy in the nineteenth century to enumerate a definite number of institutions, each having its own essential and immutable meaning; to arrange them in an order of "evolution" which corresponds with the dignity and rank of the respective meanings. The National State was placed at the top as the consummation and culmination, and also the basis of all other institutions.

Hegel is a striking example of this industry, but he is far from the only one. Many who have bitterly quarrelled with him, have only differed as to the details of the "evolution" or as to the particular meaning to be attributed as essential *Begriff* to some one of the enumerated institutions. The quarrel has been bitter only because the underlying premises were the same. Particularly have many schools of thought, varying even more widely in respect to method and conclusion, agreed upon the final consummating position of the state. They may not go as far as Hegel in making the sole meaning of history to be the evolution of National Territorial States, each of which embodies more than the prior form of the essential meaning or conception of *the* State and consequently displaces it, until we arrive at that triumph of historical evolution, the Prussian State. But they do not question the unique and supreme position of the State in the social hierarchy. Indeed that conception has hardened into unquestionable dogma under the title of sovereignty.

There can be no doubt of the tremendously important role played by the modern territorial national state. The formation of these states has been the centre of modern political history. France, Great Britain, Spain were the first peoples to attain nationalistic organization, but in the nineteenth century their example was followed by Japan, Germany and Italy, to say nothing of a large number of smaller states, Greece, Servia, Bulgaria, etc. As everybody knows, one of the most important phases of the recent world war was the struggle to complete the nationalistic movement, resulting in the erection of Bohemia, Poland, etc., into independent states, and the accession of Armenia, Palestine, etc., to the rank of candidates.

The struggle for the supremacy of the State over other forms of organization was directed against the power of minor districts, provinces, principalities, against the dispersion of power among feudal lords as well as, in some countries, against the pretensions of an ecclesiastic potentate. The "State" represents the conspicuous culmination of the great movement of social integration and consolidation taking place in the last few centuries, tremendously accelerated by the concentrating and combining forces of steam and electricity. Naturally, inevitably, the students of political science have been preoccupied with this great historic phenomenon, and their intellectual activities have been directed to its systematic formulation. Because the contemporary progressive movement was to establish the unified state against the inertia of minor social units and against the ambitions of rivals for power, political theory developed the dogma of the sovereignty of the national state, internally and externally.

As the work of integration and consolidation reaches its climax, the question arises, however, whether the national state, once it is firmly established and no longer struggling against strong foes, is not just an instrumentality for promoting and protecting other and more voluntary forms of association, rather than a supreme end in itself. Two actual phenomena may be pointed to in support of an affirmative answer. Along with the development of the larger, more inclusive and more unified organization of the state has gone the emancipation of individuals from restrictions and servitudes previously imposed by custom and class status. But the individuals freed from external and coercive bonds have not remained isolated. Social molecules have at once recombined in new associations and organizations. Compulsory associations have been replaced by voluntary ones; rigid organizations by those more amenable to human choice and purposes—more directly changeable at will. What upon one side looks like a movement toward individualism, turns out to be really a movement toward multiplying all kinds and varieties of associations: Political parties, industrial corporations, scientific and artistic organizations, trade unions, churches, schools, clubs and societies without number, for the cultivation of every conceivable interest that men have in common. As they develop in number and importance, the state tends to become more and more a regulator and adjuster among them; defining the limits of their actions, preventing and settling conflicts.

Its "supremacy" approximates that of the conductor of an orchestra, who makes no music himself but who harmonizes the activities of those who in producing it are doing the thing intrinsically worth while. The state remains highly important—but its importance consists more and more in its power to foster and coordinate the activities of voluntary groupings. Only nominally is it in any modern community the end for the sake of which all the other societies and organizations exist. Groupings for promoting the diversity of goods that men share have become the real social units. They occupy the place which traditional theory has claimed either for mere isolated individuals or for the supreme and single political organization. Pluralism is well ordained in present political practice and demands a modification of hierarchical and monistic theory. Every combination of human forces that adds its own contribution of value to life has for that reason its own unique and ultimate worth. It cannot be degraded into a means to glorify the State. One reason for the increased demoralization of war is that it forces the State into an abnormally supreme position.

The other concrete fact is the opposition between the claim of independent sovereignty in behalf of the territorial national state and the growth of international and what have well been called trans-national interests. The weal and woe of any modern state is bound up with that of others. Weakness, disorder, false principles on the part of any state are not confined within its boundaries. They spread and infect other states. The same is true of economic, artistic and scientific advances. Moreover the voluntary associations just spoken of do not coincide with political boundaries. Associations of mathematicians, chemists, astronomers; business corporations, labor organizations, churches are trans-national because the interests they represent are world-wide. In such ways as these, internationalism is not an aspiration but a fact, not a sentimental ideal but a force. Yet these interests are cut across and thrown out of gear by the traditional doctrine of exclusive national sovereignty. It is the vogue of this doctrine, or dogma, that presents the strongest barrier to the effective formation of an international mind which alone agrees with the moving forces of present-day labor, commerce, science, art and religion.

Society, as was said, is many associations not a single organization. Society means association; coming together in joint intercourse and action for the better realization of any form of experience which is augmented and confirmed by being shared. Hence there are as many associations as there are goods which are enhanced by being mutually communicated and participated in. And these are literally indefinite in number. Indeed, capacity to endure publicity and communication is the test by which it is decided whether a pretended good is genuine or spurious. Moralists have always insisted upon the fact that good is universal, objective, not just private, particular. But too often, like Plato, they have been content with a metaphysical universality or, like Kant, with a logical universality. Communication, sharing, joint participation are the only actual ways of universalizing the moral law and end. We insisted at the last hour upon the unique character of every intrinsic good. But the counterpart of this proposition is that the situation in which a good is consciously realized is not one of transient sensations or private appetites but one of sharing and communication—public, social. Even the hermit communes with gods or spirits; even misery loves company; and the most extreme selfishness includes a band of followers or some partner to share in the attained good. Universalization means socialization, the extension of the area and range of those who share in a good.

The increasing acknowledgment that goods exist and endure only through being communicated and that association is the means of conjoint sharing lies back of the modern sense of humanity and democracy. It is the saving salt in altruism and philanthropy, which without this factor degenerate into moral condescension and moral interference, taking the form of trying to regulate the affairs of others under the guise of doing them good or of conferring upon them some right as if it were a gift of charity. It follows that organization is never an end in itself. It is a means of promoting *association*, of multiplying effective points of contact between persons, directing their intercourse into the modes of greatest fruitfulness.

The tendency to treat organization as an end in itself is responsible for all the exaggerated theories in which individuals are subordinated to some institution to which is given the noble name of society. Society is the *process* of associating in such ways that experiences, ideas, emotions, values are transmitted and made common. To this active process, both the individual and the institutionally organized may truly be said to be subordinate. The individual is subordinate because except in and through communication of experience from and to others, he remains dumb, merely sentient, a brute animal. Only in association with fellows does he become a conscious centre of experience. Organization, which is what traditional theory has generally meant by the term Society or State, is also subordinate because it becomes static, rigid, institutionalized whenever it is not employed to facilitate and enrich the contacts of human beings with one another.

The long-time controversy between rights and duties, law and freedom is another version of the strife between the Individual and Society as fixed concepts. Freedom for an individual means growth, ready change when modification is required.

It signifies an active process, that of release of capacity from whatever hems it in. But since society can develop only as new resources are put at its disposal, it is absurd to suppose that freedom has positive significance for individuality but negative meaning for social interests. Society is strong, forceful, stable against accident only when all its members can function to the limit of their capacity. Such functioning cannot be achieved without allowing a leeway of experimentation beyond the limits of established and sanctioned custom. A certain amount of overt confusion and irregularity is likely to accompany the granting of the margin of liberty without which capacity cannot find itself. But socially as well as scientifically the great thing is not to avoid mistakes but to have them take place under conditions such that they can be utilized to increase intelligence in the future.

If British liberal social philosophy tended, true to the spirit of its atomistic empiricism, to make freedom and the exercise of rights ends in themselves, the remedy is not to be found in recourse to a philosophy of fixed obligations and authoritative law such as characterized German political thinking. The latter, as events have demonstrated, is dangerous because of its implicit menace to the free self-determination of other social groups. But it is also weak internally when put to the final test. In its hostility to the free experimentation and power of choice of the individual in determining social affairs, it limits the capacity of many or most individuals to share effectively in social operations, and thereby deprives society of the full contribution of all its members. The best guarantee of collective efficiency and power is liberation and use of the diversity of individual capacities in initiative, planning, foresight, vigor and endurance. Personality must be educated, and personality cannot be educated by confining its operations to technical and specialized things, or to the less important relationships of life. Full education comes only when there is a responsible share on the part of each person, in proportion to capacity, in shaping the aims and policies of the social groups to which he belongs. This fact fixes the significance of democracy. It cannot be conceived as a sectarian or racial thing nor as a consecration of some form of government which has already attained constitutional sanction. It is but a name for the fact that human nature is developed only when its elements take part in directing things which are common, things for the sake of which men and women form groups—families, industrial companies, governments, churches, scientific associations and so on. The principle holds as much of one form of association, say in industry and commerce, as it does in government. The identification of democracy with political democracy which is responsible for most of its failures is, however, based upon the traditional ideas which make the individual and the state ready-made entities in themselves.

As the new ideas find adequate expression in social life, they will be absorbed into a moral background, and the ideas and beliefs themselves will be deepened and be unconsciously transmitted and sustained. They will color the imagination and temper the desires and affections. They will not form a set of ideas to be expounded, reasoned out and argumentatively supported, but will be a spontaneous way of envisaging life. Then they will take on religious value. The religious spirit will be revivified because it will be in harmony with men's unquestioned scientific beliefs and their ordinary day-by-day social activities. It will not be obliged to lead a timid, half-concealed and half-apologetic life because tied to scientific ideas and social creeds that are continuously eaten into and broken down. But especially will the ideas and beliefs themselves be deepened and intensified because spontaneously fed by emotion and translated into imaginative vision and fine art, while they are now maintained by more or less conscious effort, by deliberate reflection, by taking thought. They are technical and abstract just because they are not as yet carried as matter of course by imagination and feelings.

We began by pointing out that European philosophy arose when intellectual methods and scientific results moved away from social traditions which had consolidated and embodied the fruits of spontaneous desire and fancy. It was pointed out that philosophy had ever since had the problem of adjusting the dry, thin and meagre scientific standpoint with the obstinately persisting body of warm and abounding imaginative beliefs. Conceptions of possibility, progress, free movement and infinitely diversified opportunity have been suggested by modern science. But until they have displaced from *imagination* the heritage of the immutable and the once-for-all ordered and systematized, the ideas of mechanism and matter will lie like a dead weight upon the emotions, paralyzing religion and distorting art. When the liberation of capacity no longer seems a menace to organization and established institutions, something that cannot be avoided practically and yet something that is a threat to conservation of the most precious values of the past, when the liberating of human capacity operates as a socially creative force, art will not be a luxury, a stranger to the daily occupations of making a living. Making a living economically speaking, will be at one with making a life that is worth living. And when the emotional force, the mystic force one might say, of communication, of the miracle of shared life and shared experience is spontaneously felt, the hardness and crudeness of contemporary life will be bathed in the light that never was on land or sea.

Poetry, art, religion are precious things. They cannot be maintained by lingering in the past and futilely wishing to restore what the movement of events in science, industry and politics has destroyed. They are an out-flowering of thought and desires that unconsciously converge into a disposition of imagination as a result of thousands and thousands of daily episodes and contact. They cannot be willed into existence or coerced into being. The wind of the spirit bloweth where it listeth and the kingdom of God in such things does not come with observation. But while it is impossible to retain and recover by deliberate volition old sources of religion and art that have been discredited, it is possible to expedite the development of the vital sources of a religion and art that are yet to be. Not indeed by action directly aimed at their production, but by substituting faith in the active tendencies of the day for dread and dislike of them, and by the courage of intelligence to follow whither social and scientific changes direct us. We are weak today in ideal matters because intelligence is divorced from aspiration. The bare force of circumstance compels us onwards in the daily detail of our beliefs and acts, but our deeper thoughts and desires turn backwards. When philosophy shall have cooperated with the course of events and made clear and coherent the meaning of the daily detail, science and emotion will interpenetrate, practice and imagination will embrace. Poetry and religious feeling will be the unforced flowers of life. To further this articulation and revelation of the meanings of the current course of events is the task and problem of philosophy in days of transition.

Lectures

THREE CONTEMPORARY PHILOSOPHERS

A Series of Six Lectures Delivered in Peking

William James (1842–1910)

FIRST LECTURE

The first of the three contemporary philosophers of whom I will speak is William James, a compatriot of mine, who was, as you all know, the pioneer of Pragmatism. The term "contemporary" means "living at the same time," and since James died in 1910, it may not be, in a strictly literal sense, correct to call him "a contemporary philosopher." However, since the effects of his thought and the development of his ideas are only now having their full impact, we can view him as a contemporary, in spite of the fact that his works were published in the twenty-year period between 1890 and 1910.

The most important among James's works is his first book, *Principles of Psychology*, which was published in 1891, and which runs to more than a thousand pages. There are two reasons why this book is so very important: first, this volume includes the bases of the philosophy which James was to develop later, since his philosophy was founded in psychology; and second, James's philosophy is scientific, not speculative, and the scientific element of this philosophy is not physics or biology, but rather psychology, the science which takes human nature as its subject matter. This fact is of the utmost importance. James's major interest was in learning about man and human nature. The psychology which he formulated is scientific; it begins with human nature and human experience. In this formulation, James eliminates with one stroke all the traditional "problems" which have interfered with man's effort to understand himself, and demon-

[First published in Chinese as "Five Major Lecture Series of John Dewey in Peking" (*Peking Morning Post*, 1920). Translated into English by Robert W. Clopton and Tsuin-chen Ou; typescript at Hamilton Library, University of Hawaii, Honolulu. The Russell lectures appeared in *Journal of the Bertrand Russell Archives* 11 (1973): 3–10, 15–20, with the title "Russell's Philosophy and Politics."]

strates that they are not, in fact, problems at all. This is the distinctive aspect of a kind of philosophy which is built upon a foundation of psychological theory which is thoroughly scientific in its nature.

James's career was primarily that of a scientist, but he was also a highly gifted student of painting, and had considerable training in painting in oils. His brother, Henry James, has, during the past thirty years, enjoyed the reputation of a major novelist, a reputation which has persisted since his death only a few years ago. James was born into a family which had a tradition of artistic achievement on a high level; he, himself, possessed both talent and training in the arts; hence his psychology is much more than a mere "anatomy of human nature." One of his unique characteristics is that, possessed of the spirit of the artist, he sees the function of the mind in terms of drama, and records his insights as though he were writing for the theatre. He rebukes traditional philosophers for having adopted the view that philosophy was argument, and succeeds in his own case in presenting philosophy as vision. When philosophy is looked upon as argument, numerous philosophical "problems" occur simply to keep the argument under way; but when we recognize philosophy as vision, it can possess both the values of art and the excitement of literature.

Since James deals with psychology as an artist-author, his psychology and his philosophy are vital; instead of being dead and dreary, they pulse with life. They are organic. James's primary dissatisfaction with traditional psychology lies in what he sees as a tendency to replace the state of mind of the participant with that of the observer, the psychologist. In his view, traditional psychologists substituted their own outlook as spectators, who, detached and uninvolved, could have no real knowledge of the process which they observed, for that of the participant, the person within whose organism these processes were taking place.

In a short article, "On a Certain Blindness in Human Beings," which he wrote late in his life, James maintains that it is impossible actually to penetrate another's mind, and that the observer can approximate the truth only by imaginatively putting himself in the place of the other; that otherwise one will understand no part of the truth. In this article James emphasizes the necessity of one undergoing the experience himself as a condition to understanding it. This was the reason that James had such great admiration and respect for the poet Walt Whitman, who had been able to discard the conventions of literature and build his poems around the common and elementary actions of every-day human beings. Our education, especially with regard to literature, has led us far afield from life as it is lived. Our literature is replete with abstract words and with figures of speech which are empty of meaning because they are so far removed from our experience and our actual responses to life. James contends that this has led us to overlook the common and elementary aspects of experience, and that it has thus resulted in "A Certain Blindness in Human Beings."

James emphasizes the common, elementary, and fundamental aspects of human behavior, while at the same time he focusses attention on distinctive characteristics of individuals. Individuality is emphasized throughout his philosophy. He rejects philosophical monism which holds that all truth is ultimately one. In his article "On a Certain Blindness in Human Beings," one paragraph reads:

> Hands off: neither the whole of the truth nor the whole of the good is revealed to any single observer, although each observer gains a partial superiority of insight from the peculiar position in which he stands. Even prisons and sick-rooms have their special revelations. It is enough to ask of each of us that he should be faithful to his own opportunities and make the most of his own blessings, without presuming to regulate the rest of the vast field.[1]

It is of the utmost importance that we keep in mind the fact that James does put so much emphasis on the common elements of human nature on the one hand, while, at the same time, he stresses the importance of individuality and rejects absolutism, because in his later period, his philosophy is based almost entirely on these two points. He coined two terms which have since come into common usage: *Radical Empiricism*, which denotes his emphasis on the fact that experiences of human beings are elementary and they cannot be subsumed under general and abstract terminologies; and *Pluralism*, which is the term he employs to denote the fact that human experiences are individualistic in character, and that they are not to be regarded as instances or

1. William James, *Talks to Teachers on Psychology: and to Students on Some of Life's Ideals.* New York: Henry Holt and Company, 1919. Page 264.

evidences of absolute and eternal principles. Late in his life James advocated a "pluralistic universe," as an alternative to monism, of which he writes with distaste as a philosophic justification for "a block universe."

After this very general introduction I shall now outline the fundamental concepts of James's psychology, and these can then serve as the basis of our next lecture in which we will discuss his philosophy. In his psychology James applies the evolutionary hypothesis to human emotions, feelings, perceptions, and so on. Darwin had published his *Origin of the Species* in 1859, just sixty years ago, the book in which he propounded the theory of evolution which precipitated a major revolution in Western thought. James, who was Darwin's contemporary, was the first man to apply the evolutionary hypothesis to psychology.

In his earlier books, James notes that very few people recognize the fact that man's intelligence derives from his practical experience of undergoing and suffering. The application of the evolutionary hypothesis to psychology seems initially to reduce all functions of the mind to the category of response. An example of simple response is closing the eyes when they are stimulated by a bright light. There must be a response within the organism whenever a stimulus occurs from without, no matter whether such stimulus is simple or complex. Another example: when someone stands in our way while we are walking, we automatically step aside and yield to him. The nature of all such responses is action, not knowledge; we respond to the external stimulus by acting.

James contends that knowledge plays only a minor role in the huge range of response to stimuli. Responses in lower animals can be easily observed, since their reactions to stimuli are of immediate practical use. The same thing is true to a lesser extent in the behavior of higher animals. When we come to the human level, the problem of knowledge is, then, not one of theory, but one of practice, which means "how to do."

James sees knowledge as a phase of mental functioning. On the one hand, there is the stimulus from the environment, while on the other there is the response by the organism. Knowledge is nothing more nor less than the mediating process which occurs between the stimulus and the organism's response to it; its function is to determine the response appropriate to the stimulus.

Knowledge is the selection of a response that can adequately cope with the stimulus. It is not independent of, but is intimately involved with both stimulus and response. Man has garnered so much knowledge from the innumerable stimulus-response activities in his experience that he has fallen into the trap of assuming that knowledge has value in and of itself. But as a matter of actual fact, we can gain knowledge only by controlling the stimulus on the one hand, and by selecting our response on the other. The importance of knowledge conceived thus as a mediating process lies in the fact that it "slows down" both the stimulus and the response, so that the organism can take time to plan. In the absence of the mediating process of knowledge, we would frequently make mistaken responses to stimuli; with the benefit of knowledge we can act more confidently. For example, a moth is attracted toward a flame, flies into it, and is burned to death; but a child knows that the flame is fire, and that if he touches it, his hand will be burned; and an adult knows that when he gets too close to the fire, his life will be endangered, so he stays away from it. A man with common sense knows that fire can be extinguished with water; and when this knowledge is refined, he knows how to take precautions by having water available where fire may occur. That's what we have fire hydrants for. The scientist studies the phenomenon of burning, and describes the chemical changes which take place when matter burns. Thus our knowledge becomes extended and enlarged, but in fact it remains the process which mediates between the stimulus and the response.

The manner in which James deals with the function of mind is evidence that his psychology is based in the evolutionary hypothesis. He notes that the functioning mind is characterized by two phenomena: first, the organism acts with reference to a future purpose; and second, it selects the methods and instruments by means of which he can hope to achieve this purpose. In the absence of these, James tells us, there is no mental function. Now these two aspects of mental function have traditionally been called "will"; and so most people call James a "psychologist of will" as opposed to a "psychologist of knowledge." But James differs from the traditional psychologists of will in that he makes use of the theory of evolution to integrate knowledge with will. When knowledge, emotion, and will are integrated, and when the organism is directed toward a future purpose, it must have been able to formulate such purpose in advance, or else it could not experience satisfaction. All surprise, happiness, pleasure, and anger arise out of the organism's success or failure in achieving this purpose through its overt activities.

We have been discussing the introductory aspects of James's psychology in rather general terms; now let us look at a concept that is uniquely Jamesian, that is, his "stream of consciousness." Before James, people looked upon consciousness as though it were some sort of mixture of individual and discrete experiences; or, at most, they regarded it as something which is "constructed" in much the same way that a house is constructed. James, however, instead of comparing consciousness to a structure of component experiences, or as an amalgam containing many individual and discrete experiences, sees consciousness as a stream which flows constantly forward. This concept is the most important single one in James's philosophy. Many of the other concepts which characterize his philosophy, his emphasis on individuality, on change, on evolution, on adventure, and on freedom of action stem from his likening consciousness to a stream of water. James notes that when people before him had treated consciousness as an accumulation of isolated and inanimate building blocks, they obviated the possibility of viewing it as a stream of water, ceaselessly flowing. These people might possibly have visualized a glass of water, or a bucketful of water, or even a large jar of water, but never a stream of unending motion. But in James's view, all impressions of the mind are incorporated into this stream of consciousness; each impression is connected with all the others, and none exists in isolation from the others. Rather they all exist as part and parcel of one inclusive stream of consciousness.

James insists that one of the greatest mistakes of the past was psychologists' practice of conceiving of mental functions in terms of physical objects; and, being misled by the fact that these physical objects were comparatively permanent and changeless, inferring that human consciousness was also permanent and changeless. They did not appreciate the fact that the stream of consciousness moves ever forward, is always in the process of changing. This desk may be the same today as it was when we saw it yesterday; but *we* have changed, so the desk cannot exist in our consciousness in exactly the same way in which it formerly

did. The consciousness of one person is never exactly identical
with that of another; and we cannot interpret either of them in
terms appropriate to physical objects. More than this, the physical
object can be separated into its parts; this cup, for example, has
a mouth, a handle, and a bottom; but our consciousness is of a
cup as a whole, and not as the sum of its parts. James employs
the example of lemonade. We know that lemonade is composed of
lemon juice, water, and sugar; but when we drink it, our consciousness is of lemonade, and not of its ingredients. A physical
object may remain the same, but our consciousness cannot. The
former can be separated into its parts; the latter cannot.

You may think that we have been speaking in trivialities, but
if you grasp the full import of this concept of "stream of consciousness," and look at the effects it is having in philosophy, you
will realize that it isn't trivial at all. There are at least two important respects in which this concept is changing philosophy. The
first is that it affords a novel way of dealing with the ancient problem of the one and the many, of unity and individuality, or of monism and pluralism. James shows us that people were laboring under a misapprehension when they feared that the concept of pluralism would lead to chaos, and when they therefore insisted
upon forcing all experience into one mold of system and unity.
But as a matter of fact, if we change our viewpoint and see human
experience as a stream of consciousness which runs ceaselessly,
there is need for both monism and pluralism in interpreting the
phenomenon. In any case, human experience has ceased to be a
"thing," a dead concept; it is a living entity, and may be examined
in a monistic frame of reference, or in a pluralistic one, as the
nature of the occasion demands.

The figure of running water is both simple and complex. To
take a single example, we may say that the water of a huge river
rushing toward the ocean also contains mud; but as it flows forward, the mud settles and the water becomes clear. When we
look at consciousness as a stream, we can see that it can be unified, but that it can also be pluralistic, according to the demands
of the occasion. For example, when we are laying out a complex
plan of action, we must take everything into consideration—and
this is a case of our consciousness being unified. But when we
are confronted with a difficulty, we must perforce analyze the dif-

ficulty point by point, and it behooves us to find out as many
methods and opinions as we can, and this instance of employing
consciousness as an instrument by means of which we deal with
our environment is pluralistic. Therefore, the question of whether
the universe is monistic or pluralistic is no longer really a problem. The only real problem is the determination of the circumstances which call for application of the principle of unity, and of
other circumstances which require application of the principle of
pluralism.

We have been dealing with the first effect of James's new
concept, what it has done to the problem of knowledge. Formerly
when people regarded knowledge as a copy or a picture, their
questions had to do with the correspondence of our impression
with the real object—the most persistent problem in the history
of epistemology. How, for example, does our impression of a cup
correspond to the real cup? James notes, however, that when we
look upon knowledge as a stream of consciousness, we need no
longer consider whether our impression of the object actually corresponds with the real object; we ask only whether the impression we have can lead us to other experience. If it can, it is
real.

Let us take one more example, this College of Law in which
we are meeting. Some people have a clear and detailed perception
of the building; some have only vague impressions; others may
not have even such vague perceptions, and may have noticed no
more than the entrance hall; blind persons may perceive only the
bell which signals the beginning of classes; and still other people
may not have any impressions even of the entrance to the building or the sound of the bell—their only perception may be of the
term, "College of Law." According to James, all such perceptions
are correct, because each offers us some experience with the College of Law. Were we to insist that our perception of the College
of Law had to correspond in every respect with the real building,
we should have an extremely difficult problem on our hands. But
the only purpose of perception is to produce anticipated consequences. This concept is of central importance in the epistemology of Pragmatism, as well as in its theory of truth, since Pragmatism regards both knowledge and truth as bridges which
enable us to approach our purposes.

In our next lecture we will discuss the application of James's psychology to philosophy.

SECOND LECTURE: WILLIAM JAMES (CONTINUED)

The problem which has been the source of the most disputation in the history of philosophy is the origin of knowledge. Some people hold that knowledge derives from experience; but many others contend that even though experience is important, the universal principles upon which truth is based cannot be derived from it, but must, of necessity, come from some other source.

Everybody agrees that certain knowledge comes from experience—such facts that sugar is sweet, that snow is white, or that fire can burn. But they will not agree that abstract knowledge, such as the axioms and laws of arithmetic, algebra, and geometry, or such things as the law of conservation of matter in physics and chemistry, or the concept of cause-and-effect in philosophy, or the moral laws of ethics, can be derived from experience. Their point is that such laws and principles are necessarily true, totally apart from experience. They point out that while the truth of such propositions as "$2 + 2 = 4$" and "the sum of the three angles in a triangle is equal to two right angles" can be verified through experience, they are not derived from it.

People who argue in this vein arrive at the conclusion that our knowledge of such universal laws and principles is innate. The empiricists were hard put to refute this conclusion until Herbert Spencer made use of the theory of evolution to show that universal truth can also be derived from experience. Spencer admitted that no one individual could arrive at absolute truth through the experience of one lifetime. But he held that as man evolved from lower animals, and made the transition through savagery to civilization, the totality of human experience through the ages has resulted in certain truths being so universal and so commonplace that man has come to regard them as absolute, and his knowledge of them as innate. Even with the change of environment certain laws and principles continue to have validity, and they are appropriately labelled "universal." Their truth, after repeated revision and restatement, becomes all but absolute, and we can utilize them to explain the regular natural phenomena within the framework of time and space. They are still, however, the products of man's total experience through the ages.

I mention Spencer at this juncture because somewhere in his *Principles of Psychology* James refers to this contribution. While James takes Spencer's argument as his point of departure, he develops the idea further. Spencer's concept is important in itself; but, far more important is the application which James makes in his philosophy. James differs from his predecessors in that on the one hand he goes far beyond the concept of empiricism which takes knowledge to be completely passive and external, while on the other hand, although he recognizes that truth comes from within, he repudiates the concept of idealism which asserts the existence of a higher, particular, and transcendental sphere from which man derives his laws and principles.

James holds that general principles originate neither in the particular nor from without, but incidentally. Initially man may have engaged in discussion and told jokes; ultimately the material of these discussions and jokes may have evolved into general principles. It is true that the mind is relatively passive in its reception of certain kinds of knowledge, such as the fact that a fish taken out of the water will die. No one, however, has ever directly experienced the principles of arithmetic, physics, or chemistry. No one would contend that our knowledge of the atom is derived from external experience; it is, rather, the result of incidental reasoning which occurs internally.

As an example, the earlier empiricists asserted that our knowledge of number is derived from experience, just because we have become accustomed to counting "one person, two persons," or "two cups, three cups." James observes that on the other hand, number is arbitrary. Let us take this teapot as an example: we can say that this is one teapot. But when we remove the cover from the teapot, we have to use the number two—one for the pot, two for the cover. And if we detach the handle from the teapot, we have three things—one the pot itself, the other two, the cover and the handle. We can count one, two, or three, even with the same teapot, depending on the way we wish to count. In the same way, if we take a tree as an entity, we say that there is one tree; but if we are concerned with the trunk and the branches, the number may become fifty; and if we are thinking about the leaves, the number may become five thousand. Thus it becomes obvious that our knowledge of number is not passive; it is, rather, the result of the connections we make between the external object on the one hand, and our internal reasoning on the other.

The practice of classification is an obvious example of an activity which goes beyond mere perception; classification is clearly an invention of man. If we had to depend on perception alone, our classifications would be very crude and elementary, and detailed taxonomy would be an impossibility. As it is, we often classify two organisms which exist thousands of miles apart in the same genus, while we place other organisms which grow side by side in entirely separate genera. The very procedure of classifying is thus not a matter primarily of perception of the external world, but a human invention, based on experience. James points out that many of the jokes of a comedian, many of the laws of a politician, or the creeds of a moralist, may turn out to be inadequate or inappropriate when their practical application is attempted. Their applicability is subject to empirical verification. Any ideal in itself is arbitrary; man cannot be confident of its utility until he has subjected it to empirical verification.

Three important points are suggested in James's treatment of the philosophical problem of whether knowledge originates in experience, or whether it is innate. The first point concerns the origins of all ideals. James rejects the position of the earlier empiricists who held that all meanings are derived from sense perception of the external world, although he does admit that some ideals do so originate. James compares the experience from without to the guest who enters the house through the front door. But, he points out that the mind has, as a house does, a back door, which also affords access. He shows that ideals and general principles have two sources: the first is the experience which enters through the front door, the second is internal reasoning, which is arbitrary, and which enters through the back door. When we hear a bell ring, our experience of the sound comes through the front door; but when we take quinine, the ringing in our ears comes in through the back door. The external object can be given the opportunity to enter our mind, but thought itself comes from within. The origin of ideals can be likened to the production of a completely new substance by mixing medicinal powders and certain liquids. All general principles in ethics, aesthetics, and science can thus be compared to the compounding of a prescription. The idealist is correct when he refuses to acknowledge that ideals and general principles arise from external perceptions; but he is wrong when he insists that there exists a higher and transcendental power from which they must derive.

James tells us that knowledge from both these sources can have significant effects. Man can invent ideals and general principles. Such ideals and general principles, coming in through the back door, as it were, and thus being arbitrarily contrived by the mind, may possibly be mere illusions; and yet there are cases in which such illusions could be more important than the guest who comes through the front door.

From this concept a second point can be derived, and this is that occurrence of incidental thought may arouse an interest or a desire which can excite the mind. Those who happen to like music may become musicians; those who react strongly to rhythm may become poets; those who enjoy observing and classifying may become scientists. Because interest is what incites someone to do something, desire and enthusiasm in mind and will are of tremendous importance.

The third point has to do with the problem of the truth or falsity of knowledge. James tells us that we need not worry about the origin of ideals and general principles; that the guest who enters through the back door may be a welcome one, and that the one who comes in through the front gate may turn out to be an enemy. The values of ethics, theology, and science cannot be determined by designating the door through which they enter; these values can be appraised only by their application in experience, by finding out whether they work as they are intended to do, by seeing whether they can help us toward satisfactory solution of our problems, by determining whether they can lead us to further experience. The theory that can do these things for us is true; the one which cannot is false. James suggests that the major difference between his predecessors and himself is that the former looked toward the origin of ideals and general principles, while he himself looks toward last things, toward fruits and consequences. It is these last things which determine the truth of ideals and principles—not their origins.

Such a concept is in harmony with James's basic concepts which we discussed in our first lecture. James is not concerned with knowledge as a copy of the original thing, but with its usefulness as an instrument. In fact, it does not matter whether our knowledge of a given object is identical with the real object. What is important is that this general idea or thought is more useful to us than another in our struggle to achieve a purpose. It makes no difference whether one idea is more nearly like the real object than another, because ideas and thoughts are meant to be applied, and are judged on the basis of such application. We can ask whether this knife can kill, or whether it can be used in preparing food, but there is no point in asking whether it is like a "real" knife or not. Its value lies in what we can do with it, and not in its resemblance to a "true" knife.

The three points we have just discussed are of fundamental significance in James's philosophy. The first point, dealing with the origin of ideals, is basic to his Radical Empiricism. The second point, concerning desire and will infused with knowledge, is developed in his *Will to Believe*. The third point, the instrumental judgment of meaning, has particularly influenced the basic concept of his Pragmatism.

As we pointed out in our first lecture, Radical Empiricism is the term James coined to indicate his recognition that all experience is real. It is a radical departure from the position of traditional empiricism which regarded experience as the passive impression of external objects upon human consciousness. In James's Radical Empiricism, experience is active, adventurous, changing, forward-moving—a conception immeasurably broader than the one it supplanted. For James, the rudeness of experience is an aspect inherent in the nature of experience itself. There can be no single concept which can embrace the entire universe. Truth and its consequences, good and evil, suffering and enjoyment, peril and safety, success and failure—all these are facts which occur in experience. James sees experience as something rude, uncertain, and transforming.

The second part, the theory embodied in James's *Will to Believe*, has been unacceptable to many people because traditionally people have believed that truth is discovered through the exercise of pure reason, not by dealing with objective facts. James defines belief as the will to act, and asserts that the more complete the belief, the stronger the will to act, and hence, the less hesitation. Behind all true theories of mathematics, physics, chemistry, and so on, there must exist the will to make the world more intelli-

gible. Underneath human reason exists irrational will. All truth
about the universe has come into being because of man's emotional satisfaction at having his world made more intelligible
when aspects of it are elucidated by new theories. Therefore, we
can say that underneath all philosophy and science, there is this
reservoir of irrational will.

Many of James's critics ask what right we have to believe if
we have only the will to believe, but no objective evidence to support our beliefs. James retorts that this begs the question, that
man could never do anything at all if he waited until he had collected all the necessary evidence. We must believe in something
first, he says, and then proceed to look for evidence. We do not
have enough evidence, for example, to know whether the world
is essentially good or intrinsically evil. The only thing to do is to
take one of the alternatives as an assumption, and seek the evidence to verify it. When we meet a new friend, we have no way
to tell whether he is a good person or otherwise; but could we
argue that we should never make new friends just because we
cannot know whether they are good or bad men? After we have
had enough association with him, we can tell whether the new
friend is one we choose to keep as a friend—but only after we
have had the association. This is a good example of the importance of the will to believe.

James elaborates this idea by another example of a man lost
in the woods who comes to a ravine. He must leap across it if he
is to continue on his way, but he does not have the evidence that
he can do it. If he believes that he can jump across the ravine, he
will take the risk and may succeed. If he hesitates, he may fail.
The greater his hesitation, the greater his danger. It is only belief
that enables us to overcome our hesitation in such situations.
James tells us that this theory is more useful in the fields of morality and religion than in others, because in these fields of experience, one must believe in something on the basis of love, not
of evidence. It is only when one believes that he is inspired to look
for evidence; the man who refuses to believe anything will not
uncover any of the evidence.

This has become the most controversial of all of James's theories, and the object of the most criticism. Some philosophers, not
content with merely rejecting James's theory, go to considerable
lengths to ridicule him. They say that according to James's theory,

a man can believe anything he wishes to believe. A man may believe that he is a millionaire, when, in fact, he is penniless. How absurd! But, of course, this is a misunderstanding. James is an essayist, and he enjoys writing. When he writes about a problem, he uses figurative language, and elaborates his point even to a degree of exaggeration. The fact that James enjoys his use of literary license has made him vulnerable to misinterpretation by unfriendly critics. But it is not necessary for me to defend James at this time. I should prefer to go on to the third point we mentioned, that is, James's advocacy of the instrumental determination of the truth or falsity of ideals and principles. And this is the guarantee of his whole theory.

This is the essence of James's Pragmatism. Initially James constructed his Pragmatism as "a theory of truth." There are two traditional theories of truth. The first is that truth is the correspondence between the perception and the external object. If the one does not correspond to the other, there is no truth, only falsity. The other theory was that the external object and its perception by the human mind are two completely different entities, and that there is no warrant for comparing the two to see whether they correspond. According to this theory, truth lies in the consistency of thought itself. When there is no contradiction in our thought, our thought is thereby true. James discredits both these traditional theories of truth, and advances the theory that the truth of all perceptions, ideas, and theories is to be determined by the degree to which the consequences they produce coincide with what they promise or predict. When they work well and produce useful consequences, they are true; otherwise they are false. This is a summary of the pragmatic theory of truth.

Some people believe that every theory has to go through the same three periods: first, a period in which everybody is sure that the theory is ridiculous; second, a period when people concede that there may be some truth in the theory, but that it is not very important; and third, a period when people insist that they have taken the theory for granted all along. James's theory has not yet reached this third stage; but I believe that the development of science will expedite its acceptance. Science itself went through the period when its hypotheses were laughed off as ridiculous; then there was a time when people agreed that "there was probably some truth in it," but that it wasn't particularly important;

now everyone takes the laws of science for granted, and their validity is not questioned. This supports the definition of truth as an
hypothesis which has been verified in practice.

In brief, James's theory is replacing the traditional concept of
absolute truth in philosophy with experimentalism. James recognizes the gradual growth and expansion of truth by means of experimentation and verification. A devotee of informal discourse
and a master of literary expression, James has never published
any orthodox philosophy; but he has exercised tremendous influence, especially in England and the United States. Since he advanced his theories, the conduct and the nature of philosophy
have undergone a radical transformation.

James has consistently opposed absolute dogmatism in philosophy, and at the same time he has repudiated utter skepticism.
Even though he recognizes that no truth can be discovered unless there is an inclination to doubt, he eschews absolute skepticism because it is not constructive. Skepticism, according to
James, can be justified only when it advances an alternative hypothesis; and if the skeptic's hypothesis is verified, we must accept it in lieu of the earlier one which gave rise to the skeptic's
doubts. What is most distasteful to James is a skepticism which
brings with it nothing that can contribute constructively to investigation. He advises us to doubt, but he warns us against an attitude of complete skepticism. He asks us to look for new truth in
the results of our past experiments at the same time that we continue to experiment and to seek for a growing area of practical
belief.

James's theories are valuable not only because they supersede
traditional dogmatism and skepticism, but even more so because
they have led to greater regard for individuality. His pet aversion
is "a block universe," which he compares to the Procrustean
bed. The reference, of course, is to Procrustes, a legendary
giant of Attica, who seized travellers and forced them into an iron
bed, cutting off their feet if they were longer than the bed,
stretching them by force if they were shorter, so that every traveller fitted the length of the bed exactly. James sees traditional
dogmatic philosophy forcing all truth into a single pattern, as
Procrustes forced his victims to fit his bed. James calls, instead,
for human life to be a continual process of re-experimenting and
re-creating.

Henri Bergson

THIRD LECTURE

Bergson, who is still teaching in Paris, was born in 1859, the year in which Darwin's *Origin of the Species* was published, and his philosophy has been a major factor in developing the philosophical implications of the theory of evolution.

Bergson's philosophy resembles James's in that both of them take psychology as their starting point, and that both have utilized the concepts of psychology in constructing their philosophies. They differ, however, in two important respects: first, in contrast to James's emphasis on experimentation, Bergson assigns a major role to introspection, and second, while James denigrates systematization in philosophy, and disclaims any interest in constructing a systematic philosophy, Bergson organizes all philosophical problems into one philosophic system. It is interesting that so many students of philosophy had assumed that Hegel had achieved the ultimate in systematization, and that after him there would be no other systematic philosophers. They did not foresee that Spencer would construct his own philosophical system, or that a later appearance on the scene would be Bergson's systematic philosophy.

But since Bergson has organized his philosophy in relation to combinations of philosophical problems, we must first identify the problems to which he directs his attention. These problems can be subsumed under three headings.

The first group of problems with which Bergson deals are those which arise out of the relationship between the noumenal world and the phenomenal world; between the existence of reality, or noumenon on the one hand, and the surface manifestations or phenomena, which are the objects of our perception on the other. Both Plato and Kant had advanced the view that human perception is limited to the phenomenal world, and that the noumenal world is unknown and unknowable. Spencer had said essentially the same thing. The problems in this group have been of fundamental importance in Bergson's philosophy. The second group of problems which have concerned Bergson are those having to do with the question of whether the universe is immutable or changing; whether it is free or pre-determined. The third group are those problems which deal with the relationship between mind and matter. These have been important problems throughout the history of French philosophy, since the time that Descartes postulated an opposition between mind and matter, basing his view on his observation that the mind is capable of thought, while matter is only extension. Since the time of Descartes this problem has concerned philosophers the world over, and it is not to be wondered at that Bergson devoted particular attention to it.

These three groups of problems were not Bergson's initial concern. He began by examining the view that all man can really know is the experience of his own mind. We can, he concluded, have clear knowledge only of ourselves, and all other experience is merely superficial. Bergson and James hold remarkably similar views of the nature of mind; as we pointed out in an earlier lecture, James views the mind as a "stream of consciousness"; Bergson also takes the view that the mind is a stream which runs without repetition and which is inseparable. "One cannot step twice into the same river." By the same token, one cannot have the same thought or perception twice. This desk which we saw the other day is no longer the same desk today, because our experience has changed, no matter how imperceptibly, since the last time we saw it. Thus, for both philosophers, the experience of the human mind is ever-changing, always transforming, and continually moving forward.

This concept of mind runs counter to the common-sense view of experience. People in general act on the assumption that experience can be separated into its constituent parts, just as we can separate the cup from the teapot, and the teapot from the book; just as we can distinguish the flame of the candle from the fire in the stove. They are thus unable to grasp Bergson's view of experience as an ever-moving stream; for them this is clearly contrary to fact. Both James and Bergson reply to this criticism by pointing out that people have traditionally viewed the human mind as though their concepts of material things could be transferred and applied to it. Just as material objects can be separated into their component parts, they think, mind can be reduced to its constituent elements. But how do people transfer their concepts of material things and try to make them apply to the mind? Bergson and James arrived at different answers to this question.

Why, Bergson asks himself, must people insist that their ex-

perience be cut into segments, if the experience of mind is like a
flowing stream? He concludes that the reason men do this is that
they want to be understood by their fellow men. The need to communicate with others forces them to segment their experience
into units which can be dealt with through language. Linguistic
symbols can portray only separated segments of experience; the
necessity for communication, therefore, requires that men slice
reality into innumerable small bits.

Working from this concept of experience, Bergson constructs
his unique and fundamental concept of "duration." Duration is,
he says, to be distinguished from time. What, then, is it? Duration
is an endless moving forward which carries all the past within
itself. Bergson compares duration to a snowball rolling down the
mountainside—a figure of speech which implies first that it incorporates within itself all that is past; and second, that because
it becomes bigger and bigger as it rolls, it is continually transformed.

Bergson bases his explanation of internal experience on this
concept of duration. In the first place, he notes, existence means
change; there can be no existence without change. In the second
place, change means growing and maturing. And in the third
place, growing and maturing involve endless self-creation. The
first point is easy to grasp; and the second, in relation to which he
employs the metaphor of the snowball, is not particularly difficult.
But what does the third point imply? Endless self-creation means
the continual addition of new meaning to existing experience.
For example, my best friend may know all my past, but he cannot
know what I am going to do tomorrow; he cannot know even
what I am going to do five minutes from now. All experience is a
result of continual creation; none of it is predetermined. Even the
most intimate knowledge of past experience cannot be a basis for
reliably predicting the future. When an artist standing before a
blank canvas picks up his brush, no one—not even he, himself—
can know ahead of time what the result will be. If he knew before
he started to paint what his painting would look like, the result
would have been achieved before the effort was undertaken—and
this would be a contradiction. Bergson has employed this example a number of times when he expounds the idea that every
experience is new, and is thus a result of self-creation.

We must accept this basic concept for the time being, so that we can explore the results which come about when Bergson applies it to the three groups of philosophical problems which we mentioned earlier. When this concept is applied to the third group, those dealing with the relationship of mind and matter, it leads to the conclusion that the two are incompatible and incommensurable. The material world is static, unchanging, fixed, and can be reduced to its component parts, right down to molecules and atoms. The material world is composed of particles; and although a material object can move in space, and although the material world can be reorganized, yet matter remains unchanged. For example, this book can be moved from here to there, but it remains a part of this room. According to the law of conservation of matter in chemistry, when this piece of paper is burned, its atoms remain unchanged, although they may be reorganized into molecules of another structure.

Bergson sees the material world solely in spatial relationships; only mental experience can be explained in terms of duration. Matter is confined within spatial relationships, and even when the element of time appears to be involved, it is only an aspect of or "disguise" for spatial relationship. Duration itself is change; the time which characterizes the material world is not duration, but pseudo-time. When, for example, we say that there will be an eclipse of the sun three months hence, it would appear that these three months represent duration; but, according to Bergson, the period of three months can be divided into any number of segments, and therefore it is pseudo-time, still a disguise of space.

An example which makes explicit the distinction between Bergson's pseudo-time and duration can be found in the clock. Here time is indicated by the hour-hand and the minute-hand; it is not duration, but is merely the spatial relationship between the two hands of the clock. Such "time" is not duration; it is a disguise of space. On the other hand, when one is hungry and waiting for food, or when he is in danger of drowning and calling for help, or when he is waiting in court for trial or sentence, he incorporates all his past experience into the moment, and moves forward to the future. This can be called "duration." We can distinguish between what Bergson means by duration and pseudo-time if we remember these examples—the clock, and the situations we have mentioned.

In brief, Bergson's material world is a matter of spatial relationships, while the spiritual world is composed of living experience, which is what he means by duration. Bergson makes the same distinction between perception and recollection. Perception results from the influence of material things; for example, this glass, when it reflects the flame of the candle, "perceives" the candle-light; a mirror, reflecting everything in front of it, is another case of perception. Thus the effect of matter is limited to the sphere of pure perception.

These examples of the glass and the mirror having perception show us that, for Bergson, perception is entirely an effect of matter. But recollection lies in another sphere; one can sum up all his past experiences and leap into the future through the processes of growth and assimilation. This unique and peculiar aspect of human nature is utterly transcendent of matter. Of course, we have become so accustomed to it that we notice nothing strange about it; but if we could actually grasp the true function and nature of recollection, we should no longer feel any need for a theory of pure materialism.

Let us take this idea to a slightly higher level of abstraction. When one material object perceives the other, as the glass perceives the candle-flame, or the mirror perceives the teapot, we may say that perception takes place, but the process is without life. On the other hand when the human mind perceives, it changes the original nature of the material object. What we perceive is determined by our conscious choice or unconscious selection. The hand held close to the eye blocks out the sight of a distant door; and Bergson tells us that this is because what is near to us is usually more important than something that is far away. The important object blocks out the less important one. But when we walk to the door, the door becomes the important object which we perceive clearly.

All of us now know that the earth is spherical; but when this idea was first advanced, people were incredulous. How, they asked, can people live on the other side of the earth when they would be upside down if the earth were truly a sphere? Bergson uses this example to show how inadequately human perception deals with matter. He tells us that man has cut the universe into tiny segments in order to deal with it and meet his needs, when, as a matter of actual fact, the universe is one and indivisible; that in spite of our need to utilize direction and position in the material world, to speak of objects as being "beneath" or "above," "ahead" or "behind," the real universe is continuous, with no part of it separated from any other part. What appear to be separate entities which combine to make up the universe, are man's arbitrary creations—creations necessary to the satisfaction of his needs, but nevertheless unreal and arbitrary.

Application and elaboration of this idea leads Bergson to hypothesize that the dead and immutable material world might well be active, changing, and alive, that is, that there is the possibility that at some time it may become identical with the spiritual world. This is, indeed, a bold assumption. But according to Bergson, there was originally no distinction between the material world and the spiritual world; the separation of this continuous universe into discontinuous and discrete units, fixed and dead, is the work of man's intelligence—something man has done to it to adapt it to his needs. Bergson indicates that this is a matter of distress to him.

This hypothesis that there is no necessary distinction between the material world and the spiritual world had never been verified until Bergson undertook verification in his *Creative Evolution*, which was published in 1907. But we must skip over this point for the moment, and go on to two cases which lend support to Bergson's concept. First, in science the distinction between mass and energy has been discarded; the scientist interprets this table not in terms of substance, but in terms of the innumerable energies which move in certain velocities and certain patterns. Scientists no longer distinguish between mass and energy, but explain mass in terms of energy. But even in his recollections, man cuts his experience into pieces, as when he takes an examination in a given subject, he concentrates on his experience with that subject to the exclusion of everything else. This is a good case in point, to illustrate how man has cut the material world into segments for his own convenience.

Let us see what happens when we apply this concept to the first group of philosophical problems we mentioned—the problems having to do with the noumenal world and the phenomenal world. Traditionally people have accorded a higher status to the noumenal world than to the phenomenal world, and have assumed that the former transcends the latter. But Bergson holds that the noumenal world is not, in fact, of a higher order than the phenomenal world, and the former really is not difficult to understand. For him, the noumenal world means duration, and this is a continuous process of creation and transformation. When man engages single-mindedly in introspection and does not segment his universe in order to satisfy his needs, he will naturally be able to enter the sphere of duration.

As he deals with this problem of the distinction between the noumenal world and the phenomenal world, Bergson utilizes two important concepts of epistemology: intellect, and intuition. Bergson and James are alike in their recognition of the close relationship which prevails between knowledge and human needs and interests, that is, that the value of knowledge lies in its utility in satisfying these needs and interests. But Bergson parts company with Pragmatism when he denigrates and distrusts knowledge, asserting that it is overshadowed by duration.

Bergson deprecates knowledge and thinks highly of intuition. He insists that when man's introspection reaches a certain level, his intuition will naturally enable him to recognize that the noumenal world is a process of continuous creation. Now obviously this sort of statement smacks of mysticism, but Bergson has always been influenced by traditional mysticism. For all practical purposes we can say that mystical strains in European philosophy all derive from Asia. Bergson is a Jew, and comes from Alexandria, a crossroads for Asia, Africa, and Europe, which has been permeated with mystical thought since the second century before Christ. It is quite interesting for us to note that Bergson, being a scientist, has his thinking shot through with mysticism.

We must not ignore the importance of this combination in Bergson's philosophy of the scientific outlook on the one hand and of a mystical aspect which can meet the religious and metaphysical desires of man on the other. I suppose that this must be the reason why Bergson has become so well-known and has attracted so many disciples. His reputation and the size of his following should not surprise us, since he bases his epistemology in Pragmatism, and combines with it other elements which satisfy needs which some people find that Pragmatism does not meet.

Now let us apply Bergson's concepts to the third and last group in the problems we listed, the problem of whether the universe is predetermined or free. Bergson concludes that the uni-

verse of duration cannot be predetermined, for it is in the process
of continuous creation, action, and transformation. Even though
man can know the past better than ever before, he will never be
able to predict the future. But, at the same time, Bergson sees the
material world within the framework of space as fixed, disjunc-
tive, and predetermined.

Bergson's concept of duration as a process of continuous
creation is highly poetic. When a poet writes a poem, he uses
numbers of separate words which might be thought of as units;
but the poem taken as a whole creative work of art is a unique
entity, not just a succession of verbal symbols. We will not find
the same poem anywhere else. The inspiration of the poet is, in a
sense, mystical. Thus it is that the real life, life which is creative,
introspective and always transforming, is free, while processes
which are mechanical and habitual are predetermined.

FOURTH LECTURE: HENRI BERGSON (CONTINUED)

In our last lecture we described some of the important concepts which Bergson employs. We noted that Bergson defines reality as psychological existence, as change which incorporates
into itself all of the past as it moves forward into the future. To
this process Bergson applies the name "duration." In his philosophy he attaches so much importance to change that he comes to
the conclusion that what is changing is change itself. Thus, the
only reality which he recognizes is change itself, nothing else.

Bergson regards material objects as remnants, or "leavings,"
which have been crowded out and left behind in the continuous
process of change. He insists that the only reality is the mental
existence of such continuous change, and that matter is that
which has been cast off, rejected, or frozen out as the process of
change continues endlessly. In his book, *Creative Evolution*, he
makes use of the evolutionary hypothesis to explain how material
things are always undergoing decay. In this book he seeks to resolve the difficulties which confront scientists as they continue to
develop the theory of organic evolution. Bergson advances an apparently simple solution. He notes that Darwin had based his hypothesis on three basic points. The first of these is his assumption
that the functional organs of creatures have come into existence
through the processes of accumulation of minor variations in the
primitive organs. The second point is that these changes have

occurred automatically and without plan in the environment
which they were to deal with. The third point is natural selection,
or the theory that creatures which cope successfully with their
environment survive and reproduce with favorable variations,
while those which fail to make successful adaptations become
extinct.

There is one great difficulty with Darwin's theory. If, as Darwin claimed, complex organs come into existence by means of
accumulation and accommodation of minor changes, and then
serve useful purposes, the question remains of what use these
organs could have been before they became complex. Darwin
notes that the eye has developed out of the creature's coping with
its environment. But the eye does not serve as a means of coping
with the environment until it has become a complex organ. When
it was still a small part of the primitive organism, it could not
function as an eye. How, then, could it have evolved? This question is a difficult one.

People who were baffled by this difficulty in Darwin's theory
countered with an alternative explanation—that the change was
not mechanical accumulation, as Darwin had claimed, but that
there had to be a Creator, who created the universe with a purpose and a plan in mind, and then constructed it step by step.
They compare this with building a house, for which we must first
draw plans, and then construct the foundations, the floors, walls,
roof, and finally add architectural embellishments. Each of these
activities proceeds on the basis of the earlier one, so the whole
thing together can be viewed as a cumulative endeavor. The advocates of this theory argue that the evolution of creatures is a
comparable process; that the evolution of the eye is a change,
planned with reference to a prior purpose. To this view we apply
the name "teleology."

In the early chapters of his book, *Creative Evolution*, Bergson
is critical of both mechanistic and teleological views of evolution.
We will note his criticisms before we talk about his own theory.
He attributes a common mistake to Darwinian mechanism and to
teleology, this being that both recognize only elements which already exist, and ignore the possibility that new elements can be
created. Darwin's view is that evolution resulted from the mechanical accumulation of minor variations, and that when such
accumulation took place smoothly, the organism or the species

survived, and that otherwise the creature perished or the species became extinct. All these variations and the mechanical laws which governed them had always existed; there had never been and could not have been any new elements, only reconstitution of the already existing. The teleologist, with his insistence on a plan comparable to that used in building a house, failed fully as completely to take account of the possibility of newly created elements.

Bergson blames both these theories for depending on intelligence and for ignoring the fact that intelligence can deal only with matter, but that it cannot serve to provide an understanding of life. The life of creatures in the process of evolution is, for Bergson, duration; and since intelligence can deal only with those things which have been sloughed off or divided into segments, it cannot enable man to understand life, which is a process of continuous change and creation. He offers the comparison of the little rock on the beach which is hit by the tide, and asks how the stone, which is dead and inert, can possibly understand the nature of the tide which engulfs it. He says that this is comparable to man's effort to use intelligence in order to understand life.

Insisting that life cannot be understood through the medium of intelligence, Bergson goes on to say that since life is a function of will, it can be understood only by action of the will. Man can employ intelligence when he dissects an organism and analyzes it in relation to its arteries and veins, its skin and muscle, and even its molecules and atoms. But no matter how minutely intelligence enables us to analyze the body of the creature, it cannot provide us with understanding of life, for life is a totality, and the more we try to analyze it, the more difficult it becomes to understand. For an understanding of life, we must resort to will. When will is the most active, that is, when we are most excited and moving forward most enthusiastically, we are best able to understand the meaning of life.

Bergson sees life as a function of will; and will is without either plan or consciousness; it is the impulse which moves life forward, and which enables it to overcome obstacles which stand in the way of its continual forward movement. This experience of the will is the true phenomenon of life; the only way to grasp the true meaning of life is to recognize that it is essentially impulse. No other theory can explain the facts of evolution.

Bergson believes that this is the only way in which we can satisfactorily explain the changes which occur in the organs of creatures in the process of evolution. He uses the term *élan vital* to designate a continuous movement toward the future. He insists that both mechanism and teleology have failed to provide a satisfactory explanation for the origins of complex organs. Bergson himself says that these complex organs have come into existence simply as a result of the will to live which exists within the organism. When *élan vital* encounters difficulty, it overcomes it and continues to move forward without plan or consideration. Our eye, Bergson says, is the result of our will to see; and as time has gone on, it has become the most satisfactory organ for dealing with our environment.

Bergson speaks of the eye as a vestige of life's constant movement into the future. Because life, by its own nature, overcomes any difficulty it encounters in its forward movement, the eye is the result of our internalized will to see. Or, to take another example, if we scatter iron filings on the table and then run our fingers along the surface of the table, our fingers will leave tracings. The mechanist would say that these traces are the result of accident, while the teleologist would say that the pattern left in the iron filings accords with a preexistent plan. Neither outlook takes account of the view that life is impulse, moving always into the future, overcoming the obstacles it meets, and leaving vestiges of the will in its wake.

We have been talking about one aspect of Darwin's theory of evolution. Now let us look at the second, which is the origin of species. Bergson is convinced that evolutionists are mistaken when they assume that plants, lower animals, and then man constitute a straight line of evolution. He insists that evolution does not occur in a straight line; that when life moves forward, it seeks the channels which allow the most satisfactory and rapid movement. It may be temporarily halted by an obstacle, but then it overcomes the obstacle and moves forward again. This is his reason for saying that the species have evolved out of a move-and-stop-and-then-move-again pattern, and for looking upon different species of plants and animals as the products of this stop-move-stop process, or as different stages in the development of life.

As life has moved forward from its beginning, it has not followed a straight-line direction. It undertakes to conquer obstacles it encounters in its progress, doing this by one experiment after another; but when no means avails to overcome the obstacle, life is halted at that point and no longer moves forward. Bergson's *élan vital* explains that some life was stopped at the stage of insects, other life continued its forward movement to become reptiles, and still other life continued its forward movement until it eventuated in man.

Bergson recognizes Spencer as the philosopher who has contributed most to the philosophical implications of the theory of evolution. Spencer explains the forms of various creatures in terms of the environment within which they live—fish are what they are because they live in the water, birds what they are because they have to fly in the air. Each species is a response to the environment in which it exists. Bergson disagrees with Spencer on this point, reversing him to say that the environment itself results from life's will to live. For example, he says, the bridges, the tunnels, and the fills on the highway which connects the city with a village are not so much a part of the environment as a result of it; their very existence results, Bergson tells us, from the will to build the highway, and the bridges, tunnels, and fills are contingent upon and derived from this will. By the same token, he argues, that species of plant and animal life cannot be determined by the environment in which they live. The only reason why a creature or species would adapt itself to a given environment, he says, is that it has the will to live.

So much for Darwin's second point; now let us look at the third, his comparison of the plant, the animal, and man. We must skip over, for the moment, what Bergson has to say about plants; but note that the distinction he makes between man and lower animals is that the latter have developed their instincts, while man has developed his intelligence. Insects, such as ants and bees, do not have intelligence, but following the impulse of life to move forward and to overcome obstacles, they have developed their instincts to the greatest possible degree.

Bergson points out three differences between the instincts of lower animals and the intelligence of man. The first difference to which he calls attention is that man uses his intelligence to deal with matter, and the lower animals use their instinct to deal with life. He supports his view with a vivid illustration of a certain species of wasp which lays her eggs inside the bodies of other animals. She stings the host animal in seven places, each of these being a vital nerve centre, so that the animal is numbed and unable to move, and so that the larvae which hatch from the eggs she has laid inside the animal can be nourished on the animal's tissues until they pupate. This is a feat quite beyond man's abilities; but the animal operates with unfailing exactitude because of the degree of development of her instincts. Bergson sees this as the most important of the three differences between man and the lower animals. Because man is inferior to other animals in the development of his instincts, he compensates by developing his intelligence.

The second difference is that man is a tool-making animal. Of course some animals also have "tools" such as their claws, their fangs, or their beaks—but these are all parts of their bodies, and they are unable to make tools which are separate from themselves. But man is different; when he wants to see more than the naked eye can compass, he makes microscopes and telescopes. The animal is warmed only by his own fur, but man makes fire—first by striking flint on metal, then in an open hearth, and now in stoves. These are examples of the ways in which man supplements his instincts by using his intelligence.

In the third place, both man and the lower animals have both strengths and weaknesses. The strength of the lower animals lies in the development of their instincts, their weakness in the absence of intelligence and in their inability to make tools. On the other hand, man can use his intelligence to make such tools as microscopes and telescopes, as we have just mentioned, but, since he cannot develop his instincts to the extent that the lower animals do, he is incapable of understanding the real meaning of life.

Bergson believes that the major problem of philosophy is that of combining the instincts of the lower animals with the intelligence of man. He notes that although man has not developed his instincts fully, he fortunately retains some of them, such as sleep, which is a heritage from the plant, and dreams, a heritage from animals. The fact that man retains these vestiges of instinct is the basis for holding out some hope for him. But it is only as he returns to the use of intuition that man can combine his instincts with his intelligence. We can see evidence that man does still have remnants of instincts when we see lower animals finding what they are seeking even though they know nothing about method, while man sometimes cannot find what he wants, even when he has developed an appropriate method. This weakness will be remedied only when man learns to combine his intelligence with intuition.

In our discussions thus far, we have assumed that matter exists. But Bergson defines reality as a psychological existence which he equates with change. Where, then, does matter come into the picture? Using his great skill with words, and appealing to his concept of evolution, Bergson has yielded to the demand that he explain the origin of matter. I shall not say much about this here, partly because we don't have much time, and partly because I, myself, do not understand it very clearly. Bergson tells us that matter originates from psychological existence. But how? He uses the example of a great poet reading one of his poems aloud. When his audience concentrates on the poem—on its meaning, its rhythm, and its over all excellence—they do not pay attention to the separate words, or to the structure of the sentences, the spelling, and so on. This is because they are concentrating on the poem, as a poem; when they get tired or their attention wanders, they hear only the separate words, and lose sight of the fact and the meaning of the poem. But when they again concentrate on the poem as a poem, they combine all the elements and what they hear is the poem.

The implication of this example seems to be that when we concentrate, we are in the spiritual world, and that when our attention is diverted, we immediately revert to the material world. Bergson explains the origin of matter in the same way: in the beginning there is only duration, or enthusiastic forward movement. Sometimes, though, we allow ourselves to relax. Life itself is duration without matter; but as we relax, we become part of the material world. He also uses the example of the sky-rocket. As it soars higher and higher, it is full of spirit; but when it falls to the earth, its burned-out shell becomes matter.

Time is running out, so I cannot give you a detailed criticism of Bergson's philosophy, but there are a few things that I do want to say. Bergson's manner of dealing with various philosophical problems is a tribute to his intellectual stature. An accomplished artist, he has performed with excellence in other fields of endeavor. The most important of his contributions is his argument that the meaning of life cannot be grasped through knowledge, that we can understand life only by living it. Behaviors cannot be the objects of knowledge; they can be understood only through behaving or acting. It is true that this concept is not original with Bergson, but he has developed it more fully and more explicitly than has anyone else.

Another important contribution is Bergson's concept of continuous creation and continuous evolution, with the ever-present possibility of adding new elements. Again, although Bergson did not originate this idea, he has developed and explicated it in competent fashion. Also we must give Bergson credit for his development of the thesis that truth can never be reached through pure reason, but only when an inner intuition is exercised.

But, because of his insistence on organizing all his ideas— many of which, in themselves, have great value, as we have seen—into one consistent system, and because of his liberal use of examples, as well as his literary style, Bergson goes to extremes and has failed in his desire to construct a philosophical system. All I can say here is that he has not succeeded in avoiding the trap into which so many of the great traditional philosophers fell—the overwhelming desire to arrange all his insights into one coherent system, and to refer everything in it to one central idea. For this reason Bergson has encountered many difficulties, and has fallen into many inconsistencies. In this particular aspect, James is more sophisticated than Bergson. Although James develops his philosophical insights along many lines, he has no wish to organize them into one coherent philosophical system. We can say that Bergson's preoccupation with building a philosophical system is his greatest weakness, and is a contributing cause to the fact that he does not enjoy the preeminence that might have been his.

Bertrand Russell

FIFTH LECTURE

This evening we will talk about the third of the philosophers with whom we are dealing in this series of lectures, Bertrand Russell, a young Englishman. A few years ago Russell was a professor of mathematics at Cambridge University, but because of his outspoken pacifism he incurred the displeasure of the British government when the European War broke out, and he resigned his professorship until the end of the war. Today we will talk about the theoretical aspects of Russell's philosophy, leaving consideration of his ethics and political philosophy for our next lecture.

It would be difficult to find another philosopher so entirely different from both James and Bergson as Russell is. As we have seen, James and Bergson share many points in common, but as far as the theoretical aspects of philosophy are concerned, Russell does not share a single point with either of them. Both James and Bergson base their philosophy in psychology, and begin their inquiries with consideration of human affairs, with the concerns of conscious, living human beings. Russell, on the other hand, starts with mathematics, the most abstract and formal of the sciences. He distrusts psychology, deeming it to be not only irrelevant to philosophy, but a source of confusion which impedes the systematization of philosophy.

Because Russell insists that knowledge must be universal, and that it can never be purely personal, he abjures psychology on the ground that its utilization in philosophy would obviate universality. Russell tells us that the reason mathematics has not earlier been used as a basis for philosophy is that it was not until recent years that mathematics was sufficiently developed to serve this purpose. But he is sure that now man has developed mathematics to a sufficiently high degree to warrant its employment as the foundation of philosophical method.

There is one point at which the philosophy of Russell resembles that of James, although this may not be particularly significant, and this is that both are pluralists. I'm sure that you know that some philosophies are pluralistic, and others monistic. A pluralistic philosopher refuses to try to embrace all reality under a single principle, while on the other hand the monistic philosopher does. James, with his great emphasis on individuality, takes the individual as the central point from which experience is to be considered, and he is thus a pluralistic philosopher. In this particular respect, Russell's basic position is like that of James, and we can also call him a pluralist.

In his writings Russell designates his philosophy "logical atomism" or "absolute pluralism." In espousing a pluralistic view,

Russell points out that pluralism does not admit of the concept of a single, unitary universe, a concept which was generally accepted prior to the development of modern astronomy. For centuries people had thought of the earth as the centre of the universe, with the sun, moon, and stars revolving about it. But the work of Copernicus rendered this concept untenable, and now astronomy has developed to the point at which it is no longer possible to think in terms of a single universe.

At this point I must make one thing clear: since Russell's philosophy is so completely founded in mathematics, which is a highly specialized area of inquiry, it would be impossible for me to give anything like an adequate introduction to it, or even a coherent outline of it, within the scope of these two popular lectures. This evening I am not going to talk about the content of Russell's philosophy at all; instead, I have chosen to discuss with you some of Russell's criticisms of other schools of philosophy, in the hope that this somewhat negative approach will suggest to you the general outlines of his own position.

Russell sees two fundamental mistakes in traditional philosophy: first, it undertook to establish the existence of a unified universe, and to subsume all reality under one principle; and second, it has been unduly influenced by religion and ethics, and has undertaken to explain the universe by use of religious and ethical terminologies. Most such philosophies have attributed inherent goodness to the universe, and have assumed that this goodness is an aspect of reality.

Many religiously oriented philosophers have utilized their religious beliefs as they have dealt with the universe or with reality; they have worked from the assumption that the universe is basically good, and that life is worth living. Even those philosophers who have rejected religion have been, at times without being aware of it, influenced by ethical and moral considerations. For example, even the evolutionists have interpreted the evolution of the universe in terms of moral concepts, presenting evolution as a process of transforming evil into good, and good into better. Russell rebukes both Spencer and Bergson for their resort to moral concepts in their explanations of evolution, and blames both for trying to explain reality in terms of what they consider to be "the better."

According to Russell not only has the progress of astronomy

undermined the concept of a single, unified universe; it has also vitiated all attempts to explain the universe in terms of ethical concepts. In the past, when people thought that the earth was the centre of the universe, and that man was the centre of the earth, and when they regarded religion and ethics as central to human existence, it was no more than natural for them to conclude that religion and ethics were of equally central importance to the entire universe. What men did was to take the criteria by which they judged their own lives, and extend these to apply to the universe as they conceived it. But now modern astronomy has made us aware of the fact that the earth is no more than a small point in the solar system, and that man is only a trivial object on the earth. How, then, Russell asks, can man's religion and his ethical systems hold any status in the universe?

After the outbreak of the European War, Russell became greatly discouraged about the prospects for world culture. In one of his articles he develops the idea of the unimportance of man in reference to the universe. He notes that the Milky Way is only a small portion of the universe; that in this small portion, the solar system is no more than a small black point, and that in this small point, the earth and the other planets could not be seen except through a microscope, and even under the microscope they would still be infinitesimal. On one of these infinitesimal points, the earth, incredibly tiny beings, composed of gas and water, busily and continually dart hither and yon, trying to extend the brief period of their lives, and killing other similar beings in their efforts to do so. Compared with the sun, man's life is brief indeed. But if they could be observed by beings on other worlds, those beings would hope that men could hasten their own destruction by killing each other.

Russell insists that men must discard their prejudices and biases before they can develop a worthwhile philosophy. For him, philosophy is a matter of pure reason; it is speculative and is not related in any way with behavior, but is concerned only with a true knowledge of the universe. Among the sciences, only mathematics is sufficiently detached from mundane concerns, sufficiently close to pure reason, to serve as the foundation for a rational philosophy. Russell says that philosophy cannot start with the results obtained by science, but that it must utilize scientific methodology. The purest and most accurate of the sciences is mathematics; hence the method of mathematics must become the method of philosophy. The objects of psychology and physics and the other sciences are existential, that is, they each exist as an object; but mathematics has nothing to do with existence. Dealing with the most abstract and universal formulae, it transcends existence. This is why the method of mathematics must be the method of philosophy.

Russell sees psychology and physics and the other sciences as being concerned with individual objects, not with universal and abstract common principles. Mathematics, on the other hand, is concerned only with the most universal and the most abstract formulae, with principles which can be applied in all fields of inquiry independently of the restrictions imposed by concrete individual objects. True knowledge can be sought only through application of the most universal and most abstract common principles—principles which apply only to the existence of truth, even without reference to their own existence as principles. Since philosophy is to be applied to the universals, its principles cannot be either verified or disproved by empirical experience. Empirical experience is materialistic; but the laws of philosophy are universal in character. These principles are eternal, no matter how much or how often the world changes. Thus only the principles of mathematics and logic can be the foundations of philosophy.

Russell takes this concept to an extreme. He even equates "love" and "hate." What he really means, of course, is that these two concepts seem to have important differences in our experience of them, but when they are subjected to logical or philosophical examination, they turn out to be relative to, rather than opposed to, each other.

There is one thing about Russell's philosophy which is strange. In its ethical and social aspects it is quite radical, and fairly consistent with democracy; while in its theoretical aspects it smacks of authoritarianism appropriate to an aristocracy. Russell exalts reason and ignores perception; he emphasizes common principles and depreciates the individual object; he assigns to reason a much higher status than he accords to experience. His philosophy in this respect resembles rationalism. This is a strange phenomenon; there is no other philosopher whose theoretical considerations reflect the outlook of aristocracy while at the same time his practical considerations are so close to the democratic ideal.

Why do we compare this attitude with that of the aristocracy? It is simply that some people are impatient with the practical affairs of life, and seek to raise themselves above mundane considerations and enter a sphere of pure reflection. Such people feel that they are "artistic," and that they belong to a higher order of being than the run of common man. It is not difficult to see that the theoretical aspects of Russell's philosophy are characterized by this tendency.

In one of his articles in which he extols the merit of pure mathematics, and deals with the distinction between the practical life of man and his ideal life, Russell avers that the most one can hope for in practical life is some sort of adjustment between the ideal on the one hand, and what is possible on the other. But in the world of pure reason, no such adjustment is needed; there is nothing to limit development or to stand in the way of continuing increment of creative activity and noble aspiration. This world of pure reason is far above all human desiring; it is immeasurably beyond the impoverished phenomena of nature; there man can construct a systematic universe for himself and dwell therein in perfect peace. There human freedom can be realized, and the sufferings of practical existence be known no more.

In Russell's more popular works we see evidence of his pessimism, amounting at times to anguish. He compares human life to a long journey in the dark, during which the traveller is beset on all sides with perils. Fatigued and tortured, man strives forward toward a destination which he knows not, and has small hope of reaching; and should he reach it, he can pause only a short time before having to resume his travels. This sort of pessimism is not infrequent in philosophy, particularly in philosophies formulated by philosophers who insist that the world of common principles must necessarily transcend the world of individual experience.

In an earlier lecture I noted that James takes the individual object as the most important and precious aspect of existence, and we may wonder why so many other philosophers accord priority to common principles. Russell's disposition is just the opposite of James's. Russell sees the universal principle as a haven of safety for man, as the ultimate and noblest goal toward which man may strive. At the same time that he acquiesces in the mystic's concept of time as an unimportant and superficial aspect of the reality, he tells us that man's first step through the door of wisdom is just to learn to find truth in the consideration of time as unimportant and superficial.

I cannot at this time deal with the details of Russell's philosophy. I have been talking chiefly about his attitude toward and his criticisms of other philosophies. It has been said that no more than twenty people in the whole world really understand mathematical philosophy—and I readily admit that I am not one of those twenty! There is one point, though, that can be discussed here. The natural sciences are means of dealing with individual objects through reference to common principles. By "common principle" in this connection we mean the scientific laws and principles by means of which we gain an understanding and grasp of our environment, even though the laws themselves are abstract and universal. The object toward which scientific endeavor is directed is the individual fact. How can science relate the two—interpret the individual fact in accordance with universal principle?

One answer to this problem is offered in modern idealism (which is to be distinguished from classic idealism). The Irish philosopher, Berkeley, held that true knowledge of the external world is nothing more than perception, and that what perception consists of is no more than sensation. For example, we see the candle as having a white light and a black wick, and when we touch it, we can tell that it is soft and greasy. A combination of these perceptions becomes our sensation, and constitutes our whole knowledge of the candle. Over and above this, there may exist a "reality" of the candle, but this is not to be known to the human intelligence; and even if it is there, it is of no concern to us. Knowledge is the combination of our various sensations; there is no call for us to concern ourselves with the problem of whether reality exists or whether it doesn't.

In one sense it seems that the progress of the natural sciences lends support to this concept. We now say that the reality of material things is actually the motion of the atoms and molecules which constitute them, and that all their characteristics are the results of such motion. But the idealist denies the reality of the material object, arguing that atoms and molecules are constructs of the human mind, and that as effects produced by our intentional and psychological assumptions, they are wholly subjective. In making these remarks, I have no intention of raising the old problem of mind and matter; my purpose is only to locate the point of dispute. Russell also explains the relationship between the scientist's atoms and molecules on the one hand, and the existence of the individual object on the other, telling us that this relationship is subject to mathematical formulation.

Russell recognizes that the object of perception is only the beginning point of our knowledge, but he is not an idealist. His approach to the problem is similar to that of Leibnitz (1646– 1716) who devised the concept of the monad. The sensation of each person is a matter of that person's point of view, and each such sensation has its own reality. With each monad having its own point of view, each person has his own private universe.

Russell holds that since the object of perception is dependent upon the point of view of the individual, and since no two persons ever have identical points of view, their perceptions may be quite different, the one from the other. But Russell permits perception to indicate real existence. For example, when we look at the table from the top, we get a perception which differs from the one we get when we look at it from underneath; but still, no two persons ever have exactly the same perception of the table. Russell would say that there is not just one table, but as many tables as there are persons perceiving it. Each person has his own table, so to speak. As with Leibnitz's monad, since each person has his own point of view, each also has his own universe. Mathematics and science function as means of communication. Insofar as your table can be demonstrated to be the same as his, a systematic universe can begin to be organized. In fact, since each person does have his own universe, the only means of communication possible to us come from logic, the sciences, and mathematics.

Bergson wrote an article in which he contends that it is not possible for human intelligence to encompass reality, change, and duration. He insists that intelligence cuts reality into segments, as the motion picture camera takes pictures of objects in movement in separate "frames," each of which is actually a still photograph. When Bergson drew this analogy, Russell had never seen a motion picture; but after reading Bergson's article, he did go to see one, and came away agreeing with Bergson that the motion picture camera had indeed divided reality into segments.

But we must also note that although Russell agrees that Bergson's description is accurate, what he means by "dividing into segments" is just the opposite of what Bergson means. Bergson insists that reality is continuous and changing, and that the separated segments are unreal; Russell, on the other hand, sees the movement as misleading, and the segments as real. Each individual object has its own existence; each individual has his own world. This is why Russell calls himself an "absolute pluralist." Reality is segmented, not continuous as Bergson contends. It is only through application of abstract laws that man can organize these segments of reality into a continuous universe. The construction of a universe is the function of science; the universe was not originally continuous. This is rugged individualism with a vengeance!

In our next and final lecture, we will talk about Russell's ethics and his political philosophy.

SIXTH LECTURE: BERTRAND RUSSELL (CONTINUED)

We mentioned in our last lecture that the theoretical aspects of Russell's philosophy differ markedly from the practical aspects. This difference is accounted for by the rigid distinctions which Russell draws between reason and experience, between knowledge and activity, and between the common principle and the individual fact. These distinctions are responsible for the sharp divergence between the theoretical aspects of his philosophy and the social aspects.

These distinctions had led Russell to apply sharply different emphases to the theoretical aspects of his philosophy on the one hand, and to the practical and social aspects on the other. When dealing with the theoretical aspect, Russell subjects human knowledge to fact, and argues that man can have only a speculative view of and a spectator's attitude toward fact—something comparable to the mirror which reflects objects as though the reflected objects were real. But when he deals with practical and social matters, Russell's philosophy is of quite another sort; he depreciates the existent individual fact, and emphasizes such concepts as creation, growth, change, and transformation.

When he deals with theoretical matters, Russell takes a dim view of impulse; but impulse takes on considerable importance when he directs his philosophical inquiry toward human behavior—an importance comparable to that of *élan vital* in Bergson's philosophy. Russell is not willing to let impulse intrude where knowledge is concerned for fear that it might disturb the quietude of knowledge; but he recognizes the importance of impulse when he deals with practical concerns. In fact, he makes it the basis of human behavior.

We cannot at this moment enter into a detailed discussion of the question of whether these such sharply divergent positions on theoretical matters and on practical matters constitute a logical contradiction; nor can we go into detail about the question of whether, or how, his theoretical philosophy has influenced his practical philosophy. We can only summarize the main points of his social philosophy. The difference between Russell's theoretical philosophy and his social and practical philosophy is not merely a matter of differing content, but is reflected in vastly different styles of writing. His writing in theoretical philosophy, with its style drawn from mathematics, is very difficult to understand; but when he deals with practical philosophy, he employs a popular style which great numbers of readers find most attractive.

The three basic works in which Russell presents his social philosophy are *Principles of Social Reconstruction*, *Political Ideals*, and *Roads to Freedom*. All three of these books were written after the outbreak of the European War, and it can be said that all of them are, directly or indirectly, influenced by the war. When the war broke out, Russell was aghast, and viewed the war as a result of the combined evil powers of man—his power to destroy, his power to detract from the meaning of life, and his power to obstruct the development and creation of life. To combat such evil powers, Russell pleads for the rapid development of man's creative and progressive abilities. This advocacy is the central theme of his social philosophy.

A word must be added here: twenty-four years ago, in 1896, Russell published his *German Social Democracy*, at a time when interest ran high in the work of Karl Marx, and in the development of social democratic theory. Russell's book was chiefly factual and historical, but it affords evidence that even that long ago he was vitally interested in social problems.

When we compare the theoretical aspects of Russell's philosophy with what he has to say about social and practical problems, we note that the theoretical aspect is based on mathematics as a universal science, and that it depreciates individual psychology as being irrelevant; but when he deals with practical matters, psychology assumes a basic and important role. In fact, Russell holds that all institutions have originated to meet psychological needs, and, even further, that these institutions cannot be adequately explained without reference to instincts. He not only erects his theories on psychological bases, but resorts to psychology as the criterion by which institutions are to be criticized, to determine which arouse higher impulses and which suppress the higher impulses and encourage the baser ones.

Russell sees human psychology as having three components: first, instinct; second, mind; and third, spirit. The parts of life which fall in the sphere of instinct include all natural impulses such as self-defense, hunger, thirst, and sex; and when we extend the concept of reproduction, the family and the state. In short, instinct is the sphere in which is determined the success or failure of the individual career, and of the family and the state. It is the part of life which we inherit from the lower animals. The life of the mind is different from the life of instinct, in that the latter is personal, while the former is impersonal. Through the life of the mind, man disregards his own benefits or sufferings, and strives to attain universal knowledge.

Russell's concept of spirit somewhat resembles his concept of mind, in that both transcend the individual aspects of life. But he has the life of the mind transcending individual knowledge, while life of the spirit transcends individual feeling. The life which has feeling at its centre finds fruition in the fine arts and in religion. The fine arts begin in instinct and ascend to feeling, while religion, arising in feeling, gradually seeps down to permeate the life of instinct.

For Russell, the ideal development is one in which these three elements are in balance. Instinct infuses us with energy; knowledge provides us with method; and spirit directs us toward purpose. When energy, method, and purpose are coordinate, a man is at his best. But such a condition is rare in ordinary life; all too often we sacrifice two of the elements in our efforts to develop a third. When we sacrifice mind and spirit for excessive develop-

ment of the life of instinct, we live the life of savages. When our
effort to satisfy desire is not sufficiently informed by knowledge,
we are barbarians, not civilized people. And when the life of the
mind becomes too critical of the life of instinct, we become skep-
tics; we distrust the world; we lose the enthusiasm which only
instinct can generate, become coldly critical and detached, and
eventually withdraw from the world of action.

Russell tells us that man has developed the life of the mind
to such an extreme that the necessity has arisen for schools of
philosophy which might come to the rescue and help him coordinate the parts that make up the whole. Among such schools of
philosophy Russell includes James's Pragmatism and Bergson's
Vitalism, both of which we have discussed in earlier lectures in
this series. But Russell rejects both approaches, because he says
that they are merely trying to adjust mind to instinct. He accuses
them of having tried to make knowledge subordinate to instinct.

Russell holds that man should be characterized by universal
feeling, so that he will not be confined and restricted by consideration of his own welfare, or the welfare of his family or his state.
Instead, a man should be concerned with the welfare of all mankind, and direct all his efforts toward the promotion of this general
welfare.

Russell lays upon social institutions the onus of individual
man's inability to develop himself to the fullest. Such obstruction
and suppression of individual development, however, is not of
fundamental importance; no matter how great influence social
institutions can wield, they cannot take away a man's internal
freedom. Far more dreadful is social temptation and bribery. For
example, an artist may have tremendous potential for artistic
creation, but society subjects him to its control with money and
the promise of fame, so that he dare not create according to his
own vision, but succumbs, and ends up by pandering to the prevailing tastes of his society—and, in so doing, is less than he
might have been. The case is no different with the writer, or with
the politician. Russell seems to distrust the politician most of all;
in his opinion there is no politician who does not prostitute himself to the whims of his constituency, and who, even after he surrenders his integrity, does not continue to subordinate his principles to the wishes of those whom he serves. Because these
tactics of temptation and bribery, of buying men's souls, can and

do stifle internal freedom beyond the possibility of resuscitation, they are more to be dreaded than forces which merely oppose or seek to suppress individual freedom.

But how, Russell asks, do such temptations and bribery, such purchase of man's soul, manage to obstruct the development of his individual freedom? Because social organization impairs the creative impulse and fosters the possessive impulse. Human activities fall into two categories, the creative and the possessive; and each is the manifestation of impulses which are creative or possessive. One cannot have such material goods as clothing, food, and other objects, and at the same time allow others to possess them. The impulse to ownership of such goods is possessive. The scientist, on the other hand, when he discovers a new scientific law, or discerns a hitherto undiscovered relationship, has no concern with the way the discovery may affect him as an individual, but immediately shares his discovery through publication. His impulse is creative. But social organizations encourage man's possessive impulse, and stifle his creative impulse.

This categorization of human impulses into the creative and the possessive is basic in Russell's social philosophy. In fact, we can say that his whole social philosophy is no more than the elaboration and application of this concept. He uses it as a criterion against which to judge social institutions, and by means of which to determine which should be cultivated and which controlled. He takes exception both to state ownership of property and to private ownership. Both these institutions are indispensable to the operation of our society as it now exists, but Russell objects that both foster the possessive impulse. To put it simply, Russell takes the central ideas of socialism and anarchism, and combines them into one concept which forms the basis of his advocacies. He says, for example, that when the possession of property is accorded central importance, the state, in protecting private ownership, helps the rich to become richer, and suppresses the poor. Extending this principle from its internal affairs to its international relations, the state lends its power to the suppression of small states, and thus contributes to the growth of imperialism.

As we have already said, the European War convinced Russell that war is an evil, a manifestation of the power to destroy. For him, war demonstrates the bankruptcy of both institutions, state ownership of property and private ownership. Private ownership, with its inherent competition in both industry and commerce, has promoted colonialism and fostered the development of imperialism. Further, the state as an institution, by protecting private ownership, vitiates individual freedom and reason, and subjects the individual to the control of and suppression by national power. As far as Russell is concerned, the European War was an irrefutable demonstration of the deficiencies inherent in both state and private ownership of property.

Aside from these two institutions, Russell says that the institutions of education, the family, and religion should have fostered the development of creative impulses, but that, in cold fact, they have failed to do so. It is not so much that such institutions are not by nature capable of fostering creative impulses as it is that they have become contaminated with possessive impulses, and have come so completely under their sway that they have fallen into decadence. Education should be a process of adventure and invention. It should be creative. But, instead, it has become an agent for possessiveness. Infiltration of the educative process by the institution of property has imposed shackles which prevent the free development of education. Thus education has degenerated into preservation of the status quo. The aim of the school as it now exists has become that of making the individual obedient and complaisant, of rendering him unquestioningly subject to the controls and regulations which surround him. Education is no longer concerned, as it ought to be, with the free development of creative impulses.

Russell charges that existing educational institutions aim not at the cultivation of thought, but rather at the cultivation of belief. Why should this be? Because education, as an institution, has been subordinated to the institution of property, and the educator is afraid that independent thought might create disturbances which would threaten property rights. Creative education should be a matter of adventure; but Russell claims that man fears thought more than anything else in the world, even more than he fears death and destruction. Thought is persistent; it is reforming; it is destructive; critical thought ignores privilege, power, existing institutions and comfortable habits; it is anarchic; it recognizes no authority and fears no law; it is great; it is quick; it is free; it enlightens the world; it is the ultimate honor of man.

Creative education should not limit itself to the preservation of the past; it should aim at the creation of a better future.

Russell brings his fundamental concept of creative and possessive impulses to bear not only on existing institutions, but on programs of social reconstruction as well. He has commented critically on all such programs that he has been able to find, and finds fatal flaws in all of them. His criticism of socialism is that it is primarily a philosophy of economics. He sets forth four criteria by which we should measure any industrial institution: first, does it provide a maximum of production? second, does it foster a fair system of distribution? third, does it accord workers reasonable treatment? and fourth (the most important), does it accelerate material and spiritual development, and bring about progress and enrichment? If an industrial institution satisfies only the first criterion, then we have over-production and our economy goes out of kilter. Socialism satisfies this criterion, and the second and third as well, but it has not yet progressed to the point of satisfying the fourth.

For another thing, when socialism is put into practice, the state as an institution must be strengthened. Russell derogates the institution of the state, blaming it for suppressing the individual and impeding his free development.

We have already talked about the negative aspects of Russell's philosophy in general. The constructive elements of his philosophy are not so much ideas which he has developed independently as they are combinations of ideas drawn from various schools of socialism. For example, he favors public ownership of the land, of mining, and of transportation facilities, and strongly supports cooperatives both for producers and for consumers. He has written in support of the guild system in industry and commerce, and in advocacy of full autonomy for professional groups. For Russell the state is no more than a judge which safeguards the rights of the people; and he says that there should be a federal government above the state to restrain it from using its power in ways contrary to the general good.

These three contemporary philosophers, James, Bergson, and Russell, represent the spirit of our time, both in their books and in the influence they have had on public opinion. Russell appears to differ from the other two, but when we examine matters closely we find that the difference is quite superficial. We find that Russell's philosophy about the state and about society is not essentially different from that of James and Bergson. Russell joins forces with them in the importance he attaches to creation, growth, change, and transformation. Even though Russell criticizes James for subordinating the life of instinct to the affairs of practical living, he himself incorporates universal feeling into knowledge. But James is more sophisticated than Russell, for while Russell takes mankind as a whole as the subject of his observations, James gives his attention to the individual person. James has consistently refused to concern himself with the concept of mankind in the abstract, and has devoted himself entirely to the life of the individual as an individual.

To conclude, each of these three philosophers has made his own contribution. James develops the concept of a dependable future which is active and flexible, and which can be freely created by those who live in it; his radical liberalism is a philosophy which invites each man to create his own future world. This is James's contribution. Bergson's emphasis on intuition adds an element of freshness to this creation of one's own future, especially when he insists that it is not a matter of rationalizing or calculating, but comes as a result of our innate impulse to forward striving. This is Bergson's contribution. Russell develops the idea of broad and universal knowledge which is not subject to the limitations of the thinking of individuals; and tells us how such knowledge can supplement intuition, so that man can give direction to his forward striving. This is Russell's contribution.

Miscellany

BOLSHEVISM IN CHINA

Service Report

Peking, China, December 1, 1920.

My dear Col. Drysdale:

In reply to your inquiry, I would say that I have seen no direct evidence of Bolshevism in China. I landed in Shanghai the first of May last year. In the year and a half since, I have been in nine provinces, including the capitals, though much the greater part of the time has been spent in Peking. I have been in Shanghai four times, however, Hangchow twice, and spent two months in Nanking having been there twice. I feel the surer of my belief that Bolshevism is lacking in China because I have been in close contact with the teachers, writers and students who are sometimes called Bolshevists, and who in fact are quite radical in their social and economic ideas.

The student body of the country is in the main much opposed to old institutions and existing political conditions in China. They are especially opposed to their old family system. They are disgusted with politics, and while republican in belief have decided that the Revolution of 1911 was a failure. Hence they think that an intellectual change must come before democracy can be firmly established politically. They have strong and influential leaders among the younger teachers. The great majority of the teachers are still, however, rather conservative in their ideas. The student body in China is proverbially undisciplined, taking an active hand in running the school, striking and demanding dismissal of teachers, etc. This is no new thing and is found in only slightly less degree in Japan, in spite of the great political docility there.

All of these things make the students much inclined to new ideas, and to projects of social and economic change. They have

[Received 2 December 1920 by the military attaché of the American Legation in China, the report was declassified by the State Department on 22 July 1960. First published in *Dewey Newsletter* 6 (1972): 7–10.]

little background of experience and are inclined to welcome any idea provided it is new, or is different from what actually exists. They are practically all socialists, and some call themselves communists. Many think the Russian revolution a very fine thing. All this may seem more or less Bolshevistic. But it has not been inspired from Russia at all. I have never been able, though I have tried to run down all rumors, to hear of Bolshevist propagandists. In the south they are said to be in the north; in the north they are said to be in the south. I do not doubt there are some in China, but I am sure they are not many. And I am absolutely certain they have nothing to do with the general tone and temper of radical thought in the country. A student was arrested two months ago in Peking for circulating "Bolshevist" literature. I investigated and found it was truly anarchistic, advocating the abolition of government and the family, but not Bolshevist.

However if the movement were practically dangerous it wouldn't be much matter whether it was inspired or directed from Russia or not. As matter of fact, it is the effervescence of school boys, being intellectual and emotional rather than practical. It is stimulated by the corruption and inefficiency of the government, and by the pro-Japanese character of the former cabinet. It is a symptom of the change of China from old conditions to new. Much of it is rather silly and superficial, but it is a sign that the students have begun to think about social and economic matters, and is a good sign for the future, because it shows that they have awakened to a realization that a mere paper change in constitution and government is not going to help China any. Radical thought has been accentuated in consequence of the war, but it has been an accompaniment of the new movement for twenty years. The first platform of the Chinese revolutionaries, adopted in 1901 or 1902, was socialistic, and so was the program of the Kuomintang, the Sun Yat Sen revolutionary party, till it was dissolved by Yuan Shih-kai. But there is no leverage in the country to bring about a social revolution or anything approaching it. The farmers are still highly conservative, and they form ninety per cent of the population. There are a good many tenant farmers, but there is much more family proprietorship. A country of peasants that will stand the famine the north is passing through now with no rioting or outbreaks of disorder is less in danger of Bolshevism than any country on the globe. Also industrialism is only just beginning. As yet it is confined to Shanghai and about a half dozen other cities. There isn't outside of these few cities any discontented "proletariat" to appeal to. In these cities unions are forming, etc., but the men are mostly interested in their wages. They are not capable of being reached by ideas of great economic changes. In Changsha a few weeks ago I was invited to attend a meeting to organize a branch of a labor association. There wasn't one actual day laborer at the meeting, mainly merchants with some students. It was much more like some civic welfare or philanthropic organization at home than any labor party, though it had been called by a national organizer sent out from Shanghai. Thus the students have no material to work upon even if they wanted to start a practical movement. Also they are still too theoretical to engage successfully in practical movements. They were quite successful in attacking some of the corrupt Anfuites two years ago, but popular opinion was strongly with them. But at present even their influence in politics where they would have a practical effect if anywhere is very slight. Most foreigners who have any contact with them wish, I think, that they were more active, and more likely to start something than they seem to be.

The sum of the whole matter is that the intellectual class is radical in its beliefs and much interested in all plans of social reform. But it is a small class, practically with little influence, and not concerned to organize itself to get more. The whole social and economic background of Bolshevism as a practical going concern is lacking. Pick ten Chinese at random who are educated and who are outside the official class (which during the Anfu regime tried to block the student movement by calling them Bolshevists) or ten foreigners in contact with the Chinese and you will get the same reply. Many hope that a political revolution is coming to throw out the present class of officials and to get a new start. There may be an upheaval of this sort which those who don't like it will call Bolshevist. But I'm afraid it won't come very soon, and when it does come it will be confined to doing over again the things that were pretended to be done in 1911.

Very sincerely yours,
(Signed) JOHN DEWEY

INTRODUCTION

Reconstruction as Seen Twenty-Five Years Later

I

The text of this volume was written some twenty-five years ago—that is, soon after the First World War; that text is printed without revision. This Introduction is written in the spirit of the text. It is also written in the firm belief that the events of the intervening years have created a situation in which the need for reconstruction is vastly more urgent than when the book was composed; and, more specifically, in the conviction that the present situation indicates with greatly increased clearness where the needed reconstruction must centre, the locus from which detailed new developments must proceed. Today Reconstruction *of* Philosophy is a more suitable title than Reconstruction *in* Philosophy. For the intervening events have sharply defined, have brought to a head, the basic postulate of the text: namely, that the distinctive office, problems and subjectmatter of philosophy grow out of stresses and strains in the community life in which a given form of philosophy arises, and that, accordingly, its specific problems vary with the changes in human life that are always going on and that at times constitute a crisis and a turning point in human history.

The First World War was a decided shock to the earlier period of optimism, in which there prevailed widespread belief in continued progress toward mutual understanding among peoples and classes, and hence a sure movement to harmony and peace. Today the shock is almost incredibly greater. Insecurity and strife are so general that the prevailing attitude is one of anxious and pessimistic uncertainty. Uncertainty as to what the future has in store casts its heavy and black shadow over all aspects of the present.

In philosophy today there are not many who exhibit confi-

[First published as the Introduction to the reprint of *Reconstruction in Philosophy* (Boston: Beacon Press, 1948), pp. v–xli.]

dence about its ability to deal competently with the serious issues of the day. Lack of confidence is manifested in concern for the improvement of techniques, and in threshing over the systems of the past. Both of these interests are justifiable in a way. But with respect to the first, the way of reconstruction is not through giving attention to form at the expense of substantial content, as is the case with techniques that are used only to develop and refine still more purely formal skills. With respect to the second, the way is not through increase of erudite scholarship about the past that throws no light upon the issues now troubling mankind. It is not too much to say that, as far as interest in the two topics just mentioned predominates, the withdrawal from the present scene, increasingly evident in philosophy, is itself a sign of the extent of the disturbance and unsettlement that now marks the other aspects of man's life. Indeed, we may go farther and say that such withdrawal is one manifestation of just those defects of past systems that render them of little value for the troubled affairs of the present: namely, the desire to find something so fixed and certain as to provide a secure refuge. The problems with which a philosophy relevant to the present must deal are those growing out of changes going on with ever-increasing rapidity, over an ever-increasing human-geographical range, and with ever-deepening intensity of penetration; this fact is one striking indication of the need for a very different kind of reconstruction from that which is now most in evidence.

When a view similar to that here presented has been advanced on previous occasions, as, indeed, in the text which follows, it has been criticized as taking what one of the milder of my critics has called "a sour attitude" toward the great systems of the past. It is, accordingly, relevant to the theme of needed reconstruction to say that the adverse criticisms of philosophies of the past are not directed at these systems with respect to their connection with intellectual and moral issues of their own time and place, but with respect to their relevancy in a much changed human situation. The very things that made the great systems objects of esteem and admiration in their own socio-cultural contexts are in large measure the very grounds that deprive them of "actuality" in a world whose main features are different to an extent indicated by our speaking of the "scientific revolution," the "industrial revolution" and the "political revolution" of the last few hundred years. A plea for reconstruction cannot, as far as I can see, be made without giving considerable critical attention to the background within which and in regard to which reconstruction is to take place. Far from being a sign of disesteem, this critical attention is an indispensable part of interest in the development of a philosophy that will do for our time and place what the great doctrines of the past did in and for the cultural media out of which they arose.

Another criticism akin to that just discussed is that the view here taken of the work and office of philosophy rests upon a romantic exaggeration of what can be accomplished by "intelligence." If the latter word were used as a synonym for what one important school of past ages called "reason" or "pure intellect," the criticism would be more than justified. But the word names something very different from what is regarded as the highest organ or "faculty" for laying hold of ultimate truths. It is a shorthand designation for great and ever-growing methods of observation, experiment and reflective reasoning which have in a very short time revolutionized the physical and, to a considerable degree, the physiological conditions of life, but which have not as yet been worked out for application to what is itself distinctively and basically *human*. It is a newcomer even in the physical field of inquiry; as yet it hasn't developed in the various aspects of the human scene. The reconstruction to be undertaken is not that of applying "intelligence" as something ready-made. It is to carry over into any inquiry into human and moral subjects the kind of method (the method of observation, theory as hypothesis, and experimental test) by which understanding of physical nature has been brought to its present pitch.

Just as theories of knowing that developed prior to the existence of scientific inquiry provide no pattern or model for a theory of knowing based upon the present actual conduct of inquiry, so the earlier systems reflect both pre-scientific views of the natural world and also the pre-technological state of industry and the pre-democratic state of politics of the period when their doctrines took form. The actual conditions of life in Greece, particularly in Athens, when classic European philosophy was formulated set up a sharp division between doing and knowing, which was generalized into a complete separation of theory and "practice." It reflected, at the time, the economic organization in which "useful" work was done for the most part by slaves, leaving free men relieved from labor and "free" on that account. That such a state of affairs is also pre-democratic is clear. In political matters, nevertheless, philosophers retained the separation of theory and practice long after tools and processes derived from industrial operations had become indispensable resources in conducting the observations and experiments that are the heart of scientific knowing.

It should be reasonably obvious that an important aspect of the reconstruction that now needs to be carried out concerns the theory of knowledge. In it a radical change is demanded as to the subjectmatter upon which that theory must be based; the new theory will consider how knowing (that is, inquiry that is competent) is carried on, instead of supposing that it must be made to conform to views independently formed regarding faculties of organs. And, while substitution of "intelligence," in the sense just indicated, for "reason" is an important element in the change demanded, reconstruction is not confined to that matter. For the so-called "empirical" theories of knowledge, though they rejected the position of the rationalist school, operated in terms of what *they* took to be a necessary and sufficient faculty of knowledge, accommodating the theory of knowing to their preformed beliefs about "sense-perception" instead of deriving their view of sense-perception from what goes on in the conduct of scientific inquiry.[1]

It will be noted that the adverse criticisms dealt with in the foregoing paragraphs are dealt with not for the sake of replying to criticisms, but primarily as illustrations of why reconstruction is urgently required, and secondarily as illustrations of where it is needed. For there is no promise of the rise and growth of a philosophy relevant to the conditions that *now* supply the materials of philosophical issues and problems, save as the work of reconstruction takes serious account of how and where systems of the past indicate the need for reconstruction in the present.

---

1. The obvious insufficiency of psychological theories on this point has played a part in developing the formalisms already noted. Instead of using this insufficiency as ground for reconstruction of the psychological theory, the defective view was accepted qua psychology and hence was used as a ground for a "logical" theory of knowing that shut out entirely all reference to the factual ways in which knowledge advances.

II

It has been stated that philosophy grows out of, and in intention is connected with, human affairs. There is implicit in this view the further view that, while acknowledgment of this fact is a precondition of the reconstruction now required, yet it means more than that philosophy *ought* in the future to be connected with the crises and tensions in the conduct of human affairs. For it is held that in effect, if not in profession, the great systems of Western philosophy all have been thus motivated and occupied. A claim that they always have been sufficiently aware of what they were engaged in would, of course, be absurd. They have seen themselves, and have represented themselves to the public, as dealing with something which has variously been termed Being, Nature or the Universe, the Cosmos at large, Reality, the Truth. Whatever names were used, they had one thing in common: they were used to designate something taken to be fixed, immutable, and therefore out of time; that is, eternal. In being also something conceived to be universal or all-inclusive, this eternal being was taken to be above and beyond all variations in space. In this matter, philosophers reflected in generalized form the popular beliefs which were current when events were thought of as taking place *in* space and time as their all-comprehensive envelopes. It is a familiar fact that the men who initiated the revolution in natural science held that space and time were independent of each other and of the things that exist and the events that take place within them. Since the assumption of underlying fixities—of which the matter of space and time and of immutable atoms is an exemplification—dominated "natural" science, there is no ground for surprise that in a more generalized form it was the foundation upon which philosophy assumed, as a matter of course, that it must erect its structure. Philosophical doctrines which disagreed about virtually everything else were at one in the assumption that their distinctive concern as philosophy was to search for the immutable and ultimate—that which *is*—without respect to the temporal or spatial. Into this state of affairs in natural science as well as in moral standards and principles, there recently entered the discovery that natural science is forced by its own development to abandon the assumption of fixity and to recognize that what for it is actually "universal" is *process*; but this fact of recent science still remains in philosophy, as in popular opinion up to the present time, a technical matter rather than what it is: namely, the most revolutionary discovery yet made.

The supposed fact that morals demand immutable, extra-temporal principles, standards, norms, ends, as the only assured protection against moral chaos can, however, no longer appeal to natural science for its support, nor expect to justify by science its exemption of morals (in practice and in theory) from considerations of time and place—that is, from processes of change. Emotional—or sentimental—reaction will doubtless continue to resist acknowledgment of this fact and refuse to use in morals the standpoint and outlook which have now made their way into natural science. But in any case, science and traditional morals have been at complete odds with one another as to the kinds of things which, according to one and the other, are immutable. Hence a deep and impassable gulf is set up between the *natural* subjectmatter of science and the *extra-* if not *supra*-natural subjectmatter of morals. There must be many thoughtful persons who are so dismayed by the inevitable consequences of this split that they will welcome that change in point of view which will render the methods and conclusions of natural science service-able for moral theory and practice. All that is needed is acceptance of the view that moral subjectmatter is also spatially and temporally qualified. Considering the controverted present state of morals and its loss of popular esteem, the sacrifice demanded should not seem threatening to those who are not moved by vested institutional interest. As for philosophy, its profession of operating on the basis of the eternal and the immutable is what commits it to a function and a subjectmatter which, more than anything else, are the source of the growing popular disesteem and distrust of its pretensions; for it operates under cover of what is now repudiated in science, and with effective support only from old institutions whose prestige, influence and emoluments of power depend upon the preservation of the old order; and this at the very time when human conditions are so disturbed and un-settled as to call more urgently than at any previous time for the kind of comprehensive and "objective" survey in which historic philosophies have engaged. To the vested interests, maintenance of belief in the transcendence of space and time, and hence the derogation of what is "merely" human, is an indispensable prerequisite of their retention of an authority which in practice is translated into power to regulate human affairs throughout—from top to bottom.

There is, however, such a thing as relative—that is *relational*—universality. The actual conditions and occasions of human life differ widely with respect to their comprehensiveness in range and in depth of penetration. To see why such is the case, one does not have to depend upon a scientifically exploded theory of control from outside and above by self-moved and self-moving forces. On the contrary, theory began to count in the sciences of astronomy, physics, physiology, in their multiple and varied aspects, when this attitude of dogmatism was replaced by the use of hypotheses in conducting experimental observations to bind concrete facts together in systems of increasing temporal-spatial extent. The *universality* that belongs to scientific theories is not that of inherent content fixed by God or Nature, but of range of applicability—of capacity to take events out of their apparent isolation so as to order them into systems which (as is the case with all living things) prove they are alive by the kind of change which is *growth*. From the standpoint of scientific inquiry nothing is more fatal to its right to obtain acceptance than a claim that its conclusions are final and hence incapable of a development that is other than mere quantitative extension.

While I was engaged in writing this Introduction, I received a copy of an address recently delivered by a distinguished English man of science. Speaking specifically of science, he remarked,

Scientific discovery is often carelessly looked upon as the creation of some new knowledge which can be added to the great body of old knowledge. This is true of the strictly trivial discoveries. It is not true of the fundamental discoveries, such as those of the laws of mechanics, of chemical combination, of evolution, on which scientific advance ultimately depends. These always entail the destruction of or disintegration of old knowledge *before the new can be created*.[2]

He continued by pointing out specific instances of the importance of getting outside of the grooves into which the heavy arm of custom tends to push every form of human activity, not excluding intellectual and scientific inquiry:

It is no accident that bacteria were first understood by a canal engineer,

2. C. D. Darlington, Conway Memorial Lecture on *The Conflict of Society and Science* (London: Watts & Co., 1948); italics not in text.

that oxygen was isolated by a Unitarian minister, that the theory of infection was established by a chemist, the theory of heredity by a monastic school teacher, and the theory of evolution by a man who was unfitted to be a university instructor in either botany or zoology.

He closed by saying, "We need a Ministry of Disturbance, a regulated source of annoyance; a destroyer of routine; an underminer of complacency." The routine of custom tends to deaden even scientific inquiry; it stands in the way of *discovery* and of the *active* scientific worker. For discovery and inquiry are synonymous as an occupation. Science is a *pursuit*, not a coming into possession of the immutable; new theories as points of view are more prized than discoveries that quantitatively increase the store on hand. It is relevant to the theme of domination by custom that the lecturer said the great innovators in science "are the first to fear and doubt their discoveries."

I am here specially concerned with the bearing of what was said about men of science upon the work of philosophy. The borderline between what is called hypothesis in science and what is called speculation (usually in a tone of disparagement) in philosophy is thin and shadowy at the time of initiation of new movements—those placed in contrast with "technical applications and developments" such as take place as a matter of course after a new and revolutionary outlook has managed to win acceptance. Viewed in their own cultural contexts, the "hypotheses" advanced by those who now bear the name of great philosophers differ from the "speculations" of the men who have made great (and "destructive") innovations in science by having a wider range of reference and possible application; by the fact that they claim not to be "technical" but deeply and broadly human. At the time there is no sure way of telling whether the new way of seeing and of treating things is to turn out to be a case of science or of philosophy. Later, the classification is usually made with comparative ease. It is a case of "science" if and when its field of application is so specific, so limited, that passage into it is comparatively direct— in spite of the emotional uproar attending its appearance—as, for example, in the case of Darwin's theory. It is designated "philosophy" when its area of application is so comprehensive that it is not possible for it to pass directly into formulations of such form and content as to be serviceable in immediate conduct of specific inquiry. This fact does not signify its futility; on the contrary, the

contemporary state of cultural conditions was such as to stand
effectually in the way of the development of hypotheses that
would give immediate direction to specific observations and experiments so definitely factual as to constitute "science." As the
history of scientific inquiry clearly shows, it was during the "modern" period that inquiry took the form of *discussion*, which, however, was not useless or idle, scientifically speaking. For, as the
word etymologically implies, this discussion was a shaking up, a
stirring, which loosened the firm hold of earlier cosmology upon
science. This period of discussion, with the loosening that attended it, marks the time of the shading off of what now ranks as
"philosophy" into what has now attained the rank of "science."[3]
What is called the "climate of opinion" is more than a matter of
opinions; it is a matter of cultural habits that determine intellectual as well as emotional and volitional attitudes. The work done
by the men whose names now appear in histories of philosophy
rather than of science played a large role in producing a climate
that was favorable to initiation of the scientific movement whose
outcome is the astronomy and physics that have displaced the old
ontological cosmology.

It does not need deep scholarship to be aware that, at the
time, this new science was regarded as a deliberate assault upon
religion and upon the morals then intimately tied up with the
religion of Western Europe. Similar attacks followed the revolution that began in the nineteenth century in biology. Historical
facts prove that discussions that have not been carried, because
of their very comprehensive and penetrating scope, to the point of
detail characteristic of science, have done a work without which
science would not be what it now is.

III

The point of the foregoing discussion does not lie, however,
in its bearing upon the value of past philosophic doctrines. Its

3. It is well worth while recalling that for quite a while Newton ranked as "philosopher" of the division of that subject still classified as "natural" in distinction from metaphysical and moral. Even by his followers his deviations from
Descartes were treated as matter not of physical science but of "natural philosophy."

relevancy for this Introduction consists of its bearing upon the reconstruction of work and subjectmatter that is needed to give philosophy today the vitality once possessed by its predecessors. What took place in the earlier history of science was serious enough to be named the "warfare of science and religion." Nevertheless, the scope of the events that bear that name is limited, almost technical, when it is placed in comparison with what is going on now because of the entry of science more generally into life. The present reach and thrust of what originates as science affects disturbingly every aspect of contemporary life, from the state of the family and the position of women and children, through the conduct and problems of education, through the fine as well as the industrial arts, into political and economic relations of association that are national and international in scope. They are so varied, so multiple, as well as developing with such rapidity, that they do not lend themselves to generalized statement. Moreover, their occurrence presents so many and such serious practical issues demanding immediate attention that man has been kept too busy meeting them piecemeal to make a generalized or intellectual observation of them. They came upon us like a thief in the night, taking us unawares.

The primary requisite of reconstruction is accordingly to arrive at an hypothesis as to how this great change came about so widely, so deeply, and so rapidly. The hypothesis here offered is that the upsets which, taken together, constitute the crisis in which man is now involved all over the world, in all aspects of his life, are due to the entrance into the conduct of the everyday affairs of life of processes, materials and interests whose origin lies in the work done by physical inquirers in the relatively aloof and remote technical workshops known as laboratories. It is no longer a matter of disturbance of religious beliefs and practices, but of every institution established before the rise of modern science a few short centuries ago. The earlier "warfare" was ended not by an out-and-out victory of either of the contestants but by a compromise taking the form of a division of fields and jurisdictions. In moral and ideal matters supremacy was accorded to the old. They remained virtually immutable in their older form. As the uses of the new science proved beneficial in many practical affairs, the new physical and physiological science was tolerated with the understanding that it dealt only with lower material concerns and refrained from entering the higher spiritual "realm" of Being. This "settlement" by the device of division gave rise to the dualisms which have been the chief concern of "modern" philosophy. In the developments which have actually occurred and which have culminated especially within the last generation, the settlement by division of territories and jurisdictions has completely broken down in practice. This fact is exhibited in the present vigorous and aggressive campaign of those who accept the division between the "material" and the "spiritual" but who also hold that the representatives of natural science have not stayed where they belong but have usurped in actual practice—and oftentimes in theory—the right to determine the attitudes and procedures proper to the "higher" authority. Hence, according to them, the present scene of disorder, insecurity and uncertainty, with the strife and anxiety that inevitably results.

I am not here concerned to argue directly against this view. Indeed, it may even be welcomed provided it is taken as an indication of where the issue centres with respect to reconstruction in philosophy. For it indicates by contrast the only direction which, under existing conditions, is intellectually and morally open. The net conclusion of those who hold natural science to be the *fons et origo* of the undeniably serious ills of the present is the necessity of bringing science under subjection to some special institutional "authority." The alternative is a generalized reconstruction so fundamental that it has to be developed by recognition that while the evils resulting at present from the entrance of "science" into our common ways of living are undeniable they are due to the fact that no systematic efforts have as yet been made to subject the "morals" underlying old institutional customs to scientific inquiry and criticism. Here, then, lies the reconstructive work to be done by philosophy. It must undertake to do for the development of inquiry into human affairs and hence into morals what the philosophers of the last few centuries did for promotion of scientific inquiry in physical and physiological conditions and aspects of human life.

This view of what philosophy needs in order to be relevant to present human affairs and to regain the vitality it is losing is not concerned to deny that the entry of science into human activities and interests has its destructive phase. Indeed, the point of departure for the view here presented regarding the reconstruction demanded in philosophy is that this entry, amounting to a hostile invasion of the old, is the main factor operating to produce the present estate of man. And, while the attack upon science as the responsible and guilty party is terribly one-sided in its emphasis upon the destruction involved and in neglect of the many and great human benefits that have accrued, it is held that the issue cannot be disposed of by drawing a balance sheet of human loss and gain with a view to showing that the latter predominates.

The case in fact is much simpler. The premise on which the present assault upon science depends is that old institutional customs, including institutional belief, provide an adequate, and indeed a final, criterion by which to judge the worth of consequences produced by the disturbing entry of science. Those who maintain this premise systematically refuse to note that "science" has a copartner in producing our critical situation. It only takes an eye single to the facts to observe that science, instead of operating alone and in a void, works within an institutional state of affairs developed in pre-scientific days, one which is not modified by scientific inquiry into the moral principles that were then formed and were, presumably, appropriate to it.

One simple example shows the defection and distortion that results from viewing science in isolation. The destructive use made of the fission of the nucleus of an atom has become the stock-in-trade of the assault upon science. What is so ignored as to be denied is that this destructive consequence occurred not only in a war but because of the existence of war, and that war as an institution antedates by unknown millennia the appearance on the human scene of anything remotely resembling scientific inquiry. That *in this case* destructive consequences are directly due to pre-existent institutional conditions is too obvious to call for argument. It does not prove that such is the case everywhere and at all times; but it certainly cautions us against the irresponsible and indiscriminate dogmatism now current. It gives us the definite advice to recall the unscientific conditions under which morals, in both the practical and the theoretical senses of that word, took on form and content. The end-in-view in calling attention to a fact that cannot be denied, but that is systematically ignored, is not the futile, because totally irrelevant, purpose of justifying the work of scientific inquirers in general or in special cases. It is to direct attention to a fact of outstanding intellectual import. The development of scientific inquiry is immature; it has not as yet got beyond the physical and physiological aspects of human concerns, interests and subjectmatters. In consequence, it has partial and exaggerated effects. *The institutional conditions into which it enters and which determine its human consequences have not as yet been subjected to any serious, systematic inquiry worthy of being designated scientific.*

The bearing of this state of affairs upon the present state of philosophy and the reconstruction which should be undertaken is the theme and thesis of this Introduction. Before directly resuming that theme, I shall say something about the present state of morals: a word, be it remembered, that stands both for a morality as a practical socio-cultural *fact* in respect to matters of right and wrong, good and evil, and for theories about the ends, standards, principles according to which the actual state of affairs is to be surveyed and judged. Now the simple fact of the case is that any inquiry into what is deeply and inclusively human enters perforce into the specific area of morals. It does so whether it intends to and whether it is even aware of it or not. When "sociological" theory withdraws from consideration of the basic interests, concerns, the actively moving aims, of a human culture on the ground that "values" are involved and that inquiry as "scientific" has nothing to do with values, the inevitable consequence is that inquiry in the human area is confined to what is superficial and comparatively trivial, no matter what its parade of technical skills. But, on the other hand, if and when inquiry attempts to enter in critical fashion into that which is human in its full sense, it comes up against the body of prejudices, traditions and institutional customs that consolidated and hardened in a pre-scientific age. For it is tautology, not the announcement of a discovery or of an inference, to state that morals, in both senses of the word, are pre-scientific when formed in an age preceding the rise of science as now understood and practiced. And to be unscientific, when human affairs in the concrete are immensely altered, is in effect to resist the formation of methods of inquiry into morals in a way that renders existing morals—again in both senses—anti-scientific.

The case would be comparatively simple if there were already in hand the intellectual standpoint, outlook, or what philosophy has called "categories," to serve as instrumentalities of inquiry.

But to assume that they are at hand is to assume that intellectual growths which reflect a pre-scientific state of human affairs, concerns, interests and ends are adequate to deal with a human situation which is increasingly and for a very large part the outgrowth of new science. In a word, it is to decide to continue the present state of drift, instability and uncertainty. If the foregoing statements are understood in the sense in which they are intended, the view that is here proposed in regard to reconstruction in philosophy will stand out forcibly. From the position here taken, reconstruction can be nothing less than the work of developing, of forming, of producing (in the literal sense of that word) the intellectual instrumentalities which will progressively direct inquiry into the deeply and inclusively human—that is to say, moral—facts of the present scene and situation.

The first step, a prerequisite of further steps in the same general direction, will be to recognize that, factually speaking, the present human scene, for good and evil, for harm and benefit alike, is what it is because, as has been said, of the entry into everyday and common (in the sense of ordinary and of shared) ways of living of what has its origin in *physical* inquiry. The methods and conclusions of "science" do not remain penned in within "science." Even those who conceive of science as if it were a self-enclosed, self-actuated independent and isolated entity cannot deny that it does not remain such in practical fact. It is a piece of theoretical animistic mythology to view it as an entity, as do those who hold that it is *fons et origo* of present human woes. The science that has so far found its way deeply and widely into the actual affairs of human life is partial and incomplete science: competent in respect to physical, and now increasingly to physiological, conditions (as is seen in the recent developments in medicine and public sanitation), but nonexistent with respect to matters of supreme significance to man—those which are distinctively of, for, and by, man. No intelligent way of seeing and understanding the present estate of man will fail to note the extraordinary split in life occasioned by the radical incompatibility between operations that manifest and perpetuate the morals of a pre-scientific age and the operations of a scene which has suddenly, with immense acceleration and with thorough pervasiveness, been factually determined by a science which is still partial, incomplete, and of necessity one-sided in operation.

IV

In what precedes, reference has been made several times to what certain human beings classed as philosophers accomplished in the seventeenth, eighteenth and nineteenth centuries in the way of clearing the ground of cosmological and ontological debris which had been absorbed emotionally and intellectually into the very structure and operation of Western culture. It was not claimed that credit for the specific inquiries which progressively revolutionized astronomy, physics (including chemistry) and physiology belongs to philosophers. It is recorded as matter of historic fact that the latter performed an office that, given the accepted cultural climate and the momentum of accepted custom, was an indispensable prerequisite of what men of science accomplished. What will now be added to that statement, in conjunction with its bearing upon reconstruction of philosophy, is that in doing their specific jobs scientific men worked out a method of inquiry so inclusive in range and so penetrating, so pervasive and so universal, as to provide the pattern and model which permits, invites and even demands the kind of formulation that falls within the function of philosophy. It is a method of knowing that is self-corrective in operation; that learns from failures as from successes. The heart of the method is the discovery of the identity of inquiry with discovery. Within the specialized, the relatively technical, activities of natural science, this office of discovery, of uncovering the new and leaving behind the old, is taken for granted. Its similar centrality in every form of intellectual activity is, however, so far from enjoying general recognition that, in matters which are set apart as "spiritual" and "ideal" and as distinctively moral, the mere idea of it shocks many who take it as a matter of course in their own specialized work. It is a familiar fact that the practical correlate of discovery when it is scientific and theoretical is *invention*, and that in many of the physical aspects of human affairs there is even now a generalized method for the invention of inventions. In what is distinctively human, invention rarely occurs, and then only in the stress of an emergency. In human affairs and in relations that range extensively and penetrate deeply the mere idea of invention awakens fear and horror, being regarded as dangerous and destructive. This fact, which is important but which rarely receives notice, is assumed to belong to the very nature and essence of morals as morals. This fact testifies both to the reconstruction to be undertaken and to the extreme difficulty of every attempt to bring it about.

The adjustment which finally moderated, without completely exorcising, the earlier split between science and received institutional customs was a truce rather than anything remotely approaching integration. It consisted, in fact, of a device that was the exact opposite of integration. It operated on the basis of a hard and fast division of the interests, concerns and purposes of human activity into two "realms," or, by a curious use of language, into two "spheres"—not hemispheres. One was taken to be "high" and hence to possess supreme jurisdiction over the other as inherently "low." That which is high was given the name "spiritual," ideal, and was identified with the moral. The other was the "physical" as determined by the procedures of the new science of nature. In being low it was material; its methods were fitted only to the materialistic and to the world of sense-perception, not to that of reason and revelation. The new natural science was grudgingly given a license to operate on condition that it stay in its own compartment and mind its own business, as thus determined for it. That for philosophy the outcome was the whole brood and nest of dualisms which have, upon the whole, formed the "problems" of philosophy termed "modern" is a reflection of the cultural conditions which account for the basic split made between the moral and the physical. These words stand in fact for the attempt to obtain the practical advantages of ease, comfort, convenience and power that were the outcome of the "application" of the new science to the ordinary affairs of life, while retaining intact the supreme authority of the old in those matters of high morals named "spiritual." The material and utilitarian advantages of the new science, rather than anything approaching acknowledgment of the intellectual—to say nothing of the moral—import of the new method, turned out to be the most dependable ally of the men who produced the new method of revolutionizing what had been taken to be a scientific account of nature as cosmos.

The truce endured for a time. The equilibrium it presented was decidedly uneasy. The saying about keeping a cake and at the same time eating it is applicable. It represented the effort to enjoy the material and practical or utilitarian advantages of the new science while preventing its serious impact on old institutional habits—including those of belief—that were accepted as the foundation of norms and moral principles. In consequence the division would not stay put. Upon the whole, without deliberate intent (though with considerable deliberate encouragement from one group of "advanced" philosophical thinkers) the consequences issuing from the uses to which the new science was put crowded in upon the activities and values nominally reserved for the "spiritual." The impact of this encroachment constitutes what is called secularization, a movement which, as it extended itself, was regarded as a sacrilegious profaning of the sacredness of the spiritual. Even today many men who are in no way practically identified with old ecclesiastical institutions, or with the metaphysics associated with it, speak regretfully and at best apologetically of this secularization. Yet the opportunity for any genuine universalization of the method—and spirit—of science as inquiry, which is perforce discovery in which old intellectual attitudes and conclusions are unceasingly yielding to the different and new, lies precisely in discovering how to give the factors of this secularization the shape, the content and the authority nominally assigned to morals, but not now exercised in fact by those morals that have come down to us from a pre-scientific age. The actuality of this loss of authority is acknowledged in the current revival of the old doctrine of the inherent depravity of human nature to account for the loss, as well as being shown in widespread pessimism as to the future of man. These complaints and doubts are warranted as long as one regards the institutional customs in action and belief of a pre-scientific age as ultimate and immutable. But they also apply, if they are employed that way, a challenge to develop a theory of morals that will give positive intellectual direction to man in developing the practical—that is, actually effective—morals which will utilize the resources now at our disposal to bring into the activities and interests of human life order and security, not only in place of confusion but on a wider scale than ever existed in the past.

Three things are intimately connected in the plaints and promulgations that are temporarily most vocal. They are: (1) the attack upon natural science; (2) the doctrine that man is so inherently corrupt that it is impossible to form morals which will operate in behalf of stability, equity and (true) freedom without recourse to an extra-human and extra-natural authority; and (3) the claim put forth by representatives of some particular kind of institutional organization, that they alone can do what is needed. I do not mention this matter here in order to subject it to direct criticism. I mention it because it presents a position so generalized as clearly to indicate one direction in which philosophy may move out of the apathy of irrelevance. By sharp contrast, it points to the other direction in which philosophy may proceed: that of systematic endeavor to see and to state the constructive significance for the future of man issuing from the revolution wrought primarily by the new science; provided we exercise resolute wisdom in developing a system of belief-attitudes, a philosophy, framed on the basis of the resources now at our command.

The issue actually raised by the assault upon the new science and its offspring by wholesale condemnation of human nature, and by the plea to reinstate in full measure the authority of antique medieval institutions, is simply whether we are to move forward in a direction made possible by these new resources or whether the latter are so inherently untrustworthy that we must bring them under control by subjection to an authority claiming to be extra-human and extra-natural—as far as the import of "natural" is determined by scientific inquiry. The impact of systematic perception of this cleavage of directions upon philosophy is disclosure that what is called "modern" is as yet unformed, inchoate. Its confused strife and its unstable uncertainties reflect the mixture of an old and a new that are incompatible. The genuinely modern has still to be brought into existence. The work of actual production is not the task or responsibility of philosophy. That work can be done only by the resolute, patient, cooperative activities of men and women of good will, drawn from every useful calling, over an indefinitely long period. There is no absurd claim made that philosophers, scientists or any other one group form a sacred priesthood to whom the work is entrusted. But, as philosophers in the last few centuries have performed a useful and needed work in furtherance of physical inquiry, so their successors now have the opportunity and the challenge to do a similar work in forwarding moral inquiry. The conclusions of that inquiry by themselves would no more constitute a complete moral theory and a working science of distinctively human subjectmatter than the activities of their predecessors brought the physical and physiological conditions of human existence into direct and full-fledged existence. But it would have an active share in the work of *con*struction of a moral human science which serves as a needful precursor of *re*construction of the actual state of human life toward order and toward other conditions of a fuller life than man has yet enjoyed.

Systematic exposure of how, where and why philosophies appropriate to ancient and medieval conditions and to those of the few centuries which have elapsed since the appearance of natural science on the human scene are so irrelevant as to be obstructive in intellectual dealings with the present scene, is itself a challenging intellectual task. As earlier intimated, reconstruction is not something to be accomplished by finding fault or being querulous. It is strictly an intellectual work demanding the widest possible scholarship as to the connections of past systems with the cultural conditions that set their problems and a knowledge of present-day science which is other than that of "popular" expositions. And this negative aspect of the intellectual activity to be performed involves of necessity a systematic exploration of the values belonging to what is genuinely new in the scientific, technological and political movements of the immediate past and of the present, when they are liberated from the incubus imposed on them by habits formed in a pre-scientific, pre-technological-industrial and pre-democratic political period.

One now fairly often runs across signs of a growing tendency to react against the view which holds that science and the new technology are to be blamed for present evils. It is recognized that as means they are so powerful as to give us valuable new resources. All that is needed, so it is held, is an equally effective moral renewal that will use these means for genuinely human ends. This position is certainly a marked improvement upon a mere assault on science and technology for the purpose of effecting a specific institutional subordination of them. It is to be welcomed in so far as it perceives that the matter at issue is moral or human. But—at least in the cases in which I have met it—it suffers from a serious defect. It appears to assume that we already have in our possession, ready-made, so to say, the morals that determine the ends for which the greatly enhanced store of means should be used. The *practical* difficulty in the way of rendering radically new "means" into servants of ends framed when the means at our disposal were of a different kind is ignored. But much more important than this, with respect to theory or philosophy, is the fact that it retains intact the divorce between some things as means and mere means and other things as ends and only ends because of their own essence or inherent nature. Thus in effect, though not in intent, an issue which is serious enough to be *moral* is disastrously evaded.

Just as this separation of some things as ends-in-themselves from other things as means-in-themselves, by their very nature, is a heritage of an age in which only those activities were called "useful" which served living physiologically rather than morally, and which were carried on by slaves or serfs to serve men who were *free* in the degree to which they were relieved from the need of labor that was base and material, so the primary need of the new state in which resources vastly different both qualitatively and quantitatively are at our command involves formation of new ends, ideals and standards to which to attach our new means. It is morally as well as logically impossible that a thoroughly changed kind of means should be harnessed to ends which at most are supposed to be changed only in the ease with which they can be reached. The thoroughgoing secularization of means and opportunities that has been going on has so far revolutionized the conduct of life as to have unsettled the old scene. Nothing is more intellectually futile (as well as practically impossible) than to suppose harmony and order can be achieved except as new ends and standards, new moral principles, are first developed with a reasonable degree of clarity and system.

In short, the problem of reconstruction in philosophy, from whatever angle it is approached, turns out to have its inception in the endeavor to discover how the new movements in science and in the industrial and political human conditions which have issued from it, that are as yet only inchoate and confused, shall be carried to completion. For a fulfillment which is consonant with their own, their proper, direction and momentum of movement can be achieved only in terms of ends and standards so distinctively human as to constitute a new moral order.

It is for the future to undertake, even in their philosophic aspect, the specific reconstructions that are involved in this carrying on to fulfillment what we have as yet attained only partially. Even a satisfactory listing of the issues that are involved with re-

spect to philosophy must, by and large, wait till the philosophic
movement in this direction has been carried beyond any point as
yet attained. But one outstanding member of such a list has just
received incidental attention: namely, the divorce that was set up
between mere means and ends-in-themselves, which is the theoretical correlate of the sharp division of men into free and slave,
superior and inferior. Science as conducted, science in practice,
has completely repudiated these separations and isolations. Scientific inquiry has raised activities, materials, tools, of the type
once regarded as practical (in a low utilitarian sense) into itself;
it has incorporated them into its own being. The way work is carried on in any astronomical observatory in the land, as well as in
any physical laboratory, is evidence. Theory in formal statement
also is as yet far behind theory in scientific practice. Theory in
fact—that is, in the conduct of scientific inquiry—has lost ulti-
macy. Theories have passed into hypotheses. It remains for philosophy to point out in particular and in general the untold significance of this fact for morals. For in what is now taken to be
morals the fixed, the immutable, still reign, even though moral
theorists and moral institutional dogmatists are at complete odds
with one another as to *what* ends, standards and principles are
the ones which are immutable, eternal and universally applicable.
In science the order of fixities has already passed irretrievably
into an order of connections *in process*. One of the most immediate duties of philosophical reconstruction with respect to the development of viable instruments for inquiry into human or moral
facts is to deal systematically with *human* processes.

Attention was earlier given in passing to some current misconceptions of the position set forth in the text which follows. I
conclude with explicit notice of a point that has received repeated
mention in the preceding text of the present Introduction. It has
been charged that the view here taken of the work and subject-
matter of philosophy commits those who accept it to identification
of philosophy with the work of those men called "reformers"—
whether with praise or with disparagement. In a verbal sense reform and re-construction are close together. But the re-construction or re-form here presented is strictly one of theory of the type
that is so comprehensive in scope as to constitute philosophy. One
of the operations to be undertaken in a re-constructed philosophy
is to assemble and present reasons why the separation once set

up between theory and practice no longer exists, so that a man like Justice Holmes can say that theory is the most practical thing, for good or for evil, in the world. One may hope surely that the theoretical enterprise herein presented will bear practical issue and for good. But that achievement is the work of human beings as human, not of them in any special professional capacity.

NOTES

14.31   S——E——P——] Either Dewey or the editors of *Dial* chose to abbreviate the title of the *Saturday Evening Post*, identified later in the *Characters and Events* republication.

22.21   Consortium] American efforts to preserve the Open Door led to the 1901 formation of an international banking consortium through which all Chinese railroad loans would be made. This consortium, from which the United States withdrew in 1913 after charging violations of China's administrative integrity, became a platform for other countries' manipulation of Chinese resources.

Textual Apparatus

Textual Commentary
Textual Notes
Emendations List
List of 1973 Variants
Line-end Hyphenation
Substantive Variants in Quotations
Checklist of Dewey's References

Index

TEXTUAL COMMENTARY

Volume 12 of *The Middle Works of John Dewey, 1899–1924* comprises nineteen items from the year 1920, all of Dewey's writings for that year with the exception of *Letters from China and Japan*. That volume is not included because it consists of personal correspondence, some by Alice Chipman Dewey and all edited by Evelyn Dewey.

Eleven of the nineteen items in Volume 12 are essays, all published in journals. Also included is one book, *Reconstruction in Philosophy*; the introduction to its 1948 reprint appears in the Miscellany section of the present volume. The remaining items are six lectures, four of them previously unpublished, delivered by John Dewey at the National University in Peking, and a service report on China, declassified by the State Department in 1960. For all nineteen items, the only authoritative appearance before this edition, whether published or not, has necessarily served as copy-text.

Although the existence of a single text eliminates copy-text problems, some commentary on the origin and reception of several of these nineteen items will clarify Dewey's writing habits and activities during this seminal year as well as provide insight into the connection of these writings with the remainder of the Dewey canon.

What began in 1918–19 as a sabbatical leave from Columbia University and a personal pleasure trip for Dewey to the Orient ended in 1921 after an extensive lecture tour and two years of teaching in Japan and China. Just before his 1919 departure from San Francisco to Japan, Dewey was invited, by cable, to lecture at the Imperial University at Tokyo. Met by reporters aboard the *Shunyu Maru* in the Yokohama Harbor, Dewey indicated that he had not definitely decided on the general topic of his lectures, "but had left the matter open till he had conferred with the people at the University."[1]

---

1. George Dykhuizen, *The Life and Mind of John Dewey* (Carbondale: Southern Illinois University Press, 1973), p. 187.

After consultation with members of the Philosophy Department at the Imperial University, Dewey embarked on a series of public lectures during February and March of 1919. His "Syllabus of Eight Lectures on 'Problems of Philosophic Reconstruction'" appears in *Middle Works* 11: 341–49. Dewey's "attempt to evaluate the modern spirit in general in contrast with that of classic philosophies"[2] in these lectures became the content of *Reconstruction in Philosophy*, published by Henry Holt and Company in early 1920.

When Dewey wrote to Columbia University colleague Wendell T. Bush about the upcoming publication, he said, "I think it has one merit; it is reasonably free from philosophic partisanship. . . . I am changing the order of some of the earlier lectures."[3] After *Reconstruction in Philosophy* was published, Dewey followed the book's progress from a distance. At her father's request, Evelyn Dewey wrote in February 1921 to Holt about sales and about the publisher's plans for the book; Lincoln MacVeagh of Henry Holt and Company replied that *Reconstruction in Philosophy* "has sold to date about fifteen hundred copies. . . . Furthermore we sold the English rights to the University of London Press, and supplied them with a duplicate set of plates. . . . We have had some very highly complimentary criticisms."[4]

Indeed, Dewey's interpretation of the reconstruction of ideas, stimulated by the hospitality and curiosity of an oriental culture eager for a fresh point of view, was warmly received by critics.[5] The favorable reviews, which found Dewey's historical analysis trenchant, were led by Boyd H. Bode's comments in *Nation*, the journal which ran *Reconstruction in Philosophy* as a premium book with subscriptions to that periodical. Said Bode, "the simplicity and penetration of the statement gives to this little book an

---

2. Dewey to Wendell T. Bush, 1 August 1919, Special Collections, Butler Library, Columbia University, New York.
3. Dewey to Bush, 1 August 1919.
4. MacVeagh to Evelyn Dewey, 25 February 1921, Henry Holt Archives, Princeton University Library, Princeton, N.J.
5. The following reviews appeared: *A.L.A. Booklist* 17 (1920): 92; John Adams, *Bookman* 60 (1921): 141–42; Ralph Barton Perry, *Dial* 70 (1921): 454–57; Horace M. Kallen, *Freeman* 3 (1921): 140–41; Clara Millerd Smertenko, *Grinnell Review* 16 (1921): 378; Boyd H. Bode, *Nation* 111 (1920): 658–60; Arthur S. McDowall, *New York Evening Post Literary Review*, 13 November 1920; Victor S. Yarros, *Open Court* 37 (1923): 596–604; George P. Adams, *Philosophical Review* 30 (1921): 519–23; *Springfield Republican*, 20 January 1921; Harry T. Costello, *Yale Review* 12 (1923): 407–10.

importance considerably out of proportion to its size."[6] While finding *Reconstruction in Philosophy* "concrete, clearly written and
unusually free from abstruse reasoning and technical diction,"[7]
reviewers also noted the pragmatic humanism of Dewey's writing, which, as Horace M. Kallen said in *Freeman*, sought "to
make eternal ideals alive by making them effectively relevant to
time, place, and circumstance."[8] Some reviewers, typified by
Harry Costello of the *Yale Review*, were disappointed that Dewey
did not offer an alternative to what he condemned in the book:
"*Reconstruction in Philosophy* is curiously unspecific in its constructive programme, and leaves the reader eager to get up and
do something, and yet very uncertain concerning just what he
ought to do."[9] Dewey himself said that he had tried to avoid "a
partisan plea in behalf of any one specific solution" (p. 79) and he
wrote to John Jacob Coss, his colleague at Columbia University,
that he "tried to sum up my past in that, and get rid of it for a
fresh start."[10]

The reception of *Reconstruction in Philosophy* by scholars
around the world indicated that they saw this book as a water-
shed, also. Besides being translated into eleven languages from
1921 to 1965,[11] *Reconstruction in Philosophy* was reprinted
twelve times in the original edition.

By 1942, sales of *Reconstruction in Philosophy* had "dropped
to approximately sixty copies a year."[12] Henry Holt and Company
released the copyright to Dewey before expiration of the first
term, and H. Bristol of that company wrote to Dewey about "the
melting of electrotype plates. . . .the result of the issuance by the

    6. Boyd H. Bode, *Nation* 111 (1920): 658.
    7. *Booklist* 17 (1920): 92.
    8. Horace M. Kallen, *Freeman* 3 (1921): 141.
    9. Harry T. Costello, *Yale Review* 12 (1923): 408.
   10. Dewey to Coss, 22 April 1920, Special Collections, Butler Library, Columbia
       University, New York.
   11. The following translations appeared: Arabic by Amīn Mursī Qandīl (Cairo,
       1957); Chinese by Ch'ung-ch'ing Hsü (Changsha, 1939), and by Shih Hu
       and Yüeh T'ang (Taiwan, 1965); Czech by Joseph Schützner (Prague, 1929);
       Iranian by S. A. Saeedi (Tehran, 1958); Italian by Guido de Ruggiero (Bari,
       1931); Japanese by Meikichi Chiba (Tōkyo, 1921), by Shin'ichi Nakajima
       (Tōkyo, 1921), and by Kokusaburō Nieda (Tōkyo, 1950); Korean by Pŏm-mo
       Chŏng (Seoul, 1960); Malay by K. M. George (Kottayam, 1955); Portuguese
       by Eugênio Marcondes Rocha (São Paulo, 1958), and by Antonio Pinto de
       Carvalho (São Paulo, 1959); Spanish by Domingo Barnés (Madrid, 1930), and
       by Amando Lázaro Ros (Buenos Aires, 1955); Tamil by A. S. Jhanasamban-
       dhan (Madras, 1957).
   12. H. Bristol, Henry Holt and Company, to Dewey, 24 August 1942.

War Production Board of their order to turn in for scrap metal any electrotype plates for which there is no assured future use."[13] Dewey chose to purchase the plates for their scrap metal value of fifteen dollars.

In 1948, at the age of eighty-eight, Dewey wrote to Sidney Hook, "am badly behind in my readings. The Beacon Press, Boston (first a Unitarian press, but now branching out) is bringing out [a] reprint of Reconstruction in Philosophy . . . and I have to write [an] Introduction."[14]

In its 1948 republication of *Reconstruction in Philosophy*, Beacon Press used the plates Dewey had purchased from Henry Holt and Company; Beacon Press also renewed the copyright at that time. Royalty statements to the John Dewey Estate show that the new publication had sold 266,445 copies by 1973.[15] Although Dewey's thirty-seven page introduction to the 1948 printing, with its invariant text printed from the original plates, will not appear in its chronological setting in *The Later Works of John Dewey*, it does appear in the present volume.

Copies of the first and last known impressions of *Reconstruction in Philosophy* have been examined on the Hinman machine and their texts found to be identical. Copy-text for the present edition is the copyright deposit copy #A597586.

Dewey's tour of the Far East was unexpectedly extended by an invitation, the result of efforts of former students of Dewey, to lecture at the National University in Peking from June 1919 to March 1920. Prior to Dewey's arrival in Peking, five Chinese progressive education organizations had asked Hu Shih, Dewey's former student and later a translator of his lectures, "to give a series of four lectures on the Pragmatic Movement, beginning with Charles S. Peirce and William James, but with special emphasis on Dewey. A series of articles on Dewey's educational philosophy was published in Shanghai under the editorship of Dr. Chiang Monlin, one of his students in Teachers' College at Columbia."[16]

13. Bristol to Dewey, 24 August 1942.
14. Dewey to Hook, 4 January 1948, Special Collections, Morris Library, Southern Illinois University at Carbondale.
15. Beacon Press Rights and Permissions division to Jo Ann Boydston, 4 June 1974. Contract files on *Reconstruction in Philosophy* were deposited at the Center for Dewey Studies, Southern Illinois University, Carbondale, at that time.
16. Hu Shih, "John Dewey in China," in *Philosophy and Culture East and West* (Honolulu: University of Hawaii Press, 1962), p. 764.

Among the lectures delivered by Dewey at the National University in Peking was a series on "Three Contemporary Philosophers: William James, Henri Bergson and Bertrand Russell," the last given at special request as an introduction to Russell before his 1920 arrival in China to deliver a number of lectures.[17] Since Dewey spoke no Chinese and delivered his lectures in English, they were interpreted in Chinese as they were given and written down by recorders for use by the press.[18] No original English manuscript for any of Dewey's lectures in China is extant; it has been conjectured that he spoke exclusively from notes.

The copy-text for these lectures in the present edition is the translation from the Chinese by Robert W. Clopton and Tsuin-chen Ou, a typescript in the Thomas Hale Hamilton Library of the University of Hawaii. These lectures, the Bertrand Russell lectures excepted, are published for the first time in this edition. The Bertrand Russell lectures appeared in a 1973 *Journal of the Bertrand Russell Archives*, which is cited in the Emendations List as the first appearance of eight corrections in spelling, capitalization, and punctuation. All revisions made in the text of the Russell lectures by the *Journal of the Bertrand Russell Archives* appear in the "List of 1973 Variants in 'Bertrand Russell.'"

These six "Contemporary Philosophers" lectures were part of what became known as "Dewey's Five Major Series of Lectures in Peking," translated into Chinese for the *Peking Morning Post* by Dewey's former student Hu Shih. Later published in book form in China, Dewey's lectures went through ten large reprintings before he left China in 1921; they continued to be reprinted for three decades in China until the Communists intervened.[19]

Dewey had told reporters, upon his arrival in the Orient, that he "wanted very much to talk with . . . leaders on matters of domestic and international importance and to report his findings in the *New Republic* and *Dial*."[20] Having arrived in China just prior to the catalytic May Fourth Movement, Dewey conferred with political leaders as well as students, professors, and members of the business and religious communities. For Dewey, the trip was the "most interesting and intellectually the most profitable thing Ive ever done."[21] "Nothing western looks quite the same any more,

17. Hu Shih, *Philosophy*, p. 765.
18. Hu Shih, *Philosophy*, p. 764.
19. Hu Shih, *Philosophy*, p. 764.
20. Dykhuizen, *Life*, p. 187.
21. Dewey to Coss, 7 November 1920.

and this is as near to a renewal of youth as can be hoped for in this world."[22]

From Dewey's extended contact with Chinese citizens emerged a series of eight articles which appeared in *New Republic*: "The Sequel of the Student Revolt," 25 February 1920; "Shantung, As Seen from Within," 3 March 1920; "Our National Dilemma," 24 March 1920; "Freedom of Thought and Work," 5 May 1920; "China's Nightmare," 30 June 1920; "How Reaction Helps," 1 September 1920; "A Political Upheaval in China," 6 October 1920; "Industrial China," 8 December 1920. Since no manuscript or typescript remains for these articles, copy-text is their first appearance in *New Republic*.

Invited to extend his visit in China for the 1920–21 academic year, Dewey wrote to John Jacob Coss in April 1920, "I have decided to stay over here and teach another year . . . to try to clinch whatever may have got started this year. . . . The students are on strike again as a protest [against] the Government's dealings with Japan, but they have excepted my lectures. Im lecturing . . . 8 hours a week altogether, but the interpretation has to come out of the time, so it is rather a lesson in selection, condensation and illustration."[23]

In addition to delivering some fifty-eight lectures in China, Dewey also found time to write two articles for *Asia*: "The New Leaven in Chinese Politics," April 1920, and "What Holds China Back," May 1920. Copy-text for these essays, in the absence of any other authoritative document, is their first appearance in *Asia*.

The final essay of the eleven in *Middle Works* 12 is "Americanism and Localism," *Dial*, April 1920. Since there is no extant typescript, the first appearance of the article has served as copytext. Before Dewey's essay appeared in print, a *Dial* editor restyled all "-or" words—neighborhood, flavor, color—to "-our" forms; these British spellings have been returned to known Dewey usage.

Apart from the eleven essays written in 1920 remains one service report which Dewey sent to Colonel Alexander Drysdale, the military attaché of the American Legation in China, in all probability at the latter's request. When Colonel Drysdale forwarded the report to the State Department in Washington, D.C.,

22. Dewey to Coss, 13 January 1920.
23. Dewey to Coss, 22 April 1920.

his attached memo read: "Dr. Dewey . . . has had unusual opportunity of getting into touch with the element in China that may
be considered as radical. I know of no one any where, better qualified to report on this important matter than Dr. Dewey."[24] Entitled "Bolshevism in China," the service report was declassified by
the State Department on 22 July 1960, and is now filed in the
National Archives, State Department Record Group 59. The State
Department typescript serves as copy-text in this edition. The report was first published in the *Dewey Newsletter* 6 (1972): 7–10;
ten emendations, mainly changes in spelling, punctuation, and
capitalization, have been adopted from that version.

B.A.W.

24. Drysdale to State Department, 2 December 1920, National Archives, State
Department Record Group 59.

TEXTUAL NOTES

68.40   China] The copy-text's usage of "Japan" instead of "China" is an obvious mistake, given the context. The error in the first printing of the article probably occurred because of the frequency of references to both countries.

235.1   outspoken pacifism] Retention of the copy-text's "outspoken" is appropriate here; although Dewey states that Russell resigned his Cambridge position, in actuality Russell was fired, or, as administrators would put it, he lacked tenure and his appointment was not renewed.

EMENDATIONS LIST

All emendations in both substantives and accidentals introduced into the copy-text are recorded in the list that follows, with the exception of the changes in formal matters described below. The copy-text for each item is identified at the beginning of the list of emendations in that item; for the items that had a single previous printing, no abbreviation for the copy-text appears in the list itself. The page-line number at left is from the present edition; all lines of print except running heads are counted. The reading to the left of the square bracket is from the present edition; the bracket is followed by an abbreviation for the source of the emendation's first appearance. W means Works—the present edition—and is used for emendations made here for the first time. For emendations restricted to punctuation, the curved dash ~ means the same word(s) as before the bracket; the inferior caret ‸ indicates the absence of a punctuation mark.

The abbreviation [*rom.*] means roman type and is used to signal the omission of italics; [*not present*] is used where appropriate to signal material not appearing in identified sources. The asterisk before an emendation page-line number indicates the reading is discussed in the Textual Notes.

A number of formal, or mechanical, changes have been made throughout:

1. Book and journal titles are in italic type; articles and sections of books are in quotation marks. Book and journal titles have been supplied and expanded where necessary.

2. The form of Dewey's documentation has been made consistent: volume numbers are uppercase roman with the following periods removed, section and chapter numbers are arabic, abbreviations have been regularized.

3. Superior numbers have been assigned consecutively throughout an item to Dewey's footnotes.

4. Single quotation marks have been changed to double

when not inside quoted material; however, opening or closing quotation marks have been supplied where necessary and recorded.

The following instances of spelling and hyphenation have been editorially regularized to the known Dewey usage, appearing before the brackets:

cannot] can not 230.21
centre(s)] center(s) 9.26, 23.30, 24.19, 30.18, 31.22, 31.30, 233.2,
    245.30, 256.13, 266.18
color] colour 15.16, 15.34, 16.11
cooperate (all forms)] co-operate 100.7, 100.14, 138.3, 153.12, 164.29,
    182.12, 193.40, 194.2, 194.6, 201.31, 273.28
coordinate (all forms)] co-ordinate 132.1–2, 193.18
deeper-lying] deeper lying 87.34
flavor] flavour 12.28
guarantee] guaranty 92.23, 134.19, 219.12
joint-stock (adj.)] joint stock 72.11, 194.21
maneuvering] manœuvering 67.8–9
matter-of-fact (adj.)] matter of fact 85.8, 86.27, 86.37–38, 87.9, 87.24,
    87.29, 92.30, 121.37–38
neighborhood(s)] neighbourhood(s) 12.12, 16.10
one hundred] one-hundred 5.9
pent-in] pent in 111.40
programs] programmes 135.11
reorganized] re-organized 224.10
role] rôle 149.35, 195.13
wage-earners] wage earners 8.31

"Our National Dilemma"

Copy-text is the first appearance of the article in *New Republic* 22 (1920): 117–18. The republication in *Characters and Events*, ed. Joseph Ratner (New York: Henry Holt and Co., 1929), 2: 615–19 (CE), is noted as the first appearance of three changes.

4.13	Doctrine] CE; doctrine
5.3	Jewish₄] W; ~,
5.9	of Americans] W; Americans
5.12	sword] CE; swords
5.30	*New Republic*] CE; [*rom.*]
6.39	supervise] W; supervises
6.39	direct] W; directs

"Freedom of Thought and Work"

Copy-text is the first appearance of the article in *New Republic* 22 (1920): 316–17. The republication in *Characters and Events*, ed. Joseph Ratner (New York: Henry Holt and Co., 1929), 2: 522–25 (CE), is noted as the first appearance of two changes.

8.14   far-reaching] CE; ~ ˄ ~
8.15   it] CE; in

"Americanism and Localism"

Copy-text is the first appearance of the article in *Dial* 68 (1920): 684–88. The republication in *Characters and Events*, ed. Joseph Ratner (New York: Henry Holt and Co., 1929), 2: 537–41 (CE), is noted as the first appearance of one change.

15.18,26   Wilkins's] W; Wilkins'
15.32   Melchizedek] CE; Melchisedek

"How Reaction Helps"

Copy-text is the first appearance of the article in *New Republic* 24 (1920): 21–22. The republication in *Characters and Events*, ed. Joseph Ratner (New York: Henry Holt and Co., 1929), 2: 815–19 (CE), is noted as the first appearance of three changes.

17.28   1918] CE; 1919
18.17   Reactionaryism] CE; Reactionarism
19.32–33   radicalism] CE; radicalicm

"The Sequel of the Student Revolt"

Copy-text is the first appearance of the article in *New Republic* 21 (1920): 380–82.

22.17   Twenty-one] W; Twenty-One
23.16   Pekingese] W; Pekinese
26.31   incident ˄] W; ~,
27.11   is its] W; it its

"Shantung, As Seen from Within"

Copy-text is the first appearance of the article in *New Republic* 21 (1920): 12–17. The republication in *China, Japan and the U.S.A.* (New York: Republic Publishing Co., 1921), pp. 9–21 (CJ), is noted as the first appearance of six changes.

30.28	Yangtze] W; Yangste
30.30	Railway] CJ; railway
30.39–40	minimum] CJ; mimimum
33.25	immeasurable] CJ; immeasurably
33.32	year (1920),] W; year, (1920) CJ; year,
34.20	China.ₐ] CJ; ~..
37.8	consciousness] CJ; consciousnes
37.34	of] CJ; in
39.1	Treaty] W; treaty

"The New Leaven in Chinese Politics"

Copy-text is the first appearance of the article in *Asia* 20 (1920): 267–72. The republication in *Characters and Events*, ed. Joseph Ratner (New York: Henry Holt and Co., 1929), 1: 244–54 (CE), is noted as the first appearance of three changes.

41.20	essence] CE; essense
48.16	hands] CE; hand
48.23	than by] W; than
49.17	Young China] CE; it

"What Holds China Back"

Copy-text is the first appearance of the article in *Asia* 20 (1920): 373–77. The republication in *Characters and Events*, ed. Joseph Ratner (New York: Henry Holt and Co., 1929), 1: 211–21 (CE), is noted as the first appearance of one change.

52.37	there] CE; this

"China's Nightmare"

Copy-text is the first appearance of the article in *New Republic* 23 (1920): 145–47. The republication in *Characters and*

Events, ed. Joseph Ratner (New York: Henry Holt and Co., 1929), 1: 193–98 (CE), is noted as the first appearance of three changes.

60.26	are] W; is
60.27–28	*The Break-up of China*] CE; [*rom.*]
61.12, 40	Twenty-one Demands] W; twenty-one demands
62.12	Bay] CE; bay
62.14	Treaty] W; treaty
62.25	Yangtze] W; Yangtse
62.28	*Break-up*] CE; "Break-up"
63.11	Treaty] W; treaty

"A Political Upheaval in China"

Copy-text is the first appearance of the article in *New Republic* 24 (1920): 142–44. The republication in *China, Japan and the U.S.A.* (New York: Republic Publishing Co., 1921), pp. 27–32 (CJ), is noted as the first appearance of four changes.

65.5	Yuan Shih-kai's] W; Yuan Shi Kai's
65.6	in 1917] CJ; three summers ago
65.8	(September 1920)] CJ; [*not present*]
66.1	Yuan Shih-kai] W; Yuan Shi Kai
*68.40	China] CJ; Japan
69.15, n.1–9	Hsu.[1] . . . [1] This was written . . . in China.] CJ; Hsu.
69n.6[1]	Government] W; Govrenment CJ; [*not present*]

"Industrial China"

Copy-text is the first appearance of the article in *New Republic* 25 (1920): 39–41. The republication in *Impressions of Soviet Russia and the Revolutionary World: Mexico—China—Turkey* (New York: New Republic, Inc., 1929), pp. 237–51 (SR), is noted as the first appearance of eight changes.

71.23–24	journals,] SR; ~ˬ
71.30	Province] W; province
72.12–13	as did . . . companies] SR; as most of the early companies did
73.10	be recorded] SR; recorded
74.22	while at the same time the] SR; while the
74.35	land ˬ] W; ~,
74.35	trade,] W; ~ˬ

74.36   mills$_\wedge$] W; ~,
75.1   a small] SR; the small
75.32,n.1–2   struggle?[1] . . . [1]The nationalistic . . . class-war.] SR; struggle?
76.20   conceivable, and only] SR; conceivable: only
76.21   best.] SR; best, not necessarily probable, to say nothing of cer-
             tain.

Reconstruction in Philosophy

Copy-text for this work is the copyright deposit copy, A597586, (New York: Henry Holt and Co., 1920).

81.1   are] W; is
99.28   through] W; though
114.10   itself,] W; ~$_\wedge$
116.27–28   governs,] W; ~$_\wedge$
120.15   Homo] W; Home
137.3   opposites] W; opposities
137.29   its] W; their
141.16   infects] W; infect
141.26–27   dialectically] W; dialectially
141.27–28   doctrine,] W; ~$_\wedge$
142.8   changeless,] W; ~$_\wedge$
151.38   matters,] W; ~.
153.3   suppose,] W; ~$_\wedge$
153.3   fanciful$_\wedge$] W; ~,
158.4   formal] W; former
183.9   other-worldly] W; ~$_\wedge$~
191.4   can] W; it can
195.33   and] W; ad
200.8   the ideas] W; will the ideas
200.9   will be] W; be

"Three Contemporary Philosophers: William James, Henri Bergson, Bertrand Russell"

Copy-text for these lectures is the translation (UH) from the Chinese by Robert W. Clopton and Tsuin-chen Ou (Honolulu: Hamilton Library, University of Hawaii, 1973). The publication of the Russell lectures in *Journal of the Bertrand Russell Archives* 11 (1973): 3–10, 15–20 (RA), is cited as the first appearance of eight corrections. Revisions made in that later publication appear in the "List of 1973 Variants in '*Bertrand Russell*'."

205.15,20,24; 206.5,25; 208.6; 210.5,16,25; 212.10; 213.1; 215.20;
216.38; 217.13,24,33; 218.7,37,39,40; 219.10,13,35; 220.4,28; 221.7,11;
240.39; 246.12; 250.18   James's] W; James'

206.4	nature.] W; ~_
206.33	a Certain] W; A Certain
208.30	stimuli] W; stimulii
210.37	changing._] W; ~..
215.28	out_] W; ~,
221.6	evolution.] W; evolution.[1] . . . [1]At this point, Dr. Hu Shih, who was interpreting, interjected the remark that Dr. Dewey, himself, was also born in this same year, and that his philosophy, as well as that of Bergson, had been instrumental in developing the philosophical implications of the theory of evolution.
226.14	the separation] W; that the separation
228.34	of] W; or
229.25	architectural] W; architectual
229.33	teleological] W; teleogical
241.32	Knowledge] RA; knowledge
243.9	his] RA; hiw
243.28	had] RA; have
244.4	*élan*] W; *elan* RA, UH
246.37	constituency] RA; constituence
248.7	War] RA; war
249.10	production?_] RA; ~?;
249.11	distribution?_] RA; ~?;
249.12	treatment?_] RA; ~?;
249.37	Russell,] W; ~_ RA, UH

"Bolshevism in China"

Copy-text is the service report received on 2 December 1920 by the military attaché of the American Legation in China. Declassified by the State Department on 22 July 1960, the report was first published in the *Dewey Newsletter* 6 (1972): 7–10 (DN), which is noted as the first appearance of ten changes.

253.6	Bolshevism] DN; Solshevism
253.7	since,] W; ~_
254.5	it has] DN; has it
254.6	able,] W; ~_
254.7	rumors,] W; ~_
254.15	not] DN; no
254.28	accentuated] DN; accentusted
254.31	1902,] W; ~_

254.32   Kuomintang] W; Kuo Min Tang DN; Kou Ming Tang
254.33   Yuan Shih-kai] W; Yuan Shih Kai DN; Yuan Shi Kai
254.39   less] DN; loss
255.2   isn't] DN; isnt
255.3   "proletariat"] DN; "proloterist"
255.4   forming,] W; ~ˌ
255.7–8   wasn't one] DN; wasnt on
255.26   at . . . educated] W; who are educated at random
255.32   don't] DN; dont
255.33   won't] DN; wont

"Reconstruction As Seen Twenty-Five Years Later"

Copy-text is the first appearance of the Introduction in the expanded reprint of *Reconstruction in Philosophy* (Boston: Beacon Press, 1948), pp. v–xli.

274.10   are] W; is

LIST OF 1973 VARIANTS IN *"BERTRAND RUSSELL"*

From the Contemporary Philosophers series, the fifth and sixth lectures on *"Bertrand Russell"* were republished in the *Journal of the Bertrand Russell Archives* 11 (1973): 3–10, 15–20, with the title "Russell's philosophy and politics." Substantive changes made in the articles for that later publication appear below to the right of the bracket. The copy-text reading appears before the bracket and does not coincide with the reading of the present edition if an emendation has been made; these readings are signaled by a grid #.

235.33   FIFTH LECTURE: BERTRAND RUSSELL] Russell's philosophy and politics/Lecture V. Russell's philosophy

236.1   outspoken pacifism] pacifism

236.9–10   as far as] so far as

237.35   and good into better] into better

238.18–19   universe. He . . . universe;] universe;

239.17   even without] without

240.12   practical] a practical

#241.32   knowledge] Knowledge

242.36–37   movement] movements

243.7   separated] separate

#243.9   hiw] his

243.19   SIXTH LECTURE: BERTRAND RUSSELL (CONTINUED)] Lecture VI. Russell's ethics and political philosophy

#243.28   have] had

244.13   question] questions

245.31   begin] being

246.26   no matter] not matter

#246.37   constituence] constituency

246.40   of buying] of buy

#248.7   war] War

248.11   and religion] the religion

248.40   free;] ~,

#249.10   production?;] ~?ₐ

#249.11   distribution?;] ~?ₐ

#249.12   treatment?;] ~?ₐ

249.29   for consumers] consumers

LINE-END HYPHENATION

I. *Copy-text list.*

The following are the editorially established forms of possible compounds which were hyphenated at the ends of lines in the copy-text.

4.19	non-participation	148.13–14	castle-building
23.3	semi-official	170.36	ready-made
29.33	today	173.38	one-sided
32.22	Today's	192.12	free-will
61.38	semi-civil	196.30–31	coordinate
73.1	egg-factories	222.23	ever-changing
81.10	resurveys	227.16	overshadowed
96.2	one-sided	258.25	ready-made
96.4	quasi-magical	267.18	pre-scientific
99.3	ready-made	269.36	pre-scientific
99.7–8	pseudo-science	269.40	one-sided
103.29	preeminently	274.17	present-day
121.22	wholehearted	274.23–24	pre-technological-industrial
134.33	readjustment	274.37	ready-made

II. *Critical-text list.*

In transcriptions from the present edition, no line-end hyphens in ambiguously broken compounds are to be retained except the following:

8.21	monkey-wrench	47.38	short-circuited
9.30	hang-over	60.8	extra-territorial
13.22	nation-wide	82.20	well-being
31.7	China-wards	99.7	pseudo-science
31.11	sea-port	113.11	full-grown
40.4	fair-play	113.19	pre-arranged
44.37	law-abidingness	113.36	so-called
47.20	re-form	119.16	well-known

143.19	self-sufficiency	259.19	so-called
143.21	self-sufficing	261.4	extra-temporal
147.6	self-enclosed	268.36	anti-scientific
160.37	self-delusion	269.22	self-enclosed
175.35	so-called	270.20	self-corrective
177.25	so-called	276.35	re-form
258.34	pre-democratic		

SUBSTANTIVE VARIANTS IN QUOTATIONS

Dewey represented source material in varying ways, from memorial paraphrase to verbatim copy, in some places citing his source fully, in others mentioning only authors' names, and, in still others, omitting documentation altogether.

Dewey's substantive variations in quotations have been considered important enough to warrant this special list. All material inside quotation marks, except that obviously being emphasized or restated, has been searched out; Dewey's citations have been verified and, when necessary, emended.

Except for required corrections noted in the Emendations List, all quotations have been retained as they appear in the copy-text. In cases of possible compositorial or typographical errors, changes in substantives or accidentals that restore original readings are noted as *Works* (W) emendations. Although Dewey, like scholars of the period, was unconcerned about precision in matters of form, many of the changes in quotations may well have occurred in the printing process. For example, comparing Dewey's quotations with the originals reveals that some editors and compositors house-styled the quoted materials as well as Dewey's own. Therefore, in the present edition, the spelling and capitalization of the source have been reproduced.

Dewey frequently changed or omitted punctuation in quoted material. When such changes or omissions have substantive implications, the punctuation of the original reading has been restored; those changes are recorded in the Emendations List. Dewey often did not indicate that he had omitted material from his source. Omitted short phrases appear in this list; omissions of more than one line are noted by a bracketed ellipsis [. . .]. Italics in source material have been treated as substantives. Both Dewey's omitted and added italics are noted here.

Differences between Dewey's quotations and the source attributable to the context in which the quotation appears, such as changes in number or tense, are not recorded.

In cases where Dewey translated the source, the reference

appears in the Checklist of Dewey's References, but no correction of the quotation is included here.

The form used in this section is designed to assist the reader in determining whether Dewey had the source before him or was relying on memory. Notations in this section follow the formula: page-line numbers from the present edition, followed by the lemma, then a bracket. After the bracket, the original form appears, followed by the author's surname, shortened source-title from the Checklist of Dewey's References, and the page-line reference to the source, all in parentheses.

Reconstruction in Philosophy

91.36   is vision] has often been defined as the quest or the vision (James, *Pragmatism*, 129.20–21)
100.22   the] a (Bacon, *The Advancement of Learning*, 294.8)
100.24   men, but as] men: as (Bacon, *The Advancement of Learning*, 294.15)
100.24   they] there were (Bacon, *The Advancement of Learning*, 294.15)
100.24   couch whereon] couch, whereupon (Bacon, *The Advancement of Learning*, 294.15–16)
100.25   wandering spirit] restless spirit (Bacon, *The Advancement of Learning*, 294.16)
100.26   tower for] tower of state, for (Bacon, *The Advancement of Learning*, 294.18)
141.28   that is perfectly] perfect, nothing genuinely (Bradley, *Appearance and Reality*, 500.3)
141.28   real moves] real, can move (Bradley, *Appearance and Reality*, 500.4)

"Three Contemporary Philosophers: William James"

207.19   the good] good (James, *Talks to Teachers*, 264.6)

Introduction to 1948 reprint of Reconstruction in Philosophy

262.30   of] and of (Darlington, *Conflict*, 3.2)
262.37   first understood] first seen under the microscope by a draper, that stratigraphy was first understood (Darlington, *Conflict*, 5.18–19)
263.1   isolated] first isolated (Darlington, *Conflict*, 5.20)
263.2   established] first established (Darlington, *Conflict*, 5.22)

CHECKLIST OF DEWEY'S REFERENCES

Titles and authors' names in Dewey references have been corrected and expanded to conform accurately and consistently to the original works; all corrections appear in the Emendations List.

This section gives full publication information for each work cited by Dewey. When Dewey gave page numbers for a reference, the edition he used was identified exactly by locating the citation. Similarly, the books in Dewey's personal library have been used to verify his use of a particular edition. For other references, the edition listed here is the one from among the various editions possibly available to him that was his most likely source by reason of place or date of publication, or on the evidence from correspondence and other materials, and its general accessibility during the period.

Bacon, Francis. *The Works of Francis Bacon.* Edited by James Spedding, Robert L. Ellis, and Douglas Denon Heath. Vol. 3. London: Longmans and Co., 1876.

Beresford, Charles. *The Break-up of China with an Account of Its Present Commerce, Currency, Waterways, Armies, Railways, Politics and Future Prospects.* New York: Harper and Bros., 1899.

Bergson, Henri. *Creative Evolution.* Translated by Arthur Mitchell. New York: Henry Holt and Co., 1911.

Bradley, Francis Herbert. *Appearance and Reality: A Metaphysical Essay.* 2d ed. rev. New York: Macmillan Co., 1908.

Darlington, C. D. *The Conflict of Science and Society.* Conway Memorial Lecture delivered at Conway Hall on 20 April 1948. London: Watts and Co., 1948.

Darwin, Charles. *On the Origin of the Species by Means of Natural Selection.* London: J. Murray, 1859.

Dewey, John. *John Dewey: Lectures in China, 1919–1920.* Translated and edited by Robert W. Clopton and Tsuin-chen Ou. Honolulu: University Press of Hawaii, 1973.

Harrison, Ernest John. *The Fighting Spirit of Japan and Other Stories.* New York: Charles Scribner's Sons, [1912].

James, William. *Pragmatism: A New Name for Some Old Ways of Thinking.* New York: Longmans, Green, and Co., 1907.

————. *The Principles of Psychology*. New York: Henry Holt and Co., 1890.

————. *The Will to Believe*. New York: Longmans, Green, and Co., 1897.

————. "On a Certain Blindness in Human Beings." In *Talks to Teachers on Psychology: And to Students on Some of Life's Ideals*, pp. 229–64. New York: Henry Holt and Co., 1919.

Kant, Immanuel. *Critique of Pure Reason*. Translated by Francis Haywood. London: W. Pickering, 1838.

Lippmann, Walter. "The Political Scene: VI. A World Pool; VII. Alternatives." *New Republic* 18 (22 March 1919): 7–9.

Miner, Luella, ed. *Two Heroes of Cathay*. New York: Fleming H. Revell Co., [1903].

Oppenheim, James. "Poetry—Our First National Art." *Dial* 68 (1920): 238–42.

Russell, Bertrand. *German Social Democracy; Six Lectures*. New York: Longmans, Green, and Co., 1896.

————. *Political Ideals*. New York: Century Co., 1917.

————. *Principles of Social Reconstruction*. London: G. Allen and Unwin, [1916].

————. *Roads to Freedom: Socialism, Anarchism, and Syndicalism*. London: G. Allen and Unwin, [1918].

Shakespeare, William. *Shakespeare's Comedy of "A Winter's Tale."* 14th ed. London: J. M. Dent and Co., 1906.

Wilhelm II. *The Kaiser's Letters to the Tsar*. Edited by N. F. Grant. London: Hodder and Stoughton, 1920.

INDEX

Absolutism, 135, 189; Kant and, 98–99
Abstractions, 166–67, 179
Achievements, 191
Action, 125–26
Adams, Henry, 13
Alcmaeon of Croton, xiii
Alexander, Samuel, xxx
Allies, 35, 63, 66
Alsace-Lorraine, 60
Americanization, 12–16
Anarchism, 247
Anfu Club, 65–69, 255. *See also* China
Animals, 81–82, 232–34, 245
Antiquity, 97–98
Anwhei faction, 69–70
Apology, xii
Apprehension, 161–62
Aquinas, Saint Thomas, 111, 140
Argumentation, 97, 132–33
Aristocracy, 239–40
Aristotle, xvii, xxi, xxvii, 87, 89, 90, 111; Bacon's charge against, 96–97, 99–100; on change, 141; and distinction in ends, 177–78; on experience, 125–26; on forms, 140; on knowledge, 142, 143; on Potentiality, 112, 113; on slavery, 189; on the state, 104; and ultimate reality, 140–41
Armistice Day, 4, 17
Art, 98, 139, 200–201, 228; fine, 152; localism in, 15–16; military, 88
Art as Experience, xv
Artisans, 86–88, 116, 143
Asia, 227; national consciousness of, 35–36, 37; as Yellow Peril, 35

Astronomy, 116–17, 122–23, 144–45, 237, 262, 264
Athens, Greece, 86–87, 90, 258
Atomism: defined, xiv; "logical," 236
Augustine, Saint, 143–44
Authoritarianism, 239
Authority, 106–7, 160, 191–92; final, 172; seat of, 171
Autonomy, 249

Bacon, Francis: criticism of learning of his day, 95–96; on experience, 135–36; "Knowledge is power," 95–96, 103, 108; summary of ideas of, 95–96, 126
Balance of qualities, xiii
Balfour, Arthur James, 3
Being, 260; and non-being, 141; perfect, 143–44; spiritual realm of, 266
Belief, 86, 94, 217–18, 256, 261
Bentham, Jeremy, 174–75, 184, 187
Beresford, Charles, 60, 62
Bergson, Henri: compared with James, xx, xxvii–xxix, 221, 227–28, 235; compared with Russell, 236, 242–43; contribution of, 249–50; on creation, xxviii, 120, 235, 242–43; and criticism of views of evolution, 229; on impulse of will, 230–31; on life understood by living it, 235; and problem of universe as immutable or changing, 221, 227–28; on reality as psychological existence, 221–28; and relationship between mind and matter, 222, 224–26; and relationship between noumenal and

Empirical: and rational, 126, 130; theory of knowledge, xiv, 259
Empiricism, 124, 126, 136, 213–15
Ends: conflicting, 175; fixed, 119–20, 174; "higher," 178; intrinsic and instrumental, 177, 178–79; means and, 121; moral, 175–76; values and, 180
Energy, 226, 245. *See also* Science
England. *See* Great Britain
Enlightenment: thinkers of, in England and France, xiv, 107
Environment: coping with, 229, 231; and formation of ideas, 85, 232; life and the, 128
Epistemology, xxix, 107, 119–20, 150, 152, 227. *See also* Intellect; Intuition
Estheticism: and environment, 117, 146–47, 182; reconciling science and, 152–53
Ethics, 172, 237
Etiquette: in Japan and China, 55–56. *See also* Crowd
Europe: intellectual revolution in, 100–103; nationalistic movement in, 195
European aggression: in China, 28, 34–37, 62; for financial ends, 36. *See also* Western civilization
European War. *See* World War I
Evil: cause of, in political China, 49; problem of, 181; science and technology responsible for, 274
Evolution: in Aristotle, 112–13; Bergson on, 228–32, 235, 237–38; of the state, 194–95
Existence, 92, 223
Existentialists, xxi
Experience, xi, xiv, xv, xvi, 97, 129, 139; classic and modern notions of, 106, 125–27, 132–34; empirical, 239; evil as result of conception of, 137–38; as guide in science and moral life,

124–25, 131–34; James on, 217, 222; separation of, 222, 226; as source of knowledge, 133–34, 213
Experience and Nature, ix
Experimentalism: James on, 220; method of, 87
Exploration, 101–3
Extra-territoriality, 46–47

Facts, 85, 135–36, 160–62, 243
Family: in China, 72, 253; as developer of creative impulse, 248; principle, 114–15, 188
Fanaticism, 176
Farmers: in China, 254
Faulkner, William, xxvi
Fear, 101–2
Feudalism, 103–4, 113, 114–15, 184
Fighting. *See* Conflict
Final good, xiii, xx, 172–74, 184. *See also* Good
Finite: or Imperfect, 141; and infinite, 117
Fire, 85–86, 111–12, 129, 209
Flux, 112, 141–42
Foo-chow, China, 22, 23, 39
Foreigners: in China, 44–49, 74. *See also* United States; Western civilization
Formalism, xxiii
France: agreements of, with Japan, 35; and Alsace-Lorraine, 60; demands for concessions by, 62; history of philosophy in, xiv, 107, 222; and Versailles Conference, 5, 18
Freedom: of franchise, 10–11; internal, 246–47; law and, 198; realization of human, 240; religious, 105; secured by vigilance, 17–18; of thought, 8–11; of will, 192
"Free Man's Worship," xxix
Freudian psychology, xxvi
"Frontier Defense" army, 66
Fukien, China, 22, 23

India, 6, 35, 102
Individual, 99–100, 104–5, 108;
James on, 236, 250; in social
and moral sense, 190–94; state
and the, 189
Individualism: in modern philosophy, 107–8; political, 104–5; religious and moral, 105; rugged,
243; in Young China, 75
Induction, 98
Industry: in China, 71–76, 254;
guild system in, 48, 249; labor
in, 9–11, 75–76; movements in,
100–106; science and, 100–
101, 102, 103; unjust institutions of, 8
Infinite, 117, 118
Initiative, 105, 199–200
Inquiry: development of, 179,
265–77; free and impartial,
163–64; mathematics as, 237;
methods of, 89, 177, 270; scientific, 179, 262, 264, 266–68
Instinct, 245–46
Institutions: claims of, 273; industrial, 249; inquiry about, 192–
93; meet psychological needs,
245–46; states as, 247–48
Instrumentalism, xviii, 177–78
Intellect, 82–83; related to intui-
tion, 227; somnambulism of,
160–61. See also Epistemology
Intellectualism, 147
Intelligence, 99–100, 108; de-
fined, 134–35, 258–59; devel-
opment of, 208; functions of,
173–74, 226, 230
Interest, 191–92
Internationalism, 14, 197
Introspection, 192, 227
Intuition, 227, 234
Invention, 101, 103, 108, 149–50,
270
Investigation, 164–65
Ipse dixit method, 174–75
Isolationism, xxi, 2–7

James, William: basis of philosophy of, ix, xxv–xxviii, 205–20;

compared with Bergson, xxx,
221, 222, 235; compared with
Russell, xxx, 236; contributions
of, 249–50; on experience, 217,
222; on individuality, 236; on
knowledge, xxv, 208–9, 215–
16; opposes dogmatism, 220; on
philosophy as vision, 91, 206;
pragmatism of, 100–101; "radical empiricism" of, xi, 207, 217
Japan: army of, 22, 32–34; corruption of, 66, 68–69; diplomacy of,
39–40; economic development
of, 34–40, 74; propaganda of,
45, 63; relationship of, with
China, 22, 27, 29–40, 45–46,
63–68; and Russia, 60–64; as
successor of Germany, 26, 29–
30, 34–37; and U.S., 36–37
Joyce, James, xxvi
Judgment: in logic, 156–57;
moral, 180–81; standards of,
179–80

Kant, Immanuel, xi, xxixn, 28,
107–8, 127, 197; on limitation
of perception, 221; philosophy
of, and German character, 136–
37
Kiangsu, China, 71, 73
Kinship, 115
Knowledge: Bergson deprecates,
227; degrees of, 141–42; empirical, 121–22; functions of, xix,
149, 150, 208–9; modern views
of, xxvi, 144–45, 262–63; old
conception of, 144–47, 214; origin of, 213, 215–16; positive vs.
traditional, 86, 88–89; is Power,
95–98, 103, 108; Russell on,
236, 238–39, 243–44, 246; sensations and, 129–31; truth or
falsity of, 216
Köhler, Wolfgang, xxvi
Korea, 6, 28, 31, 33, 62, 64
Kuomintang, 254

Labor: in China, 255; European
democracies and, 6; in industry,